D0938893

JONAH

A PSYCHO-RELIGIOUS APPROACH
TO THE PROPHET

STUDIES ON PERSONALITIES OF THE OLD TESTAMENT
James L. Crenshaw, *Editor*

DANIEL IN HIS TIME
by André LaCocque

JOSEPH AND HIS FAMILY:
A LITERARY STUDY
by W. Lee Humphreys

EZEKIEL:
THE PROPHET AND HIS MESSAGE
by Ralph W. Klein

NOAH: THE PERSON AND THE STORY
IN HISTORY AND TRADITION
by Lloyd R. Bailey

JONAH: A PSYCHO-RELIGIOUS
APPROACH TO THE PROPHET
by André LaCocque and
Pierre-Emmanuel Lacocque

J O N A H

A PSYCHO-RELIGIOUS APPROACH
TO THE PROPHET

ANDRÉ LACOCQUE
and
PIERRE-EMMANUEL LACOCQUE

Foreword by Mircea Eliade

UNIVERSITY OF SOUTH CAROLINA PRESS

Copyright © University of South Carolina 1990

Published in Columbia, South Carolina, by the
University of South Carolina Press

Manufactured in the United States of America

Library of Congress Cataloging-in-Publication Data

Lacocque, André.
    Jonah : a psycho-religious approach to the prophet / André
Lacocque and Pierre-Emmanuel Lacocque : foreword by Mircea Eliade. -
- 1st ed.
      p. cm. — (Studies on personalities of the Old Testament)
    Rev. ed. of : The Jonah Complex.
    Includes bibliographical references.
    ISBN 0–87249–674–0 (alk. paper)
    1. Bible. O. T. Jonah—Criticism, interpretation, etc.
I. Lacocque, Pierre-Emmanuel, 1952– II. Lacocque, André. Jonah
complex. III. Title. IV. Series
BS1605.2.L33 1990
224'.9206—dc20   89–28569
                                              CIP

To David, Rebecca, Jonathan, Natalie,
Daniel, and Jeremy

*And if we obey God, we must disobey ourselves,
and it is in this disobeying ourselves, wherein the
hardness of obeying God consists.*

*From the sermon of Father Mapple,
in Herman Melville,* Moby-Dick
*(New York: Holt, Rinehart &
Winston, 1957), p. 41.*

CONTENTS

EDITOR'S PREFACE

Critical study of the Bible in its ancient Near Eastern setting has stimulated interest in the individuals who shaped the course of history and whom events singled out as tragic or heroic figures. For example, Rolf Rendtorff's *Men of the Old Testament* (1968) focuses on the lives of important biblical figures as a means of illuminating history, while Fleming James's *Personalities of the Old Testament* (1939) addresses the issue of individuals who function as inspiration for their religious successors in the twentieth century. Other studies restricted to a single individual—e.g., Moses, Abraham, Samson, Elijah, David, Saul, Ruth, Jonah, Job, Jeremiah—have enabled scholars to deal with a host of themes and questions: psychological, literary, theological, sociological, and historical. Some, like Gerhard von Rad's *Moses*, introduce a specific approach to interpreting the Bible, hence provide valuable pedagogic tools.

As a rule, these treatments of individual figures have not provided books accessible to the general public. Some such volumes were written by thinkers who lacked an expert's knowledge of biblical criticism (Freud on Moses, Jung on Job) and whose conclusions, however provocative, remain problematic. Others were targeted for the guild of professional biblical critics (David Gunn on David and Saul, Phyllis Trible on Ruth, Terence Fretheim and Jonathan Magonet on Jonah). Few such books have succeeded in capturing the imagination of a wide audience in the way fictional works like Archibald MacLeish's *J.B.* and Joseph Heller's *God Knows* have done.

The books in this series are written by specialists in the Old Testament for readers who want to learn more about biblical personalities without becoming professional students of the Bible themselves. The volumes throw light on the imaging of deity in biblical times, clarifying ancient understandings of God. Inasmuch as the Bible constitutes human perceptions of God's relationship with the world and its creatures, we seek to discern what ancient writers believed about deity. Although not necessarily endorsing a particular understanding of God, we believe such attempts at making sense of reality contribute something worthwhile to the endless quest for knowledge.

James L. Crenshaw
Duke Divinity School

FOREWORD

What is striking in the history of religions is not the almost universal presence of some important rituals, myths, and symbols, but the fact that their significance is never *exactly* the same. Of course, this considerable variety of meanings is not immediately evident to the nonspecialist. Thus, many followers of the three "religions of the Book" are sometimes embarrassed to discover that a belief, symbol, or rite considered to belong exclusively to *their* faith is in fact profusely distributed throughout the world. On the other hand, agnostics, atheists, or religiously indifferent scholars emphasize triumphantly the almost universal presence of some central symbols and ideas that characterize the biblical and Christian traditions. Thus, when solar mythology was in vogue, scholars and dilettantes discovered solar elements in the Old and the New Testaments and, as a matter of fact, everywhere else in the world. After the publication of *The Golden Bough*, corn-mothers, fertility demons, and dying gods were identified in numberless religions and folklores and, of course, in the Jewish, Christian, and Muslim myths, rituals, and beliefs.

It is useless to multiply examples. Suffice it to say that, leaving aside the grotesque exaggerations of many partisans of solar mythology and of Frazerian or "Myth-and-Ritual" schools, these researchers were correct in pointing out the analogies and the similarities of a great number of mythological themes, symbolisms, and religious structures. In fact, it is difficult to imagine the situation otherwise. As far as we know, from the very beginning prehistoric man was *homo religiosus*, *homo faber*, and *homo ludens*. That is to say, the "sacred" is an element in the structure of consciousness and not a stage in the history of consciousness. Furthermore, the experience of the "sacred" is expressed in a limited number of acts, images, ideas, and narratives. In the case of the three "religions of the Book," their "pagan" analogies are explained by the fact that they developed historically in the context of ancient Near Eastern, Mediterranean, and Hellenistic syncretistic cultures. As a matter of fact, we cannot understand them outside their historical context.

But as I said, for a historian of religions, even more important than the similarities between *religious expressions* belonging to different cultures and periods is the inexhaustible variety of their *significance*. To cite an example: in all the higher cultures of Asia, as well as among archaic societies, the images of cosmos, house, and human body were equivalent; moreover, all of them present, or are susceptible to receive, an "opening" that allows passage into another world. To the "hole" in the sky through which the *axis mundi* passes corresponds the smoke-hole of the house or the "eye" of the dome and, in Indian speculations, the "opening" at the top of the head (*brahmarandhra*), through which the soul escapes at the moment of death.

But Gautama Buddha gave a new and more profound meaning to this traditional anthropocosmic imagery. To express the passage from a conditioned existence to an unconditioned mode of being (*nirvana, samadhi,* etc.), the Buddhist texts utilize a double image, that of breaking through the roof and flying through the air. *Arhats* shatter the roofs of their "houses" (i.e., the skull) and fly up into the sky. This means that the transcending of the human condition is figuratively expressed by the imagery of the destruction of the "house," that is to say, of the personal cosmos that has been chosen for a home. Every "stable dwelling" wherein one is "installed" is equivalent, in Indian thought, to an existential situation that one assumes. But the Buddhist interpretation of "breaking through the roof" proclaims that the *Arhat* has now *abolished* every "situation" and has chosen *not* installation in the world but the absolute freedom that implies the annihilation of every conditioned world.

We may also recall the Christian revalorization of two archaic and universally distributed cosmological symbolisms: the waters (and the immersion in water) and the world tree. In a great many religious contexts, waters are creative, purifying, and regenerative. The church fathers did not fail to explore some of the pre-Christian and universal values of aquatic symbolisms, but they enriched them with new meaning. For Tertullian (*De Baptismo* III–IV), water was the "first seat of divine Spirit," and it was water that "first produced that which has life." Through the descent of the Holy Spirit, waters were sanctified and "in their turn impregnated with sanctifying virtue . . . and procured salvation in eternity." According to John Chrysostom (*Homil. in Job* XXV, 2), baptism represents "death and entombment, life and resurrection. . . . When we plunge our head into water, as into a sepulchre, the old man is immersed, altogether buried; when we come out of the water the new man simultaneously appears." But the valorization of baptism as a descent into the waters of death was made possible, for the Christian, by Christ's descent into the Jordan, that is to say, by an episode in "sacred history." Moreover, the baptism of Christ in the Jordan was compared by the church fathers with Noah, rising victorious from the waters to become the head of a new race, and with Adam (baptismal nakedness being the abandonment of the old vesture of corruption and sin in which Adam had been clothed since the fall).

Likewise, Christianity has utilized, amplified, and revalorized the symbolism of the cosmic tree. A Homily of pseudo-Chrysostom speaks of the cross as a tree that "rises from the earth to the heaven. A plant immortal, it stands at the center of heaven and earth; strong pillar of the universe, bond of all things, support of all the inhabited earth," and so forth. The Byzantine liturgy sings even now, in the day of exaltation of the Holy Cross, of the "tree of life planted in Calvary . . . , which springing from the depths of the earth, has risen to the center of the earth and sanctifies the Universe unto its limits." Many texts compare the cross to a ladder, a column, or a mountain—and these are universally attested images of the "Center of the World," the *axis mundi*. It is as a symbol of the "Center of the World" that the cross has been likened to the cosmic tree. But, of course, for Christians the cross was sanctified through the agony and death of Jesus: it became the instrument of salvation. (We may add, however, that the idea of salvation prolongs and completes the notion of perpetual renovation and cosmic regeneration, of universal fecundity and sanctity, of absolute reality and, in the final reckoning, of immortality—all of which coexist in the symbolism of the world tree; see my *Images and Symbols,* [New York: Sheed & Ward, 1969], pp. 44ff., 161ff.)

The book of Jonah—considered by some theologians to be the most important text of the Old Testament—brilliantly illustrates the revalorization (one is tempted to say re-creation) of some archaic and universally distributed symbols and mythico-ritual scenarios. Apropos of Jonah's flight to Tarshish, one may compare the resistance of the future shaman against his "call," his election by supernatural beings. One need not insist on the rich symbolism of the sea and the tempest. In regard to the swallowing of Jonah by a marine monster, the historian of religions can evoke not only parallel stories (Herakles, the Finnish shaman-sage Vainamoinen, a number of Polynesian heroes, etc.), but also many initiation rites in which the novice is symbolically placed in the body of a giant snake or a marine monster. The significance of such rites is obvious: the novice "dies" to the "natural" life in order to be reborn as a new "spiritual" (i.e., initiated) person.

From a certain point of view, the swallowing of Jonah, and the three days and nights in the whale's belly, can be compared to a *descensus ad infernos,* thus to an initiation rite. But the comparison with the well-known pattern of initiatory death and resurrection (= rebirth) stops here, for Jonah is not *existentially changed* when the whale, on God's order, vomits him on the shore.

André and Pierre-Emmanuel Lacocque do not only elaborate a comparative analysis of such universal themes as resistance to God's call, the sea and tempest, or the symbolism of being swallowed and regurgitated by a marine monster, but their hermeneutical endeavor also concentrates on the new, more complex, and deeper meanings susceptible to decipherment in the book of Jonah. The great merit of their work resides in the minute, delicate, and multilateral analysis of this enigmatic narrative. They critically examine the different interpretations elaborated by Jewish and Christian exegetes from antiquity to our days; they further discuss a number of contemporary evaluations of Jonah's narrative structure, psychological implications, and religious message. It is this interdisciplinary approach—from textual criticism and theology to contemporary psychologies and historical events—that confers a unique value on the work of André and Pierre-Emmanuel Lacocque.

One may wonder why the authors invited a historian of religions to write a foreword to a book manifestly involved in the problems of, and the crises provoked by, the confrontation of the Judeo-Christian message with the contemporary Western world. Perhaps they are aware of the growing risks of "provincialization" of the Judeo-Christian, as well as the entire Mediterranean and Near Eastern, heritage. Although they honestly acknowledge their fidelity to Christianity, perhaps they too ask themselves the question that today obsesses every responsible Western individual: What significance may Jewish-Christian theologies have (in our case, Jonah's saga and its religious and ethical implications) for a Hindu, a Buddhist, or a member of the Third World? We do not know the answer because a genuine and free dialogue among the religions of the world has hardly begun. But in order to pursue a meaningful dialogue with the representatives of non-Western religions, it is indispensable to know at least some of the "universal" symbols, myths, and religious ideas. Certainly, as I said, there is a discontinuity between the shaman's resistance to his "call" and the flight of Jonah to Tarshish as well as between the archaic myths and rites of initiation and Jonah's being swallowed by the whale. But this means that, in a very remote past, *there was a continuity,* interrupted by what the Israelites and the Christians consider as their "sacred history." Nevertheless, if one day Jonah's adventure should interest *religiously* a Hindu or a "primitive," it will be thanks to their "old myths" of the ocean and the marine monsters, of their initiation rituals, and of the sacred stories of shamans and saints who vainly tried to resist the "call" of a divine Being.

Mircea Eliade
University of Chicago

PREFACE

The present edition is an in-depth reworking of our *The Jonah Complex* (Atlanta: John Knox Press, 1981). Anyone familiar with this former version of our study will find differences that go far beyond such matters as style, clarity, and substance. The different dimensions of the biblical book are more pointedly delineated. Using literary criticism and its synchronical and diachronical approach as the royal avenue to the understanding of the work, we again realized how hermeneutically determinative is the discernment of Jonah's literary genre. Even its date is thereby affected. Today we are convinced that the composition of Jonah is from the third century B.C.E.—a difference of some 200 years from the results of our former inquiry. Much is thus changed in the authorship, the audience, the setting in life, the environment, the problematic, even the message. In third-century Palestine, the issue is the Hellenization of the Near East, and the subjects of conversation are universalism and individual salvation. The nagging problem is the nonfulfillment of exilic prophecies for restoration. Internally, the situation is going from bad to worse, and externally the nations are far from humiliated. Many in Jerusalem find a semblance of comfort in the thought that Israel receives the exclusive attention of the living God, while the non-Jews are all but abandoned. The tale of Jonah comes in that context as a protest against such an arrogant isolationism. It is, at any rate, out of the question to see in the narrative something other than fiction. Jonah is a problem story. Once a historicist reading is dismissed, it becomes more evident how much Jonah is dependent upon a universal mythical fount. A synoptic view of the parallels accumulated by historians of religion is illuminating.

Ethnology and depth psychology have therefore something to contribute to an intelligent reading of Jonah. One readily thinks of a name like Carl G. Jung. We shall here speak of his collective unconscious and of its images (in dreams, myths, phantasms). We shall review Jung's developments on the hero and his struggle with the unconscious, a fight that popular epos symbolically describes as a highly expensive quest for a treasure. In the process, the hero is swallowed by monsters or by the netherworld. He may be dismembered and scattered to the four corners of the world, like Osiris or Tammuz. But pious hands gather his *membra disjecta* and reanimate him for the fulfillment of his task. The important interpretive contribution of psychoanalysis will be assessed. We shall follow the leadership of Sigmund Freud, Melanie Klein, Donald Winnicott, Jolande Jacobi, Erich Neumann, Harold Searles, and others. Our hope is to understand better the rich symbolism in the book of Jonah, such as the ship, the fish, the tree, the booth, the threshold, the wind. . . .

As we shall see in the course of this study, however, the authors have consciously kept at bay the fatal snare of "psychologizing" the biblical text. Such was the mistake, for example, of Freud in his *Moses and Monotheism.* Instead of patiently being receptive to the canonized report of Israel, he short-circuited the revelation of the dialogical relationship of Jewish soul with God. He prematurely proceeded to a psychological analysis of religious representations, bringing them together with clinically obtained results. As Paul Ricoeur says in *The Conflict of Interpretations* (Evanston: Northwestern University Press, 1974; p. 349), "He found, at the end of his analysis, only what he knew before undertaking it."

It was imperative not to offer the flank to similar criticism in this book of ours. More decisive yet was not to abstract the tale of Jonah from its biblical context, including all it conveys in terms of theological reflection on history. Jonah is no international fiction although it has borrowed from folktales and myths specific elements and themes. It belongs to Israel's heritage. We had thus to show its deep originality in contrast to other formally parallel stories. Then it becomes feasible to envisage anew the profound human issues of Jonah's narrative. Psychology is interested in the fear of engulfment; the fear of success; the resistance to integrating new discoveries about the self; the ambivalence of intuition; the withdrawal from commitment, from introspection, from loneliness—in short, in all that constitutes the complex of Jonah; and those problems are not foreign to philosophy and theology. These human sciences, in their turn, focus on the narrative's fundamental issue of human and divine justice. They show that, within this framework, it becomes even more risky rigidly to delineate the parameters of human vocation, as well as of human ethics or politics. To shed more light on this question, a comparative study of the narratives on the prophet Elijah in the books of Kings will be attempted. It shows the kinship of the two traditions, and allows one to understand better the issues that the book of Jonah tackles with so much tact and wisdom.

In other words, the present essay on Jonah is not only cross-disciplinary by virtue of the individual expertises of its authors, it is also and above all pluridimensional. One will find here historical criticism (ch. 1–2), literary criticism (ch. 1–2, app), exegesis (ch. 4–7), history of religion (foreword, ch. 3), existential and depth analysis (ch. 8–9), social politics (ch. 1, 6), and, throughout, theology and hermeneutics.

But, of course, to take into consideration such a pluralism in the text makes the task of reading Jonah a complicated endeavor, as well as justifying at the same time the interdisciplinary approach that is ours here. There must be a balanced integration of hermeneutics, exegesis, politics, and psychology. The reader is thus taken sometimes through rough ways as they are not always familiar to him or her. There is, however, no imperative reason why one would stumble upon one or another detail of the exposé. True, in the opinion of the authors, the harmony of the totality is gained through the relationship among all the details, but they are all transcended by the finality of the message, and we come ceaselessly back to it.

This brings us to some reflection upon the composition of this study. Writing a book is always an adventure. It is also an enormously expensive proposition—in time, effort, research, and especially expectation. The personal investment is immeasurable; this is even more true for the authors of this book, for they are father and son. What they have here produced was dear to them even *before* anything was put in writing, for a miracle was occurring, which both will always remember—they were dialoguing, they were experiencing the authentic encounter.

PREFACE

When we started it was not clear to the biblicist that psychology was not some sort of disguised narcissism. The psychologist, on the other hand, was not sure that theology was not a sophisticated way to kid oneself with empty concepts having no real bearing on humanity and the world. Indeed the dialogue started in part because of that mutual curiosity about our respective vocations. For the rest, we started to speak to one another because of a deep mutual respect.

Conversation is never more real than when a terrain is found where each of the two partners has to cover one-third of the distance—one-third for the one, one-third for the other, and one-third for the terrain itself, which, the two partners should acknowledge in advance, will always transcend their reflections and formulations. It is indeed the last third, lying in the center, that allows for the encounter of the other and, perhaps, of God.

The terrain was, we knew, all-important. We decided on Jonah, a biblical book that we thought could be "interesting" for a psychologist and a theologian. We did not know at that time how profoundly moved and enthusiastic (literally, filled with the numinous) we would be through a regular commerce with that unassuming, tongue-in-cheek, understating narrative. From the outset Jonah had features that claimed our attention. A short story told with disarming simplicity by the "singer of tales," its purpose is far from obvious, though its language is familiar to the Bible student. It speaks of the God of Israel, of a Jewish prophet, of well-known places, of an oracle, of attributes of God celebrated in biblical liturgies, of movement of repentance in people and even in God—themes appearing frequently elsewhere in the Scriptures.

The psychologist also felt attuned to Jonah as a popular narrative, a folktale, a parable in a skillfully symbolic form, and he readily recognized this literary piece as a mirror of the soul. Jonah as a character is very human, confronted like an epic hero by extraordinary events and phenomena (not even the dragon is absent), but he is more an antihero than a model of courage and virtue. Such a picaresque personage—some twenty centuries before that literary genre was invented in Europe[1]—was all the more fascinating, since he is the antipode of the Greek "oversized" hero—the hero usually selected by psychological scientists to exemplify the complexes, syndromes, neuroses, and psychoses of John Does confronted in reality by neither father-assassins nor mother-whores, by neither powerful soothsayers nor cryptic sphinxes, but more generally (and it may appear, trivially) by the call (the urge, the drive, the inner necessity)[2] to become what they actually are.

So, is Jonah a "theological" pamphlet or a "psychological" symbolic tale? The literary critic looking at the Bible as literature may consider the religious overtones of the story as culture-bound "externalia." The biblicist, on the contrary, may have the tendency to play down the literary genre and stress the theological construct. But form and content are one, and they must be received together. The story of Jonah is a *story* that happens to belong to a canonical literature, to Israel's Bible. Jonah can be understood only if those two components (biblical and narrative) are equally appreciated. In other words, the exegete, in order to read Jonah, must be more than a biblical theologian, and the literary critic or the psychologist also must reach beyond the usual boundaries of those disciplines.[3]

We had thus to start with the *given:* Jonah is a biblical narrative. What it means for a text to be in the Bible and what it means for that text to be a story had to be appraised from the outset. Further, the historical "setting in life" (*Sitz im Leben*) of the "parable"[4] had to be carefully pondered, since there are texts whose meaning heavily depends upon their setting in life. For example, Jonathan Swift's Gulliver stories must be read as critiques of eighteenth-century England.

Similarly, Jonah is no "world citizen"; he is a Jew. The city to which he is called is not just any metropolis; it is a source of hostility to his people. The message he is commissioned to proclaim is not just any curse; it describes the fate of Sodom and Gomorrah. The denouement is unimaginable outside the Israelite parameters within which the story is told, and the absence of a normal ending tells something about the creative milieu of such tales.

From this perspective, Jonah cannot be confounded by means of a cheap theological anti-Judaism with a petty stiff-necked Jew; nor by means of a facile psychological typology, à la

Molière, with "the coward," or "the reluctant missionary." The singer of the Jonah tale had much more on his mind than a caricature of his own race, and indeed he had too great a respect for his audience to waste their time with a shallow polemical satire, so general in its sway as to be addressed finally to no one. As said above, the historical circumstances of Jerusalem then were not conducive to the light-headed vanities that prevailed at the court of Louis XIV. Jonah was written long after the return from exile, when prophetic promises were not realized. The subsequent frustration in Jerusalem caused some to turn to religious isolationism and to proclaim the advent of theocracy in Zion, while others wrote prophecies like Joel or Zechariah and stories like Ruth or Jonah, protesting against the complacency and the lack of theological vision of the conservative party. The author of Jonah could easily have been so provincial in his interests and so narrow in his scope as to render his story unusable for other times and other peoples. But he was a genius. He molded his specific message to specific opponents in such universal categories that the tableau he painted reveals a profound human character—a character as relevant today as it was then.

Others before us have written about the so-called Jonah syndrome. They intuited in Jonah the presence of profoundly human feelings, but they were content with the stereotyped interpretation of the biblical book in vogue in the Christian church. Jonah thus was a *type*, a caricature, a foil for human virtues. From that perspective, the Jonah syndrome designated a distorted human behavior prompted by narcissism, parochialism, greed, envy. The authors of the present book felt it necessary to reassess the humanity and indeed the universality of the Jonah character, which had been so badly disfigured by preconceived notions. What resulted is expressed especially in our final two chapters.

It has been said above that the interpretation of Jonah depends largely upon the literary genre to which it belongs. As a work of fiction, it is underpinned by the three functions of the discourse, according to Ricoeur: the function of *reference* to world—to a world that is not necessarily ours—raises the *hermeneutical* and fundamental problem of the difference of horizons that must fuse together (cf. Gadamer). The function of *communi-*

cation between the narrator and the reader establishes again a hermeneutical situation, but also a *political* one. Furthermore, to the extent that the communication between individuals is indeed mediation of the divine communication itself, it implies a *theological* level. The third narrative function is the one of *self-understanding*. There is reading only when there is conscious awakening. There is understanding of the narrative only when there is transforming reception of the message. The text is revealing. It forces me to face myself. In a way it re-presents me; it gives me a presence I lacked before. We then pass on to a *psychological* level.[5]

In this respect, the book of Jonah is particularly illustrative, hence the very title of this essay that combines the tasks of explanation and understanding. A true reading opens up the way to many more right readings. Already from that point of view, the scope of our inquiry, although clearly defined by the four chapters of a straightforward biblical story, transcends its boundaries. Not only is the tale of Jonah illustrative, it is also exemplary. That is why we confess that our ambition in this book goes beyond the limits of reading the book of Jonah. The brief biblical book, when considered in its entirety and in an uncompromising hermeneutical fashion, is a paradigm for the whole biblical narrative genre. On the other hand, to the extent that we succeeded in "weeding out" the theological language, and in "substantializing" the psychological idiom thanks to the theological contribution, there is here a conscious effort to express biblical concepts in nonreligious language—as Dietrich Bonhoeffer said. This is one of the aims of our book: the demonstration that existential and depth psychology in cross-cultural rapport with biblical disciplines is able to provide a language that can be understood by our contemporaries.

Such language conveys a message respectful of its audience. The author of Jonah did not become tactless in his polemics against the conservative party in power in Jerusalem. The least that modern expositors can do is to learn that lesson from Jonah and not to indulge in a cheap reduction of its hero to the dimension of a contemptible dwarf. No indeed, Jonah has nothing to do with a petty insubstantial Jew conceived by the deranged mind of an anti-Semite. Jonah is Everyman, and like Everyman he is under the commandment to respond to his human vocation. Jonah must not become Moses, he must become Jonah, which recalls a profound Hasidic story. If he is unwilling to yield to the call, it is not because he is subhuman, the by-product of an obstinate race, but simply because he is a human being. What he imagines about himself has become more important, more attractive, than what the commandment (vocation, call) tells him he actually is. It even happens that the Being-Object, which has no voice other than his own, is to him dearer than the Being-Subject, who speaks and says things he finds repulsive (see Jon. 4:2).

Unless . . . yes, unless all this be only a surface reading. In the image of this extraordinary narrative that comes to an inconclusive end, we must perhaps leave open the possibility that all is not said at the close of the literary, exegetical, psychological, and theological analysis. Perhaps the story of Jonah escapes all psychoanalytical or hemeneutical encircling. It may be that the resistance of Jonah to the "outer voice" is not just a manifestation of a universal complex but—as in the story of Job—the daring ultimate act of a man opposing his justice to the justice of God in the name of the countless Jewish victims—at the hands of Ninevites, at the hands of Nazis—of a paradoxically merciful God.

NOTES

1. We shall discover below the intermediary link.
2. St. Augustine speaks of the "inner master."
3. Among Bible scholars there is reluctance to use psychological categories. Such a dictate of an unwarranted principle betrays "a curious fundamentalistic survival within critical scholarship," as Heikki Räisänen says (*Paul and the Law*, [Tübingen: J. C. B. Mohr 1983], p. 232). There is certainly a danger in "psychologizing" a text or a symbol. There is psychologization when such text or symbol is "judged ultimately by its emotive or conative affects" (P. Wheelwright, *The Burning Fountain* [Bloomington: Indiana University Press, 1954], p. 45). Psychology, like history or sociology, is but one dimension of the symbol. It must not be overstated (so as to become the "ultimate judge"), but its underestimation blocks the road to existential appropriation.
4. The term is provisionary; it designates a genre that is always world-subverting, says John D. Crossan (see below, chap. 2).
5. See Paul Ricoeur, *Time and Narrative*, vol. 1 (Chicago: University of Chicago Press, 1985).

ACKNOWLEDGMENT

We express here our thanks to so many people who contributed to the creation of this book. More particularly, we want to mention our respective wives, Claire and Vickie, and also the Chicago Theological Seminary, which organized courses on Jonah that we taught together, and helped us financially to produce this essay.

André LaCocque
Pierre-Emmanuel Lacocque

JONAH

A Psycho-Religious Approach
to the Prophet

THE BOOK OF JONAH:
A Translation

Once upon a time the word of the Lord came to Jonah ben Amittai, saying: "Arise! Go to Nineveh, the great city, with the proclamation against her that her evil has flown in my face."

But instead Jonah rose to flee to Tarshish from the Presence of the Lord! He went down to Joppa where he found a ship bound for Tarshish. He paid its fare and went down inside to go with them to Tarshish, from the Lord's Presence. Then the Lord hurled a great wind toward the sea, and it became such a great sea storm that one thought the ship was being wrecked. The sailors became frightened and they cried out to their respective gods; they hurled into the sea the ship's wares to lighten it. Meanwhile Jonah had gone down to the vessel's hold. He was lying there sound asleep.

(6)   The captain came near to him and asked him, "How can you sleep so soundly? Arise! Call to your god. Perhaps that god will notice us and we won't perish."

Then the sailors said one to another: "Come, let's cast lots to find out why this evil is upon us." So they cast lots and the lot fell on Jonah. They thus said to him, "Tell us now, whose fault is it that this evil is upon us? What is your job? Where do you come from? What is the name of your country and of your people?" He

1

said to them, "I am a Hebrew, and I fear the Lord, the God of heaven, who has made sea and land alike." Then the men became very frightened and they asked him, "How could you do this?" For the men knew from Jonah's own admission that he was flee-ing from the Lord's Presence. They said to him, "What should we do to you that the sea may calm down—for the sea grows stormier." He said to them, "Pick me up and hurl me into the sea; then the sea will calm down. I know that it is on account of me that this great storm is upon you." However, the men started to paddle hard toward the shore but without success, for the sea grew still stormier against them. Then they called to the Lord and they said, "Please, Lord, let us not perish on account of this one man. Do not place upon us the onus of innocent blood, for you are the Lord, and you do as you please." They then picked up Jonah and hurled him into the sea—and the sea stopped its raging. Then the men feared the Lord greatly; they offered a sac-rifice to the Lord, and bound themselves by oaths.

Chapter 2

But the Lord appointed a great fish to swallow Jonah, and Jonah remained in the fish's bowels for three days and three nights. And Jonah prayed to the Lord, his God, from the fish's bowels and said:

I called in my distress to the Lord, and He answered me;
From the belly of Sheol I cried for help—You heard my voice.
You cast me into the depth, into the heart of the seas.
A current whirled around me;
Your breakers and waves all swept over me.
Then I thought, "I am driven away from Your sight,
    But I persist in gazing at Your holy Temple!"
Waters choked me to death; the Abyss whirled around me;
    Weeds were tangled about my head.
(7)   To the base of the mountains I descended;
    Of the earth the bars were forever locked on me.
Yet You lifted my life from the pit, O Lord, my God.
As my soul was faint within me, I remembered the Lord;
    My prayer came unto You, unto Your holy Temple.
Those who adhered to futile idols may abandon their loyalty,
But as for me, with a song of gratitude

A TRANSLATION

I shall bring offerings to You;
what I have vowed I will fulfill.
Salvation is the Lord's!

Then on the Lord's order, the fish spewed Jonah out on the shore.

Chapter 3

So the word of the Lord came to Jonah a second time, saying: "Arise! Go to Nineveh, the great city; let her hear the proclamation I am telling you." Jonah arose and went to Nineveh as he had been told by the Lord. Now Nineveh was a city of huge dimensions; it took three days to walk across it. Jonah entered the city and walked for a day; then he made this proclamation: "Yet forty days and Nineveh shall be overthrown!"

(5) The people of Nineveh believed God, and they proclaimed a fast and donned sackcloth, from the greatest to the least of them. And when word reached the king of Nineveh he rose from his throne, stripped himself of his royal vestment, and, covered only with sackcloth, he sat in ashes. Then he had it promulgated in Nineveh: "By order of the king and his court: Neither man nor beast in herd or flock shall even taste anything; they shall neither graze nor drink water; they are to cover themselves with sackcloth, both human and beast, and fervently to invoke God. Everyone must repent from his evil way of living, from the violence of his deed. Who knows but that God may repent and be forgiving, for if He turns away from His burning wrath, we shall not perish!"

(10) God considered what they were doing, how they repented from their evil way of living; so God relented concerning the evil He had thought to do to them, and He did not do it.

Chapter 4

But Jonah resented this greatly and was incensed. He prayed to the Lord and said, "Now Lord, is not this what I thought while yet on my own turf? That's why I fled in the first place to Tarshish, for I knew all along that You are a gracious and merciful God, slow to anger, rich in kindness, and forgiving of evil intention. Now then, Lord, take back my life, for I'd rather die than live." And the Lord said, "Is it fair for you to be angry?"

(5) Jonah left the city and sat to the east of it. He made himself a booth on the spot to sit under its shade until he would see what

3

was going to happen to the city. Then the Lord God appointed a plant to grow up over Jonah to form a shade over his head and relieve him from his discomfort. And Jonah had an immense joy on account of the plant. But at dawn on the following day, God appointed a worm to attack the plant so that it withered. Moreover, when the sun rose, God appointed a stifling east wind; the sun beat upon Jonah's head and he became faint. So Jonah asked for death, saying, "I'd rather die than live!"

(9)

And God said to Jonah; "Is it fair for you to be incensed about the plant?" He answered, "Till my last breath, it is fair!" Then the Lord said, "You, you found it a pity about a plant for which you did not labor nor did you make it grow, and which from one night to the next lived and then perished. And I—shall I not take pity upon Nineveh, the great city, in which there are more than 120,000 people who do not know their right hand from their left, and many beasts as well?"

PART I

HISTORICITY, GENRE, AND SYMBOLISM

ONE

HISTORICITY, SETTING, AND LANGUAGE

In trying to decide what a great man meant by his original formulations, it is always good to find out what he was talking *against* at the time.

Erik H. Erikson, *Young Man Luther: A Study of Psychoanalysis and History* (New York: W. W. Norton, 1961), p. 218.

The book of Jonah is unique in Scriptures. It bears the name of a prophet of Israel, but the only "oracle" it reports consists of a single sentence: "Yet forty days and Nineveh shall be overthrown." More important is the person of the prophet, which, by contrast with a general situation in the Bible, comes to the fore with a negative attitude toward vocation, as he becomes the mouthpiece of his God in a far-away and ill-famed city. There are a number of elements that distinguish this book from all other prophetic books, and which might lead one to conclude that Jonah is not representative of the prophets in the Bible and is perhaps even unimportant. In fact, however, in the words of Elias Bickerman:

> The Book of Jonah contains only forty-eight verses according to the reckoning of the ancient Hebrew scribes. But the name of no prophet is better known to the man in the street. Jonah is that man who was swallowed alive by a whale and was spewed up three days later, unhurt. . . . Celsus . . . suggested that the Christians should worship not Jesus but Jonah or Daniel, whose miracles outdo the Resurrection.[1]

7

HISTORICITY, GENRE, AND SYMBOLISM

Thus, despite the fact that the episode of the "whale" occupies only a couple of verses and is by no means central to the book, it is precisely this motif that struck the imagination of readers. Its popular nature easily touched deep fibers, and it is not in the least paradoxical that so many attempts have been made to "prove" its historical character. Bickerman continues:

> In modern times exegetes have often tried to vindicate the episode by quoting sailor yarns. Two years after the publication of Darwin's *On the Origin of Species* Canon Pusey collected some such old salt's tales in his commentary on Jonah (1861). . . . Despite the discomfort the story arouses in the faithful, its literal historicity was declared as late as 1956 in a Catholic encyclopedia, and admitted albeit half heartedly, in a Protestant biblical dictionary in 1962.[2]

So the problem of "authenticity" is one of the main questions at the outset of our study. It is directly dependent upon the literary genre of the book. Should we understand the story of Jonah as history or as fiction? James D. Smart puts forth several arguments to show that the latter possibility is the only viable one. We shall, below, indicate how still other elements prove that he is correct. First he calls attention to the fact that we have in the book of Jonah a complete absence of historical data. The monarch of Nineveh is not named; rather, he is called "king of Nineveh," an unusual and indeed unique expression in biblical and extrabiblical annals. The narrative is but a sequence of miracles (the sea calmed, the psalm in the fish's belly, the message of Jonah uttered in a foreign language, the conversion of the whole city, the tree that grew in one night and its destruction by a worm, the dimension of Nineveh, etc.). Besides, asks Smart, what would be the nature of such a record whose ostensible aim lay in demeaning a prophet of Israel? Who would write this, and for what purpose?[3]

If, however, we consider the possibility that the tale of Jonah be some kind of parable, we find abundant and striking parallels elsewhere in the Bible (e.g., 2 Sam. 12:1ff.; Isa. 5; etc.). But if it is a parable, that is, a literary vignette making a specific point, then the object of that parable becomes a moot and complicated question. According to Smart, the aim of Jonah is to express caustic opposition to the hostility toward the non-Jews in Israel after the exile. Jonah, as the main character of the narrative, appears "absurd," "idiotic," "ludicrous in the extreme," as a "sulky child," and the like, and the text of 4:2 would constitute the point of the whole parable, that is, Jonah's rejection of the God of the fathers because of his mercifulness.

As it is, Smart's reading is widely accepted in the church. It has become customary to see Jonah as a petty, narrow-minded, and stiff-necked representative of his stubborn people, and anti-Semites have always found in this book a fertile ground for their poisonous seeds. Even as careful an exegete as Gerhard von Rad—whom we quote here as a foil to anti-Semitism—called Jonah a "religions-psychologisches Monstrum"![4]

On the contrary, Bickerman entitled one of his chapters "Jonah as Friend of Israel." He sees in the reluctant attitude of the hero an unwillingness to betray his own people for the sake of speaking the word of God to the archenemies of his nation.

> And why should he be pained to death at the display of divine mercy? . . . The traditional Jewish explanation was that Jonah, being a prophet, knew in advance that Nineveh would repent and be saved. But that would put to shame stiff-necked Israel. "Since the heathen are nearer to repentance, I might be causing Israel to be condemned." The prophet knew, says Jerome, that "the repentance of the Gentiles would be the downfall of the Jews."[5]

Such is the reading of Jonah by the synagogue on Yom Kippur,[6] and one will remember that the New Testament puts the story in the same light: the Ninevites shall raise up an accusation against Jesus' generation . . . (Matt. 12:41 and parallel). Compare *Midrash on Lamentations,* Intr. No. 31: "I sent one prophet to Nineveh and he brought it to penitence and conversion. And these Israelites in Jerusalem—how many prophets have I sent to them!"[7]

Be that as it may for now, it is clear that the bulk of the evidence leans toward the fictitious character of the book of Jonah.[8] There is, however, at least one element in the narrative that re-

vives the whole problem, namely, the presentation of the hero in
1:1: "And the word of the Lord came unto Jonah the son of Amittai. . . ." This name comes directly from 2 Kings 14:25 where we
read, "Jeroboam II restored the border of Israel from the en-
trance of Hamath unto the sea of Arabah, according to the word
of the Lord, the God of Israel, which he spoke through his servant Jonah the son of Amittai, the prophet, who was of Gath-
Hepher." This is the only reference in the Bible to an eighth-
century prophet by the name of Jonah under the reign of
Jeroboam II. This king, as is well known, is condemned severely
by the Deuteronomistic historians, authors of the books of Kings,
and it is all the more surprising that he receives the promise, by
an oracle of the prophet Jonah, that his country would extend so
far as to reach the dimensions of the Davidic empire. Evidently
Jewish tradition could not read 2 Kings 14:25 as a mere prediction of bliss to a wicked king. Was there no way to suspect the
prophet Jonah ben Amittai of being a false witness? No, for he is
mentioned in the text of 2 Kings as God's "servant" and
"prophet." The midrash (cf. *PRE* 10; *Midrash on Jonah* 96) then
imagines that Jonah had had the task of proclaiming the destruction of Jerusalem, but his prophecy did not materialize and
Jonah was therefore known as "the false prophet." When sent to
Nineveh to prophesy the downfall of the city, he knew in advance
that the heathens would do penance and decided not to go. This
rabbinic development is all the more interesting in that modern
scholars have, on the basis of 2 Chronicles 13:22; 24:27, suggested that the tale of Jonah is a midrash on the books of Kings.[9]
Hans Schmidt, for example, thinks that Nineveh is a substitute
for Jerusalem, a literary device used by the poet in order to render
his argument more cogent by selecting a pagan city that God for-
gave because of the presence of just ones in its midst.[10] The book
of Jonah, continues Schmidt, must be read together with the prophecies of Jeremiah and Ezekiel, who had condemned the city before 586; Jonah's composition also is to be dated before the exile.
    Such a stance is, however, unwarranted. We shall show below
(chap. 2) that this dating is impossible, if only because Jonah's
literary genre was invented centuries after the exile in Babylon.

Suffice it for now to notice, with Adolphe Lods,[11] that prior to 586 the problem was not the inefficacy of repentance; on the contrary, the prophets made their oracles of doom conditional. But the illusion of the nation was precisely that repentance was unnecessary. It may be that people took refuge in interpreting texts such as Genesis 18, speculating that there always would be some righteous people in the city to repent and thus save the community at a low price for all. But Jonah's argument takes us in another direction. It shows the repentance of a whole city, even a pagan and wicked city. Moreover, it would be at least strange to see Jonah balking at the idea of announcing the destruction of Nineveh (Jerusalem?[12]), while it is pointed to by critics how many parallels exist between the prophet and Jeremiah-Ezekiel.

A slightly different version of the preceding historical thesis focuses on the character of Jonah himself. It is assumed that he may have been a nationalistic prophet of the north who backed up even such a wicked king as Jeroboam II because of his policy of expansion.[13] This version is a variant of the one mentioned earlier. Here the one who passes through conversion is Jeroboam II, thanks to the ministry of Jonah, and the latter is thus rightly called "prophet" and "servant" in the text of 2 Kings. The two versions have, in fact, a single meaning. The tale found in the book of Jonah would involve a shift from wickedness to righteousness by means of a dramatic conversion. Either way a negative note would be followed by a positive one. A refinement of the theory sees the eighth-century prophet speaking to Jeroboam II in order to bring him to repentance even though he himself was displeased both by his commission and by the outcome of his message to the king. Much later, the author of the book of Jonah transposed the historical situation into a fictional one in which a prophet of Israel was sent to the wicked Ninevites to proclaim their doom. Unexpectedly, however, he brought them to their knees and they turned to the living God, but in this the storyteller radically altered the nature of his model. Leaving history behind, he resorted to the story—indeed to a parable with symbolic meaning. Even the name "Jonah" leaves the realm of actuality and enters the universe of symbols (cf. below).

None of these solutions seems to us right. With them, however, our inquiry has gone one step further. If it is taken for
granted now that Jonah is no historical report, are we permitted
then to read the tale as symbolic and even as allegorical?[14] In the
latter case, Jonah would represent Israel, and Nineveh the world,
while the fish would be the symbol of the exile in Babylon.[15] We
shall take exception to this reading on several counts, but it seems
to us incontestable that there are a certain number of symbols or
metaphors in Jonah, while the book as a whole is itself a metaphor or parable. We shall discuss this point more fully below.
This view is not new; the rabbis saw in Jonah a personification of
Israel, playing even with the word *yônāh* ("dove"), which in the
Song of Solomon designates Israel. In the Talmud the same symbolism is found in *Shabbat* 130a.[16] This and other textual evidence
of the metaphoric meaning of the name "Jonah" point in a direction that is worthy of exploration.

Before we do this, however, we must first explore another issue. The unity of composition of the book has been disputed in
the recent past. W. Boehme feels that it is a mixture of four main
sources—in many respects on the model of the Pentateuch—
namely J, E, an addition to J, and a redaction of JE.[17] Hans
Schmidt also sees a series of additions, as for instance the psalm
of 2:3–10 (inserted there because the shift from the prayer in vs.
2 to the Lord's pardon in vs. 11 was deemed too abrupt); in 3:6–9
(on the king of Nineveh); in 1:4a, 5a, 9b, 13–14 and all the details
concerning Jonah's sleep and his dialogue with the skipper.[18]

Today, however, only the psalm in chapter 2 is thought to be
a later addition. We call attention to the absence of Aramaisms
there in comparison with the rest of the book. Moreover, there
are in the Psalter close parallels to that psalm of thanksgiving,
and the occasion of the parallels is often a narrow escape from
fatal danger. In the course of our commentary we shall defend
another stance, convinced as we are that the psalm has been inserted where it now stands by the author himself. The differences
in style and vocabulary are owing to the difference of genres
(from prose to poetry with many loans from older psalms).

The book of Jonah presents, indeed, a remarkably balanced
structure, which makes it "a model of literary artistry, marked by

symmetry and balance."[19] To wit, the outline of the tale proposed by Leslie C. Allen:

I. A Hebrew sinner is saved (1:1–2:end)
  A. Jonah's disobedience (1:1–3)
  B. Jonah's punishment; heathens' homage (1:4–16)
  C. Jonah's rescue (1:17–2:10 [Hebrew 2:1–11])
    1. God's grace (1:17)
    2. Jonah's praise (2:1–9)
    3. God's last work (2:10)
II. Heathen sinners are saved (3:1–4:11)
  A. Jonah's disobedience (3:1–4)
  B. Nineveh's repentance (3:5–9)
    1. God's grace (3:10)
    2. Jonah's plaint (4:1–3)
    3. God's last word (4:4–11)

Moreover the leitmotif of the book is found in all of its parts, with the notable exception of the psalm in chapter 2, for obvious reasons. So, we read "Nineveh the great city" in 1:2; 3:2–3; 4:11, while the attribute "great" is used about other things: wind (1:4); storm (1:4, 12); fish (2:1); fear (1:10, 16); wickedness (4:1); joy (4:6); see also 3:5, 7; 4:10. One finds paronomasia in 1:16; 3:2; 4:6; 3:10–4:1; repetition in 1:7, 11–12; 3:10; 4:5; cf. 2:1–11. . . . Even the divine names as used in the book contribute to the cohesion of the whole, a point missed by Boehme. In association with Jonah, God appears always as YHWH (with the exception of 4:6–9; see below). In relation to the sailors, God is Elohim (1:6), but after being presented to them by Jonah, he becomes YHWH (1:14–15). In relation to Nineveh he is, of course, Elohim (3:5–10), and the condemnation is made on the basis of general ethical crimes, that is, wicked relations between people and their neighbors—4:6–9 constitutes an exception; there God appears to Jonah as Elohim. It is noteworthy, however, that the context is one of nature. As God of nature, God is Elohim (as in the book of Job, chaps. 38–42, for instance).[20] He becomes YHWH again when nature is replaced by history and when God's mercy is again emphasized (4:10).

The unexpected coupling of YHWH and Elohim as a composite name occurs, on the model of Genesis 2:4ff., in Jonah 1:9; 2:2; and 4:6. There is no problem with 1:9 and 2:2; in 4:6 it is both the God of nature, Elohim, and the covenantal God of Jonah, YHWH, who permits a *qîqāyôn* tree to grow in order to test Jonah (as in Gen. 22, for instance).[21]

The book is thus a whole and, following the lead of Gabriel H. Cohn, we shall speak of "aspects" of a holistic work rather than "parts" or "elements" or even "layers."[22] Is it possible to fix the date of composition of this tale? Indeed, the question can be answered with a high degree of certainty. For, despite the absence of historical allusions in the book, its literary appertaining is decisive, as we shall see in chapter 2, below. Moreover, it is evident that Nineveh is described in terms that seem to be mythical rather than historical, indicating that the city had been destroyed long before Jonah was written, and thus had become the occasion of fantastic speculations as to its dimensions and power. The size of Nineveh according to Jonah 3:3 does not correspond with the relatively modest measurements proposed by archaeologists. Nineveh, which was utterly destroyed in 612, by Cyaxarus, did not exceed eight miles in circumference. However, André Parrot has suggested that Nineveh as described in the book of Jonah may have designated a triangular territory with an uninterrupted succession of cities from Chorsabad in the north to Nimrud in the south on a stretch of forty kilometers. In this case 120,000 human beings would not be an exaggerated estimate of population.[23] We must therefore turn to other evidence in order to determine the date of Jonah.

More decisive are arguments based on vocabulary and style. The book presents numerous examples of late Hebrew and of Aramaic forms of Hebrew words. For example, in Jonah 1:4 the term translated "to be thought to" (+ verb) is used in classical Hebrew strictly for persons, never for inanimate objects. In 1:9 the expression "God of Heavens" is coined on the model of Zoroastrian formulas[24] and its use is confined mainly to texts written in Persian times and after (see Neh. 1:4–5; 2:4; Ezra 1:2; 5:11–12; 6:9–10; 7:21, 23; Dan. 2:18, 37, 44; 4:34; 5:23; 2 Chron. 36:23). In 4:2 the preposition translated by "when" or by "while" is a Hebrew preposition with an Aramaic meaning absent in classical Hebrew. In 1:5 the term translated "mariner" or "sailor" appears elsewhere only in Ezekiel 27. The term translated "vessel" (1:5) is a *hapax legomenon* in Hebrew but is common in Aramaic and Arabic. In 1:6 the verb translated "to care" or "to think upon" is found with this meaning only in Daniel 6:3. In 2:1; 4:6; 4:7a, 7b, the verb "to prepare" is found only in late Hebrew and Aramaic. As a final and quite convincing example, we note 3:7 where the verb "to cause" or "to command" is found only here in a Hebrew text, while it is frequent in the Aramaic of Ezra and Daniel (Ezra 4:19, 21; 5:3, 9, 13, 17; 6:1, 3, 8, 11, 12; 7:13, 21; Dan. 3:10, 29; 4:3; 6:27).

From a grammatical and syntactic point of view one notices the use of the particle *še* (1:7, 12; 4:10), which comes from Syriac and Aramaic. In 4:6 the verb "to save" is followed by a preposition with the dative instead of the accusative as in classical Hebrew.

It has recently been suggested that some of these peculiarities are owing to Phoenician influence rather than Aramaic because of the sea setting of the story,[25] but this explanation does not help in dating Jonah. In some respects this argument recalls the rabbinic opinion according to which Jonah was from Zebulun (see 2 Kings 14:25 [Gath-Hepher]; cf. Josh. 19:10, 13 [Zebulun]). So believed R. Levi (d. ca. 300 C.E.). R. Johanan preferred to think of the tribe of Asher.[26] But in order for the linguistic argument to hold, the Phoenician influence should be felt only where the story has a sea setting, namely, chapters 1–2. Why would it also be the case in chapters 3–4, which are set in Mesopotamia? Moreover, it seems wrong to view Jonah as a Phoenician tale adapted to Israelite conditions, since Jonah is too typical a Jewish story, understandable only within a Jewish *Weltanschauung*.[27]

Linguistic information is not the only evidence to be considered with respect to the question of the date of the book of Jonah. We have noted before the expression "God of Heavens," which makes the reader think of Persia. Another clue is provided by the participation of animals in mourning rites, which recalls what Herodotus said about the Persians (*Hist.* IX, 24). Furthermore, the association of the nobles with the king in decision-making is a markedly Persian procedure hitherto unknown in the histories of Israel or Assyria (see Ezra 7:14; Dan. 6:16; Esth. 1:13; Herodotus, *Hist.* III.31). On the other hand, such a consulting of the elite by the king or the head of an assembly is, of course, richly illustrated among the Greeks.

More important, the anthological character of the book of Jonah contributes to the solution of the problem of dating the work. The parallel with the books of Kings has been noted, and we referred to 2 Kings 14:25, which introduces the eighth-century prophet Jonah ben Amittai. There are, moreover, parallels between the prophet Jonah and the prophet Elijah. Some of those parallels may appear to be accidental, such as Jonah 4:5–6 in parallel with 1 Kings 19:9, 14. But others seem to be intentional and carry an ironic tone that is hard to miss. So Jonah 4:2–3 parallels 1 Kings 19:4, and Jonah 4:9 parallels 1 Kings 19:14. That connection is all the more interesting in that Elijah and Elisha are the only prophets who were sent to pagans, according to 1 Kings 17; 2 Kings 7ff. (cf. 8:7–15, Elisha in Damascus).[28]

The parallelism with the book of Jeremiah is still more impressive. Besides the fact that Jeremiah is called "prophet of the nations" (1:5), and that he appears as one of those prophets who try to escape their mission (see 9:1; 20:9), the parallel between Jonah 3 and Jeremiah 36 is especially striking. The two texts envision the possibility of the nonfulfillment of divine oracles in the case of conversion (Jer. 36:2–3; Jon. 3:8–9). Moreover, the very pattern of events in the two texts is parallel. To the threat expressed in Jeremiah 36:7b and Jonah 3:4 corresponds a fast in Jeremiah 36:9 and Jonah 3:5, where the same expression is used (whereas Joel, for instance, uses another one; see 1:14 and 2:15); the king with his court is addressed in both texts (Jer. 36:12, 20; Jon. 3:6); and the response of the king of Nineveh in Jonah 3:6–8 and that of Jehoiakim in Jeremiah 36:24 stand in direct opposition to each other (Jon. 3:10 and Jer. 36:29–31).

On the literary level also, the parallels between Jonah and Jeremiah are numerous. "Make the proclamation" of Jonah 3:2 (cf. 1:2) is in parallel with Jeremiah 2:2; 4:5; 7:2; 11:6; 19:2; and 20:8. The expression in Jonah 3:5 "from the greatest of them even to the least of them" is found in the reverse order in Jeremiah 6:13; 8:10; 42:1, 8; 44:12. The expression "man and beast" of Jonah 3:7–8 and 4:11 has textual parallels in Jeremiah 7:20; 21:6; 27:5; 31:27; 32:43; 33:12. The pathetic question of Jonah 3:9, "Who knows?" corresponds to similar expressions in Jeremiah 21:2; 26:3; 36:3–7; 51:8 ("perhaps," says Jon. 1:6). The expression of Jonah 3:9 "his burning wrath" occurs in Jeremiah 4:8, 26; 12:13; 25:37, 38; 30:24; 49:37; 51:45. "Nineveh the great city" in Jonah 1:2; 3:2; 4:11 stands in parallel with Jeremiah 22:8, which speaks of Jerusalem.[29] Jonah 1:14 "do not place upon us the onus of innocent blood" finds its parallel in Jeremiah 26:15 "if you put me to death, you will bring innocent blood upon yourselves, and upon this city, and upon the inhabitants thereof." Thus, in the conclusion of a detailed study of the sources of the book of Jonah, André Feuillet can state: "Jeremiah, the prophet of the nations, constitutes the main source for the author of Jonah."[30]

The book of Jonah also borrows from Ezekiel. In the Hebrew Scriptures there are only two shipwreck narratives besides Jonah 1:Psalm 107:23–32 and Ezekiel 27. Chapters 26–28 of Ezekiel forecast the fall of the city of Tyre through the allegory of a splendid ship armed by all nations, which eventually founders "in the midst of the seas." From this passage in Ezekiel, Jonah has borrowed several words and expressions. The term "mariners" of Jonah 1:5, as we saw, is found elsewhere only in Ezekiel 27:9, 27, 29. The word "pilot" of Jonah 1:6 is found elsewhere only in Ezekiel 27:8, 27, 28, 29. Ezekiel 27:25–28 especially seems to have been used by the author of the book of Jonah. In both places we find expressions such as "Tarshish," "an east wind" (cf. Jon. 4:8), "to be broken" (cf. Jon. 1:4), and "cries" recur no fewer than six times in Ezekiel 27 and 28 (cf. Jon. 2:4). André Feuillet is correct, however, in calling attention to the sharp contrast introduced by the author of Jonah. Whereas Ezekiel described the fate of the foreign and adverse city of Tyre, here it is the Israelite hero himself who is lost in the "heart of the seas."[31] This reversal of situation is a feature that will come up again in the discussion below of the cultural setting of Jonah (see chap. 2, below).

There is probably no conclusion to be drawn from the textual parallels between Jonah and Joel (cf. Jon. 3:9a with Joel 2:14a;

Jon. 4:2 with Joel 2:13); the common expressions are liturgical and can be found in a number of other texts (see Exod. 34:6; Pss. 86:15; 103:8; Neh. 9:17). However, we have left unmentioned until now the parallel that seems to be the most important one, although it has never been invoked by critics so far as we know. It is an oracle of Third Isaiah, which will also clarify the symbolic meaning of the name "Jonah." For the name of the prophet unmistakably evokes the figurative meaning of *yônāh*, "the dove," as found in quite a number of biblical texts. True, they represent different points of view. The dove is noted for its plaintive cooing (Isa. 38:14; 59:11), for its foolishness (Hos. 7:11), for its power of flight (Ps. 55:6), and for its loyalty to its mate and its gentleness (Song of Sol. 2:14; 5:2; 6:9). In general it is a "clean" animal mentioned with affection, and in many cases it designates metaphorically the people of Israel (Pss. 68:13; 74:19; Hos. 7:11; 11:11). In *Targum Song of Songs* 2:12 "the voice of the turtle dove" is understood as meaning "the voice of the holy spirit of redemption" (cf. Matt. 3:16). George A. F. Knight goes even further and renders the whole name "Jonah b. Amittai" as the Dove Son of Truth.[32] The "Dove" is Israel (see especially Hos. 11:11; in Pss. 55:6 and 56:1, the Masoretic text has *yônāh*, but the Septuagint translates "congregation" or "people") and the "Truth" is the Torah (see Ps. 119). Thus the dove filled with truth is invited to share the Torah with the nations, according to Knight, but he refuses. He is punished by exile to Babylon (Jer. 51:34, 44 shows clearly that the fish in Jonah represents just that).

Provocative as these suggestions are, we propose here a more potent motive why the author chose the name *yônāh* for his hero by invoking Third Isaiah. Isaiah 60 proleptically celebrates all nations with their kings, their riches, and their animals coming to the light of Jerusalem. They come like doves (*yônim*, vs. 8) and at their head are ships (*oniyoth*, cf. Jon. 1:3) of Tarshish (vs. 9)! The borrowing goes much further. It implies at times what Albert Lord calls "compositional themes," that is, recurring elements with a high degree of similarity in wording. At times also the parallels fall rather in the category of "type-scenes," namely, repeated elements or details that are not always found in the same order or to the same extent as their duplicates, "but enough of which are present to make the scene a recognizable one."[33] Each of the imperatives in Isaiah 60:1 ("arise," "shine") belongs to one of these categories. "Arise" is used in Jonah 1:1, so that both texts have the same beginning. "Shine" is clearly reminiscent of Second Isaiah's "light of the nations" (42:6; 49:6) and is here illustrated by the prophet Jonah's going to Nineveh. In Isaiah 60:3 the nations go toward the light, that is, toward Jerusalem. Jonah reverses the formula: the prophet goes toward the darkness of Nineveh. Isaiah 60:5 is about the joy of Jerusalem, Jonah about the bitterness of the prophet. As hinted at above, Isaiah 60:8 provides the key for understanding the symbolism of the name "Jonah." It is ironic in our book. According to Isaiah 60, the nations fly like "Jonahs" (*yônim*) to Jerusalem, and Jonah is ordered to fly like a *yônāh* from Jerusalem to Nineveh. But if he stands up as ordered, it is to flee away and go down (1:3), while, in going to Jerusalem, one always goes up. In another similar contrast, the wickedness of Nineveh is going up to God. Jonah goes even deeper into the ship's, and eventually into the fish's, entrails. The "dove" has become a crouching dog!

Isaiah 60:10 mentions the *bene-nekar* ("strangers") among those who come to Jerusalem and then "their kings" in that order. Jonah 3 also mentions the Ninevites, then their king. "For in my wrath (*qeṣep̄*) I smite them," says God, according to Isaiah; Jonah 4:1, 9 uses another word to describe Jonah's anger (*ḥarah*, three times) but the parallel is unmistakable. Isaiah 60:19–20 was the inspiration for Jonah 3:5ff. Isaiah 60:21 reads "your people . . . shall be a branch of my planting"; it becomes a *qîqāyôn* tree in Jonah 4:6. At the end, Isaiah 60:22 uses metaphorically the term "a little one" and "a young one," whereas Jonah 4:11 explicates that the little and young ones are such because "they cannot discern their right hand from their left hand"!

The dependence of Jonah upon Third Isaiah is important, not only from the point of view of a *terminus a quo* for the book's date, but also because both documents, Isaiah 55ff. and Jonah, belong to the same postexilic literature of *subversion*.

Third Isaiah is, right after the return from Babylon, a witness of the underground struggle in Jerusalem against the ideology of the party in power under Zerubbabel. The conservative doctrine finds its herald in the Chronicler, even if his composition comes later (fourth century B.C.E. and after). Decisive for the party of opposition was that the twelve tribes had not been re-united, national independence was a long way off, economic conditions were disastrous instead of paradisiac according to prophetic promises, and the nations had never displayed more contemptuous indifference to God's city and to his Lordship. To feign to ignore the situation in Jerusalem was only delusion. Far from being of little import, the nations were to come and pledge their allegiance to YHWH; this would indeed constitute the eschatological event, the crowning of history. The claim to exclusive election on the part of the Temple "establishment" was just arrogance. Rather, run to Nineveh and witness there the God-given gracious reversal of the course of history—the changing of wolves into lambs, of rogues into saints—than to stick one's head in the sand and pretend not to see the world out there. The book of Jonah, like the opposition literature of that epoch, puts its stock in miracle, the only alternative to foolish complacency and blind triumphalism. God will have mercy and spare Nineveh, and thus also Jerusalem![34]

Jonah points in that direction. For this book also the *terminus a quo* is the return from exile in the second half of the sixth century B.C.E. And as it seems to have been known by Ben Sira (see Ecclus. 49:10; cf. Tob. 14:4, 8 [Codex S]), the *terminus ad quem* is the second century B.C.E. Between 538 and the time of Ben Sira, it is possible to propose a more precise chronology for the book.

The examination of the book's terminology has led us to conclude comfortably in favor of a postexilic date. What were the main problems in Jerusalem immediately following the return from Babylon? No doubt the most vexing question was the apparent nonfulfillment of exilic prophecies. Instead of being a messianic era, the times were hard and the readjustment to Judean conditions difficult. Specific promises of Isaiah, Jeremiah, or Ezekiel could not be reconciled with the dire reality. Zion, far from being restored as promised, was under the yoke of triumphant nations. The failure of the forecast restoration of Jerusalem entailed the obsolescence of the oracles of doom against the foreign nations. Even, since the latter were not eliminated by divine wrath but were prosperous, it was to be concluded that the prophecy of restoration, initially addressed to Israel, had shifted to "Nineveh," and conversely, by implication, the threat initially brandished against "Nineneh" had now shifted to Jerusalem![35]

This logic, so to speak geometrical, seems to vindicate the position of Bickerman, according to whom Jonah is taking an opposite stance to Jeremiah's and Ezekiel's. These exilic prophets had declared that the impending destruction would be suspended by God on the condition that the culprit repent (cf. Jer. 18:7–10; Ezek. 3:16; 33:1–9). Is it now the case that Jonah personally believes that such a relenting on the part of God in behalf of his people is scandalous and inopportune? A comparison of the text of Jonah 3:8–9 with Jeremian texts shows that the answer is No. Jeremiah 25:5; 26:3; and especially 18:11 emphasize the possibility: "perhaps they will hearken and turn every one from his evil way, so that I repent of the evil which I purpose to do to them because of the evil of their doings" (26:3). What are the parameters of the conjecture?

In fact, a closer study shows that the economy envisaged by the exilic prophets invariably concerns Israel. In all the texts quoted above, *Judah* is specified as the object of the liberation from the chains of determinism. This is especially clear in Jeremiah 18:11: "now therefore speak to the people of Judah and to the inhabitants of Jerusalem saying. . . ." The new disposition is thus valid only for God's people. Jonah's dealing with a foreign nation brings about a new problem. For Jeremiah and Ezekiel it was a question of comforting the Jews in exile, explaining that they were not the victims of the determinism of punishment. In God's economy, if "a nation" (meaning they themselves) repents, God also will relent and forgive. In short, the restoration is possible and at hand.

On the contrary, Jonah's story completely reverses the situation envisaged by his predecessors. Jeremiah and Ezekiel had in mind the salvation of Israel and the curtailment of the nations' success at Israel's expense. But Jonah's author broadens the prophetic principle to include the salvation of "Nineveh" and by implication the curtailment of the success of the Jews who returned to Zion. It is therefore understandable that Jonah resist with all his strength that extension of God's "graciousness and compassion" (4:2). This cannot be; it would be too unjust. Israel has been put down by the wickedness of the nations in the past—would Israel now be put down by their repentance?

In other words, there is here no theoretical opposition to Ezekiel or Jeremiah, but the author of Jonah uses irony and satire.[36] Jonah 3 is ironical because, in Jeremiah 36 the individual Jehoiakim refuses to repent after a lengthy exhortation of the exilic prophet, whereas all the Ninevites of one accord repent after a few words (five in Hebrew) uttered by a foreign prophet. The contrast is further emphasized by the similarities in detail between the two documents. Nineveh is "the great city" in Jonah, as Jerusalem was in Jeremiah 22:8. Also on the point of the theology of God's forgiveness, Jonah is in ironic contrast to Jeremiah. In Jonah 1:14, which stands in parallel with Jeremiah 26:15, the sailors are better than the Jerusalemites in the time of Jeremiah (cf. Jon. 1:16; 2:10). And in Jonah 3, the conversion of the Ninevites is of the type advocated by the exilic prophets to their fellow Jews—namely, penance, fasting, prayer, avoidance of sin. Furthermore, Jonah 4:2—the veritable center of gravity of the whole book—presents a liturgical formula that is normally reserved exclusively for the relations between God and his people (see Exod. 34:6; Ps. 103:8; etc.). In Jonah, however, we find it used within a universalistic framework in sharp contrast to the former usage in the Israelite liturgy.

This very point of universalism is helpful for dating, approximately, the book of Jonah—before we suggest a precise date in chapter 2, below. The scope of Micah and First Isaiah, for example, is universalistic but centralized in Zion. Only during the exile do we find a decentralized universalism in Jeremiah and in Isaiah 40–55. Both prophets make requisite only a general conversion of the hearts. With the return from exile, however, there is a new attempt at recentralizing the universalism in Zion—so Haggai, Zechariah, and even Third Isaiah. An exceptional note is struck by Malachi 1:10–11, which goes very far in the interpretation of God's universal kingship. Finally, in Hellenistic times, the priestly orthodox writing of Ben Sira returns expectedly to a more conservative universalism, in reaction to pagan "humanism" (cf. Ecclus. 1:25f.; 33:7–14; 36:1–17). The book of Jonah takes the stance of a decentralized universalism. We are, then, at a much later time than the era of Haggai, Zechariah, and the Chronicler. Such vagueness must suffice for the time being. For more chronological precision, we must scrutinize further the problem of the literary genre. We now turn to this point.

NOTES

1. Elias Bickerman, *Four Strange Books of the Bible (Jonah/Daniel/Koheleth/Esther)* (New York: Schocken Books, 1967), p. 3.

2. Ibid., pp. 3–4. It is the opinion of P. Alberto Vaccari, S. J., in "Il Genere Letterario del Libro di Gioni in Recenti Publicazioni," *Divinitas* 6 (1962): 231–52. In part, the argument rests upon the picaresque character of the hero. Vaccari says that there is no parallel in other ancient literatures.

3. J. D. Smart, *The Interpreter's Bible* (Nashville: Abingdon, 1956), vol. 6, pp. 871ff.

4. G. von Rad, *Der Prophet Jona* (Nürnberg: Laetare, 1950), p. 11. See also L. C. Allen, *The Books of Joel, Obadiah, Jonah, and Micah,* New International Commentary on the Old Testament (Grand Rapids: Eerdmans, 1976), p. 229: "What religious monster is this?"

5. Bickerman, *Four Strange Books,* p. 15; he quotes Jerome, *Commentary on Jonah* 1:3.

6. Cf., e.g., L. Ginzberg, *The Legends of the Jews* (Philadelphia: Jewish Publication Society, 1955), vol. 6, pp. 348–52.

7. Quoted by J. Jeremias, *ThDNT,* vol. 3, p. 408n17 (s.v. Ionas).

8. As Montaigne said (*Oeuvres* [Paris: Pléiade, 1976], I, 21, p. 194), "Whether or not it happened, in Paris or in Rome, to John or to Peter, it is always a feat of human ability" (our trans.). It can also be said, as Jonah is a poetic piece, that the book offers a "truth" commensurable with poetry, or, in the words of George Steiner, the book presents an "internal consistence and psychological conviction" (*The Death of Tragedy* [New York: Oxford University Press, 1980], p. 240).

9. This midrash is designated by 2 Chron. 13:22 as "the story of the prophet Iddo," and by 2 Chron. 24:27 as "the story of the book of the kings."

10. H. Schmidt, *Jona, eine Untersuchung zur vergleichenden Religionsgeschichte,* FRLANT 9 (Göttingen: Vandenhoeck & Ruprecht, 1907). Cf. Karl Budde, *ZAW* (1892): 40ff., followed by O. Loretz, K. Marti, G. A. F. Knight (midrash on texts of Jeremiah and Deutero-Isaiah). Sellin-Fohrer say "midraschartige Lehrschrift." Ten righteous may save Sodom (Gen. 18:22–23; cf. Jer. 5:1), but cf. Gen. 31:29.

11. A. Lods, *Histoire de la Littérature Hébraique et Juive* (Paris: Payot, 1950), ad loc.

12. Although H. Schmidt's stance is ungrounded, it is advisable not to dismiss too lightly the possibility of a symbolic substitution of Nineveh by Jerusalem. The tale of Jonah is meant for Judeans.

13. See P. R. Ackroyd, *Israel under Babylon and Persia* (London: Oxford University Press, 1970), p. 338.

14. For the allegorizing theory, cf. Kleinert, Bloch, Cheyne, König, Smith, Ackroyd.

15. See P. R. Ackroyd, *Exile and Restoration* (Philadelphia: Westminster Press, 1968), pp. 244–45. (Isa. 65:1 provides a parallel to Jonah: God is found by those who sought him not.)

16. We shall note here as a curiosity Jacques Ellul's connection with the *yônāh*, which brought back to Noah the sign of the end of God's wrath in Gen. 8:11. See "Le livre de Jonas," *Foi et Vie* 50 (1952): 84. F. Weinreb, *Das Buch Jona, der Sinn des Buches Jonah nach der ältesten Jüdichen Überlieferungen* (Zurich: Origo, 1970), also draws the parallel with Noah (pp. 126, 132). Let us recall also the identification made by the New Testament with the Holy Spirit (see Matt. 3:16). A notable rabbinic interpretation sees the dove as representing Israel unjustly persecuted, in *Baba Qamma* 93a (on the basis of Ps. 74:19), where the word is not *yônāh* but *tôr*. It is also interesting that for C. G. Jung (*Psychology and Alchemy*), the dove is a symbol of Mercurius whose ornithological form is the one of *spiritus*, in parallel with the Holy Spirit.

17. "Die Komposition des Buches Jona," *ZAW* 7 (1887): 222–84. Boehme grounds his argument concerning the model of the Pentateuch on the most unreliable basis—the variation of divine names in the book. As a matter of fact, God is sometimes called YHWH (hence source "J" for Boehme), sometimes Elohim (hence his source "E"), or even as, for example, in Gen. 2, YHWH-Elohim (1:9, 2:2, 4:6, hence Boehme's JE redaction).

18. "Die Komposition des Buches Jona," *ZAW* 25 (1905): 285–310. The same methodology has been used in 1976 by L. Schmidt, *"De Deo," Studien zur Literarkritik und Theologie des Buches Jona, des Gesprächs zwischen Abraham und Jhwh in Gen. 18:22ff., und von Hiob 1, BZAW* (Berlin: De Gruyter, 1976), p. 143.

19. Allen, *Joel, Obadiah, Jonah, and Micah*, p. 197. The outline is on p. 200.

20. In Jon. 1:4, therefore, one might have expected the use of Elohim rather than YHWH, but it is made clear by the author that the storm on the sea concerns Jonah exclusively. It is a *historical* gesture in the disguise of a natural phenomenon.

21. On the preceding development, see G. H. Cohn, *Das Buch Jona im Lichte der biblischen Erzählkunst* (Assen: Van Gorcum, 1969); see also below, n. 36.

22. Cohn, *Das Buch Jona*, p. 37.

23. A. Parrot, *Nineveh and the Old Testament*, trans. B. E. Hooke (New York: Philosophical Library, 1955).

24. With the possible exception of Gen. 24:3, 7 (J).

25. See G. M. Landes, "The Kerygma of the Book of Jonah," *Interp.* 21 (1967): 3–31; and before him O. Loretz, "Herkunft und Sinn der Jona-Erzählung," *BZ* 5 (1961): esp. 19–24.

26. See *Genesis Rabbah* 98 (ed. Theodor-Albeck, p. 62a).

27. In a pointed philological study of Jonah, G. M. Landes dismisses all linguistic and syntactic arguments generally invoked for dating the book. He finally keeps only the verb "to notice" in 1:6 as a sign of a postexilic composition. Also the order of words in the expression "gracious and merciful" in 4:2 points in the same direction, as well as the book's preference for the plural form of a number of terms used in the singular in preexilic texts. By themselves, however, those signs are insufficient for a firm dating of Jonah. Landes agrees with Jack Sasson

that the literary and linguistic phenomena here are, at this stage of our knowledge, too narrow a basis for dating Jonah. See G. M. Landes, "Linguistic Criteria and the Date of the Book of Jonah," *Eretz-Israel* 16 (1982): 147–70; and J. Sasson, *Ruth: A New Translation with a Philological Commentary* (Baltimore: Johns Hopkins University Press, 1979), p. 244.

28. See our development on Elijah, below, chap. 7.

29. To recall, H. Schmidt believes that here Nineveh represents Jerusalem (see above).

30. A. Feuillet, "Les Sources du livre de Jonas," *RB* 54 (1947): 176.

31. Also Feuillet, "Jonas," *SDB* 4, col. 1126: Jonah refers to the oracles of Ezekiel on Tyre (Ezek. 26–28; 29:17–21).

32. G. A. F. Knight, *Ruth and Jonah*, Torch Bible Commentaries (London: SCM, 1950).

33. A. Lord, *The Singer of Tales* (Cambridge, Mass.: Harvard University Press, 1973), p. 207.

34. According to T. H. Robinson, the book of Jonah reacts against a way of thinking too narrowly nationalistic in Jewish masses (*Die Zwölf Kleinen Propheten* [Tübingen: Mohr-Siebeck, 1954], p. 118). E. Haller also diagnosed a "narrow orthodoxy, almost pathological" ("Die Erzählung von dem Prophet Jona," *ThEH* (1958): 6. But Millar Burrows reminds us that the Jews in question are former exiles and that it is natural that they be concerned with their Hebraic descent, see Ezra 9–10 and Neh. 13:1–3, 25–28 ("The Literary Category," *Translating and Understanding the Old Testament* [Nashville: Abingdon, 1970], p. 105). It is psychologically understandable to have a reaction of defense before an imminent danger from outside. It is, after all, thanks to this historical inner centeredness that Judaism could survive. The price to pay, though, was enormous, for the dialectical tension between survival and openness toward others was sacrificed.

35. We shall come back to this issue in the appendix, below.

36. The use of irony by the author of Jonah has been stressed by various commentators (see below, chap. 2). Along the same line, Allen (*Joel, Obadiah, Jonah, and Micah*) sees also parodies of 1 Kings 19:4 in Jon. 4:4, 8; of Jer. 18:7, 8, 11 in Jon. 3:9, 10; of Joel, esp. 2:13–14, in Jon. 3:9; 4:2. On the use of Joel in Jonah, see H. W. Wolff, *Studien zum Jonabuch*, Biblische Studien 47 (Neukirchen-Vluyn: Neukirchener Vlg, 1947; Köln, 1965).

TWO

JONAH,
A MENIPPEAN SATIRE?

The menippea is a genre of "ultimate questions."
Mikhail Bakhtin, *Problems of Dostoevsky's Poetics*
(Ann Arbor, Mich.: Ardis, 1973), p. 95.

The main characteristic of narrative according to Paul Ricoeur[1] is that is disorients and reorients our imaginations. The disorientation occurs because the message conveyed by narratives—or by events before they are narrated—is a demonstration that we have misinterpreted the world. The reorientation is putting our attentiveness to creation back on the track. It constitutes a real breakthrough in the circularity of our existence because the message, heard in reality for the first time, indicates a direction, an orientation, to our life movement. With such a direction, one leaves the rut in which the same phenomenon is perpetually interpreted by the same person according to the same rules with the same unsatisfactory result. For example, the message lifts one up from the oppression of distributive justice (in which even Job is still enmeshed), or of unchecked natural compulsions (by which Eli's sons are controlled, according to 1 Sam. 2:12ff.). The biblical narrative reorients as it proclaims the irruption of the extravagant grace of God, which is a "how much more" (see Gen. 7:17ff.; 8:13ff.; Matt. 5:38ff.; Rom. 5:6ff.), the disconcerting superabundance of the word that brings about what it says (Isa. 55).

The message is multiform. It is the creator of an endless literary tradition if only because of the ineptness of each attempt to encompass the incredible. In the concert of those attempts, however, no literary genre is better suited to reshaping the imagination than fiction, and in particular the parable. It is, according to J. D. Crossan, a "story subverting the world," for the structure of expression on the part of the speaker lies in diametrical opposition to the structure of expectation on the part of the reader.[2] Readers want a text to be "readable," said Roland Barthes, meaning a text that does not disturb them in their habits. In brief, in order to be comfortable, the hoped-for text must confirm the options of the past and the projects for the future of the reader.

But such is not fiction when it disorients and reorients. "One of the functions of fiction . . . is retrospectively to free certain possibilities that were not actualized in the historical past," says Paul Ricoeur.[3] What would happen if the prophet Jonah ben Amittai of the eighth century B.C.E., of whom we do not know much, had gone to Nineveh to proclaim an impending catastrophe? What would happen if, at his word, the whole city were to repent? And if this unexpected outcome were to indispose the prophet to the point that he would wish to die? And if God had decided to choose between justice according to Jonah and justice according to his compassion? Ricoeur adds:

> The *quasi past* of fiction thus becomes the detection of *possibilities interred in the actualized past.* What could have happened—the verisimilar according to Aristotle[4]—covers at the same time the potentialities of the "real" past and the "unreal" possibilities of pure fiction.

The gap between history and fiction is thus less deep than it has been claimed by historicism. The historian must have recourse to the imaginary in reconstructing history, and the teller to the verisimilar in his or her poetic description. That is why, on the side of fiction, a novel such as *Der Zauberberg* is dated with precision by Thomas Mann. Similarly, Jonah is "ben Amittai" and he goes on board a ship in the well-known harbor of Joppa in order not to go to the famous Assyrian capital, Nineveh.

The story of Jonah intends to apprehend the existential reality.[5] It fulfills this task in collapsing personages and incidents, and this is a characteristic of epics. But the genre of epics is here broken. We shall come back to this point. Let us note here that the real author is truly endowed with ubiquity. He identifies himself with his hero although he is also in another sense fighting with him. He oversees the whole stage as the crow flies[6] and thus appears as a *deus ex machina*. He is judging his prophet from the point of view of the other characters in the tale (the sailors, the Ninevites) and even more subtly from the point of view of his readers. Such a distance that he keeps from Jonah never slackens, so that it is possible to say that Jonah is an antihero in an antiplot.

Further on this point, the book cannot be technically listed as classic comedy, characterized by a happy ending. The historical tragedy of Job ends as a comedy; the historical comedy of Jonah might end as a tragedy. For this it suffices that eventually Jonah be not convinced by God's arguments. And this brings us to another element of distancing from the epos: Jonah appears as a "picaresque" character.[7]

As is well known, that literary genre puts on stage a *picaro* ("scoundrel"), mixing, according to an anonymous definition of the seventeenth century, *burlas y veras,* "fun and truth." It is clearly a genre subversive for the surrounding ideology, for it introduces contingency within the monolithic dogmatism of faith and order. The picaresque novel frees itself and also the reader of all fear. It plays with the scary, and the "whale" of Jonah becomes here a comical monster. It scorns kings and bishops. In the book of Jonah, the prophet himself is the laughing stock. As Roland Barthes says, the indexee is of another nature than the indexing. Jonah is marked with a *sign* of prophecy, but not with its index. The sign "provides the ground for the order of representation (but not of the determination of the creation, like the index), the two parts swap between them, signified and signifying are spinning in an endless process."[8]

True, Jonah belongs to mimetic genre, but at the antipode of myth.[9] The quest of Jonah is not for a Grail, but for his own identity. Jonah is one of those "great realistic narratives [that] combine the tragic concern of the individual with the comic concern for society . . . inserting . . . tragic characters in comic situations."[10]

The terms "comedy" and "comical" put us on the right track for the decisive discovery regarding the book of Jonah. Jonah be-

28

longs to irony,[11] that is why there is distance between the author and his personage, as we saw above (as there is between Shakespeare and his heroes). There is specifically irony when the narrator's point of view does not coincide with the point of view as expressed by the narrative's hero. Or when the narrator's voice is raised in the midst of a milieu that is proper to him (first cultural milieu) and is addressed to a listener of whom he knows that the environment is different from his (second cultural milieu).[12] It is what happens in the book of Jonah where the prophet's point of view is the one of a personage who is "marginalized" by the author, as Franz K. Stanzel says.[13]

Boris Uspenski sees in irony the noncoincidence of ideological and phraseological points of view. So, he says, in *The Brothers Karamazov* Dostoevsky pretends to adopt the viewpoint of the student Kolya Krasotkin. He adopts his style but not his ideology. Krasotkin does not represent in the least Dostoevsky. There is "irony," says Uspenski, "when one speaks from a certain viewpoint while judging from another one."[14]

In general, as a matter of fact, the reader is well disposed toward adopting the different viewpoints of the author (see below). In irony, on the contrary, the author deliberately avoids such coincidence in adopting a role that is not at all his, through the intermediary of a personage who is "judged and not judging."[15] This very distinction between the author and the author's personages (so that the author can even go so far as to mock the latter) is called by Dorrit Cohn "dissonance."[16]

Coming back to Uspenski, the Russian formalist distinguishes, on the psychological level, a first type of description, which consists in "seeing the described person from outside," and a second type, which consists in "seeing him from inside."[17] Only the first type is represented in the book of Jonah (and generally in the Bible). According to this type, all the events are described with objectivity without reference to the state of the soul of the characters. So all verbs expressing an intimate consciousness are avoided (*verba sentiendi*).[18]

But that which is true of the gap between the viewpoints of the narrator and the personage is still more so regarding the real author and the implied author. One recognizes in Jonah the hand of the implied author, but the real author remains unknown, anonymous; he remains hidden behind his narrative. This phenomenon, present in the literature of all ages, takes on, in the book of Jonah, a particular turn. In general, as we said, the implied author is deserving of trust, that is, he tacitly enters into a compact with the reader by which the reader decides a priori not to fend for himself or herself, but to trust at least provisionally the narrator. Samuel T. Coleridge said that there is a "willful suspension of disbelief." Here, however, as we have seen above, instead of wishing to be "trustworthy," the ironic author wants to be "not worthy of trust."

"The case of the *unworthy* narrator," says Ricoeur, "is particularly interesting from the point of view of the appeal to freedom and responsibility of the reader." For the narrator disorients the expectations of the reader in leaving the reader "in the uncertainty on the point to know whither he eventually wants to go." This makes of this type of literature a "dangerous," "venomous," or yet "corrosive" literature, for it produces "a suspicious reader, for whom the reading stops being a trusting trip in the company of a narrator who himself is trustworthy, to become a fight with the implied author, a fight which brings the reader back to himself."[19]

But, if there is indeed a fight, it is essentially with a world order that is fundamentally questioned. This is an issue that particularly interests Mikhail Bakhtin, especially in his study of Dostoevsky[20] or Rabelais.[21] It is well known how important carnival folklore is in Bakhtin's eyes. No one has been able to distinguish the literary characteristics of the "carnival behavior before the world" better than the Russian formalist. Humor opposes "all powerful relations in society based on hierarchy."[22] But here the humorous is *serious comic* art. The laughter is restraint, it is a pitiless, facetious truth, a cruel unveiling in the guise of a joke. Satire is the effective weapon of the dispossessed, the biting retort of the *sans-culotte* to the authoritarian well-to-do. The literary genre thus implies a sociological environment of popular anticonservative milieu. It flowers in periods of crisis, when the differences in social status are large and their injustice intolerable. Satire is the alternative to violent revolution and is sometimes even more subversive. It takes shape in a time of decadence in the tradition of a nation and of destruction of the ethical norms that previously had established an ideal of beauty and nobility, at a time of strife between heterogeneous parties from the point of view of religion and philosophy.[23]

The central pivot of the genre of serious comic art is the *present time,* that is, there is no chronological hiatus between reader and personages and situations described by the narrative, as was the case in epics and tragedies. To be sure, Jonah ben Amittai is a personage of the past (eighth century B.C.E.). But the author of the book makes of him a contemporary. For another characteristic of the fiction is that it is not based on legendary information but on experience and free imagination.[24]

Finally, we must note the mix of the genre, for its style is a mixture of the elevated and the vulgar, the serious and the comical, prose and poetry, classic language and dialect (cf. the terms of navigation in Jon. 1 or the description of the tree by the word *qîqāyôn* in chap. 4).

It behooves this literary genre to bring the hero down to such earthy proportions that he becomes "picaresque" like Don Quixote or Eulenspiegel, as we have seen. That is why, in this book, we repeatedly qualify Jonah as "antihero."[25] The antihero may be the only one to know the truth although considered by all as a fool. To exemplify this, Bakhtin cites the short story of Feodor Dostoevsky "The Dream of the Ridicule Man," where, from the onset, the personage says, "Oh how difficult it is to be the only one to know the truth!"

This could be applied to Jonah at Nineveh, but now Jonah is not considered a fool by the Ninevites, and this is the first surprise. He himself, furthermore, is endowed with wisdom only through his mission. The irony is therefore not where Dostoevsky put it in his tale, but somewhere else, in the very character of the prophet. It is here a working device of the satirist that he puts in the mouth of the "hero" the very arguments that condemn him. Hence the victim of irony is none else but that antihero who personifies a worldview that the author of the satire rejects.

Irony in the book of Jonah is everywhere. It is in his very name, so little fitting his attitude. For he is a hawk rather than a dove, and suspicious rather than trusting. Everything he does seems inappropriate. He promptly reacts to his call, but runs in the wrong direction. He preaches to the Ninevites, but he is so ill-willed that the effect of his words is, rather, in spite of than thanks to them. The very low profile that he chooses for himself is confronted with the deafening enormity of divine means of persuasion. The tempest at sea is Homeric, the descent to the abyss is Dantesque, the reaction of the prophet to Nineveh's repentance is bombastic. Everything here is disproportionate, exaggerated, parodic. The threat that Jonah utters against Nineveh is the unparalleled devastation of Sodom and Gomorrah. The conversion is also absolute, total, without residue, even the animals go through the motion. The missionary's disappointment is to death. The heat is scorching. The *qîqāyôn* grows to the stature of a tree in no time; it also withers overnight. The wicked city is immense, its population fantastic in number and in "illiteracy." But, more than all this combined, the personage of Jonah is a mixture of tragedy and comedy. More pointedly, he is tragic in his own eyes and he deals with life-and-death issues. In short, he is deadly *serious*. To the reader, however, he appears as an *alazon* ("braggart") manipulated by the *eiron* (the "ironic" author). He is unconsciously *comic*.[26]

That is why Jonah is a "strange book" in the Bible, as Elias Bickerman says. It is strange because the reader is deliberately made uncomfortable. However, the feeling is not unpleasant, as the reader is challenged to engage in a quest for the real author. Satire must be handled with care by the reader. It combines indirection of attack with definite targeting. It aims especially at hypocrisy, and the earnest reader is never positively sure of being beyond suspicion on that score.

It is clear that the narrative-reader (narrator-recipient) relationship is infinitely complex. The tale does not respond directly to the reader's expectation, but only indirectly and sometimes after many detours. That this be not necessarily to displease the reader is proved by the pleasure one has in reading a suspense novel that endlessly accumulates clues for the solution but delays the latter indefinitely. That is why Thomas Mann wrote, about irony, that it is "without exception the deepest and the most fascinating problem of the world."

JONAH, A MENIPPEAN SATIRE?

But if the reader's interest is thus sustained, it is at the price of constant frustration. The author of Jonah brings this to its paroxysm in leaving the story unfinished! In short, the satirical narrative is the counterpart of the normal discourse where, as has been correctly seen by Roland Barthes, the reader lends his or her voice to the author and lets him say things he is interested in.[27]

One would be wrong to read Jonah as if it were a monologue, that is, a work in which the dialectical development is at the service of a unified spirit.[28] In fact, the book is and remains until the end dialogical. Two "worlds" are confronted, the one is God's world, the other Jonah's world.

If, at the beginning of chapter 3, Jonah seems to adopt God's viewpoint (he goes to Nineveh), the agreement between the two worlds is, however, illusionary. Jonah has not surrendered, as is clear from chapter 4. Until the end communication does not occur.

So the expectation of the reader remains unfulfilled. It is of no avail to readers to turn the pages and read the end to see what is the denouement and so reassure themselves. For there is no end and thus no reassurance before the problem raised by two contradictory conceptions, the one of justice in the world and the one of compassion toward humanity. Jonah therefore is a "polyphony," meaning that the different viewpoints expressed or alluded to are essentially equal in import, as in the "polyphonic" *Brothers Karamazov*.[29]

Starting with Bakhtin's notion of "counterpoint," Ricoeur writes, ". . . along with the dialogue comes a dimension of unendedness and incompleteness which affects deeply the personages and their world view; the whole composition is, it seems, condemned to remain '*open ended*,' even 'endless.' "[30]

The actual absence of an end in the tale of Jonah is of the utmost importance. That it is not due to an accidental loss of the final page is confirmed by biblical parallels to this phenomenon of abrupt conclusion as found in Genesis 8:32–33, and especially in the book of Job. The attempts to explain through external causes the incompleteness of Jonah's tale are useless; they are also a significant mistake. For, as Barthes writes, "in imposing upon oneself to spell out *the end* of all action (conclusion, interruption, closure, denouement) the readable [derogative word in Barthes] asserts its historicity." (Hence we never pass to the mythic time in which there is no before and no after; cf. Barthes, *S/Z*).[31]

Jonah is endless and its very incompleteness fits perfectly the main feature of the personage, namely, his reluctance, which participates in the hermeneutical code of delays in the flow of the discourse, "that delaying space, of which the emblem could be 'reluctance,' that rhetorical figure which interrupts, suspends, or derails the sentence."[32] Here the reluctance takes on a much greater importance than simply stylistic. It is in many ways the central characteristic of biblical narrative. Not only Moses and several prophets "drag their feet" when called, but the patriarchs earlier have recourse to expediencies to turn the events to their advantage rather than to what they know is God's will. If there is a constant lesson to learn from biblical narrative in general, it is this one: the divine design is fulfilled despite and, paradoxically, through the multiple and tortuous reluctance of the agents of the *Heilsgeschichte* ("history of salvation"). Few modern critics have better understood this than Robert Alter.[33] In a chapter that he significantly calls "Characterization and the Art of Reticence," he writes:

> Causation in human affairs is . . . brought into a paradoxical double focus by the narrative techniques of the Bible. The biblical writers obviously exhibit, on the one hand, a profound belief in a strong, clearly demarcated pattern of causation in history and individual lives, and many of the framing devices, the motif-structures, the symmetries and recurrences in their narratives reflect this belief. God directs, history complies. . . . The very perception, on the other hand, of Godlike depths, unsoundable capacities for good and evil, in human nature, also lead these readers to render their protagonists in ways that destabilize any monolithic system of causation, set off a fluid movement among different orders of causation, some of them complementary or mutually reinforcing, others even mutually contradictory.

Further on in his book, Alter speaks of the

> intersection of incompatibles—the relative and the absolute, human imperfection and divine perfection, the brawling chaos of historical experience and God's promise to fulfill a

design in history. The biblical outlook is informed, I think, by a sense of stubborn contradiction, of a profound and ineradicable untidiness in the nature of things.[34]

Irony knows no border. It has been used in the West and the East, in the North and the South. It is found in all human literatures. As regards satire, however, its territory is more strictly limited in time and space. As a means of expression, it goes back, in Greece at least, to the time of Aristophanes of Athens (448–380? B.C.E.). And, as a bona-fide literary genre, it was a Greek invention in the third century B.C.E. As such, it became right away a powerful subversive tool in the hands of Cynics. A particular brand of satire was produced at the same epoch at Gadara, Palestine, a city that Josephus called "a Greek city" (*Ant.* 17.11.4; *War* 2.6.3). In an epitaph for one Apio, the town is said to be "*chrestomousia*," that is, "lettered, cultured." Its structure was definitely Greek, with its two theaters, its basilica, its arcades, its baths. Meleager, who also was a Gadarene and became a renowned poet in the second century B.C.E., says of himself that he was born in "an Attic fatherland among Syrians—Gadara" (*Greek Anthology* VII. 417).

It is worth our while to develop this point, for, as will be shown hereafter, the book of Jonah presents remarkable parallels with a special strand of satire created in Gadara of Palestine by Menippos in the first half of the third century. This fact is only meaningful, of course, if Jonah is to be dated during the process of Hellenization of the Middle East. In disfavor of it, one stresses the absence of Greek words in the text. Contrasting Jonah's language with Esther's, for example, some critics consider it as generally classical. But we shall call attention in what follows to the presence of at least one Greek idiom in Jonah (the *qîqāyôn* of chap. 4). Other clues to Hellenistic influence will be noticed. Furthermore, the alleged classicism of Jonah presents particularities that cannot be considered as such. Presently, it is important to pinpoint what kinds of ideas were on the educated Jews' minds in the third century. A look at the literature of the period tells us much about it.

Toward the time of Alexander the Great's death, Greek genius invents two ideological and literary novelties: "the new philosophies" and "the new comedy." Both productions shared a common stance: anything can happen to anyone, anytime. "New comedy" is particularly illustrated by Meleander (342–292 B.C.E.), whom Paul quotes in 1 Corinthians 15:33. His characters come from lower classes of society. Meleander treats also with equanimity Greeks and Barbarians, freemen and slaves. His mode of expression is comic.

Similarly, comedy and dialogue characterize the satire of Menippos or Menippean satire around the same time. Its creator was of Gadara and the genre owes much to "new comedy," even from an ethical and social point of view. Like "new comedy," the Menippean satire believes that evil can be eradicated through its mere revelation. It suffices to ferret out evil from its hidden places. The Menippean satire is a medley of farce, fable, diatribe, comic and serious moods, laughter and melancholia.

Menippos of Gadara was a slave in Sinope where he became a pupil of the Cynic philosopher Metrocles. He somehow amassed a fortune in commerce and died as a freedman in Thebes. He was called *spoudaiogeloios* (or *spoudogeloios*), that is, literally "prompt to laugh," but as a technical term, it designates the serio-comic mentioned above. In other words, Menippos was fond of doing what later the Romans would call *ridendo dicere verum* ("to say the truth while laughing"). Menippos mocked people's follies, especially their greed for power and money. He was antiestablishment, even antisociety, denouncing religiously or philosophically sanctioned clichés of all kinds. As a Cynic, he exalted the poor and the oppressed. Only the poor and the Cynic enjoy happiness, because they are free from illusion in this world and the next. But more important still was the Cynic defiance of convention. This Cynics did with harshness, snarling like "dogs" (in Greek, *kynos* is the genitive of *kyon*, "dog"). Their main slogan was *paracharattein to nomisma*, which means "to falsify the currency." This demanded a great liberty of language (*parresia*), and the rhetorical genres they deemed fit for this were "diatribes" (dialogues), sermons—those of Menippos influenced a number of Christian preachers—and satires.

The "new philosophies" were brought to the Middle East by the Macedonian conquerers of the fourth century. But there were indeed very few true philosophers among the colonists. Thus the new ideas that found their way to Palestine were, rather, a popularized and eclectic type of philosophy. Besides, Cynicism itself was already a democratized brand of doctrine, more at home with ethics than with metaphysics. Its teaching of the populace throve, rather, in diatribe and apothegm, in sharp words and memorable illustrations, than in dialectic. Parenthetically, let us recall that prophetic discourse in Jonah is reduced to five Hebrew words! In the Gospels as well, Cynic influence is evident.

Missionary by its nature, the Cynic teaching betrays its popular roots. The stage is provided by the street, the market place, the ship deck, the jailhouse, the netherworld. The Cynic holds himself as sent by God (*angelos*) to all people without exception; his task is to show to all that they are going astray. Like an explorer (*kataskopos*), he must unveil what is good and what is bad in humankind (see Dion Chrysostom, *Orationes* lxxvii, par. 35–45).

Parallels in Jonah are evident. Topography corresponds here and there. Even ill-famed places and the netherworld are present in Jonah. Below, we shall insist on the negative meaning of Nineveh in the whole Hebrew and Jewish tradition. To go to Nineveh is not very different from going to hell. Besides, Jonah as an *angelos* sent to all to denounce their weaknesses, or as an explorer of humankind's deep baseness, would look familiar to any Cynic. A remarkable feature is that the patron-god of the Cynics was Herakles; the god was represented as being in the belly of a whale.

We said earlier that the Greek ideas as spread in Hellenized Palestine were a medley of eclectic popular ideas with a veneer of philosophy. It is therefore difficult to label with any certainty which Greek philosophical school influences a given non-Greek writing during the Hellenistic period. We shall show that the literary genre of Jonah reminds one of the Menippean satire (invented by a Near Eastern man). But influences from other quarters will also be clear in other parts of the biblical book, Stoic for instance (whose founders are also people of the Near East). This we shall see especially in dealing with Jonah 4. Also in that chapter, we shall recognize ideas that come straight from Greek mystery religions. Furthermore, as we are mentioning the vast cultural and ideological commerce between near and far countries of the time, we must emphasize the fact that Jonah is the oldest known aretalogy outside Egypt.[35]

There is no reason to wonder about this, provided that Jonah's date is the Hellenistic period.[36] The Hellenization of the Middle East pervaded all milieus. It created a time spirit, an irresistible *Geist*.[37] It had become totally impossible to think and to live, after Alexander the Great, in the same way that one had before him. The language had changed; the issues were not the same anymore, their solutions were novel. A book of Jonah inaccessible to the epochal ideas would be not only anachronistic but totally unintelligible. True, its author raises a problem that already in the past proved irritating for the Jewish soul, namely, the problem of universalism, but he does this in new terms and with the intimation of an unprecedentedly daring solution.

It was appropriate to set the stage first on a ship deck. The shipping business never attracted the Israelites, but long travels overseas had become popular. To wit, the remarkable development of the "Greek novel," a Hellenistic new literary genre whose two axes were eroticism and voyage. It told about fantastic trips to faraway and mysterious countries. We here refer to the classic *Der griechische Roman und seine Vorläufer* of Erwin Rohde, already mentioned above in a note. Before the appearance of the Greek novel, the setting of an Israelite character upon a ship is unthinkable. Jonah is, here again, unique in the Hebrew Bible. Before the fourth century, no Israelite storyteller would have thought of placing one of his heroes at sea. For this was the home of demons and chaotic monsters—represented in Jonah by the "big fish"—but certainly not the place for a divine dialogue with a prophet.

In chapter 1, above, we mentioned that the vocabulary of Jonah has been attributed to a Phoenician origin, especially as regards maritime terms. Such was, for example, Oswald Loretz's opinion. He spoke of "North-Israelitic-Phoenician peculiarities of the [Jonah] language." He therefore saw the place of its composition as being "most likely the area of the Phoenician coast or a region under its direct influence."[38] It is noteworthy that this very region is the birthplace of Zeno and Chrysippos, the founders of the Stoa. Zeno was born in Citium, a Phoenician city whose patron-god was Herakles-Melkart, depicted there as riding a winged seahorse![39]

Stoic (and Cynic) influence can be seen, among other places, in the dialogue between sailors and Jonah on the ship deck. It is part of Stoic and Cynic ways of arguing to ask people who they are, what way of life they are called to, what kind of happiness they look for.[40] To the sailors' question, Jonah says that he is a Hebrew. We could contrast that statement with the one of Diogenes the Cynic who proclaimed himself a *"polites tou kosmou"* ("citizen of the world"),[41] but the opposition between the two men is only surface deep. Jonah adds immediately that he is the servant of a universal God, thus venting his stance that God is the Lord of all and of each. This conception falls in parallel with the cosmopolitan view of the Stoa. The whole world is a "megalopolis" and everyone is a citizen of the world.[42]

There are other parallels that will appear below in this chapter and in chapter 7 on Jonah 4. But we must return to the Menippean satire. From the study that is made by Bakhtin in his book on Dostoevsky, we select the following points:

1. The Menippean satire is free from any historical moorings, and even from any character of verisimilitude, although the heroes are occasionally historical. The satire gives free reign to philosophical invention. (Jonah is a historical character set by the author in situations deprived of all credibility in order better to ground the philosophical or theological argument.)

2. Fantasy is here omnipresent, but it is subservient to the quest for truth. That is why the hero climbs up to heaven or descends to the netherworld if need be, in order to test not so much himself as the truth. (Jonah, thrown in the midst of raging waters or of another Sodom, goes down as well to the netherworld, so that he may witness, however reluctantly, a truth that is not only his but God's.)

3. Symbolism here goes side by side with realism. The plot is unwinding on roads, on a ship deck, in inns, in places of ill repute, in short, where the visionary must confront baseness, depravity, wickedness. (Everything in the book of Jonah is

symbolical, even the prophet's name. The hero constantly faces more or less mythological monsters, unless they are perverted human beings.)

4. The Menippean tale is a literary genre dealing with ultimate problems, with life-and-death questions. The satire is here at the service of philosophical universalism.

5. The topology is here the market, as we saw, but also the "threshold," the city gate (or the gates of heaven, or the netherworld). (The parallels in Jonah are evident. That the scene is here, at least occasionally, liminal in the proper sense of the word, is indicated by Jon. 3:4a, for example.)

6. The storyteller's viewpoint is unusual; for example, he watches, like Jonah, from the top of a mountain what is happening to a city.

7. The hero is presented as moved by passions that border on folly—they bring him, for example, to desiring death, even to suicide. As Bakhtin says, "He stops coinciding with himself." He is the man of the extraordinary, often of the extravagant.

8. The author multiplies the oxymorons: the king acts as a slave, the bandit as a noble man, the prostitute as a saintly woman! (In Jonah, the prophet acts as an infidel; the sailors act like saints; the sea monster like a "sea taxi"; the king of Nineveh dons a sack and sits on ashes; a gang of thugs convert and go through repentance. . . .)

9. The Menippean tale is a genre open to all other genres. Poetry goes with prose. (In Jonah, the hymn and the prophetic oracle are both present but not without undergoing, as expected, a certain caricaturing.)

True, the alternation of prose and verse is a normal phenomenon in Semitic literature. There is thus nothing peculiar in the narrative of Jonah being interspersed with the hymn of chapter 2. It is, however, noteworthy that the intermingling of verse and prose is Menippos' innovation in Greek literature and without precedent in the classical period.[43] All students of late biblical literature know how often an originally Israelite feature is reinforced by a similar phenomenon from Babylon, Iran, or Greece. To give just one example, Jewish apocalyptic eschatology is at the crossroads of Israel and Iran.

10. The Menippean tale includes elements of social utopia in the form of travels to unknown lands, for example.

11. The Menippean tale holds a mirror to the mores and the passions of the time. By nature polemical, it shows the oddities of contemporaries.

12. Born, as we saw, in a period of decadence, the Menippean satire is perhaps the best vehicle of the preoccupations of the time.

Apropos these latter three characteristics, it is to be remembered that the third century B.C.E. is a time of party strife in Judea between the "Hellenized" (or modernist) Jews, and the Hasidim (or orthodox), strongly opposed to foreign influence on ancestral tradition. To an ideology of theocracy centered on the Jerusalem Temple as the earthly throne of God, the Hasidim opposed their utopia of an eschatological coming of the kingdom of God, a belief that actually relativized considerably the Judean social and religious institutions.[44] From this perspective, God's relationship and Israel's dealing with the non-Jews were invested with a decisive importance for the eschatological advent of the kingdom. Far from condoning the national isolationism of the governors Nehemiah and Ezra, the Hasidim demanded that the relationship with foreigners belong to the Jewish consciousness of their identity. Such a viewpoint can be found in popularly composed narratives like Ruth, the Moabitess,[45] and Jonah, the prophet, sent to the nation most hated by Israel. All nations, say Third Isaiah and Second Zechariah, are to come to Jerusalem to worship God with the Israelites. Some among them will even become priests and Levites (Isa. 66:21), and all will celebrate the Festival of Booths in the Temple of Jerusalem (Zech. 14).

The book of Jonah, as an instrument of propaganda for the party of opposition, presents a satiric aretalogy of an obscure prophet of the eighth century.[46] Lucian of Syria (ca. 125–192) also uses the Menippean model of the false aretalogy in *Philopseudes* and, indirectly, in *True History.* "The most memorable episode in the *True History,*" says Moses Hadas, "is its hero's adventures in the belly of the whale, and this inevitably recalls Jonah in the Old Testament. The curious thing about the book of Jonah," he continues, "is that it conforms so well to the pattern of the aretalogy.

The absolute universalism of Jonah, so directly opposed to the particularism of Ezra, for example, gives it a definitely Stoic coloring. Jonah's career, the wonderful things that befell him and their lesson, is exactly in the mode of the aretalogy."[47] Let us add that the Jonah aretalogy is parodic. The hero is an antihero; his theological stance is at the antipole of the author's.

Jonah is a book of protest against the isolation of some Judeans in Jerusalem. One cannot understand the book out of its historical context. As a matter of fact, Jonah raises anew the question of election. Israel alone is elected; if not, there would be no divine choice (cf. Num. 23:9; Deut. 7:7f.; 10:15; Amos 3:2). Israel has been called to separate itself from the rest of the nations (Lev. 20:26; 18:3f.; 20:23; Isa. 40:20; 52:11; Jer. 51:6, 45). At the antipode, there is Nineveh, the type of nonelection, the foil to election, because it is that which Jerusalem has chosen not to be (cf. Jon. 1:2; 3:8). In the negative, Nineveh is the justification of Jerusalem's election. It is the night in contrast to which light has its whole raison d'être. But Jonah cannot admit that night could sometime be called to become day, for, at the minimum, it would relativize the divine choice of Israel. If Jonah rejects his mission (1:3), it is not so much because of his hatred for the Ninevites as because of his puzzlement before the attitude of God (4:2). In short, Jonah represents the party of the "ideologists" in Jerusalem whose attitude vis-à-vis the nations is highly ambiguous.[48] They show themselves permeable to the ongoing Hellenization of the Near East and behave like citizens "liberated" by modern ideals, while keeping jealously the Temple privileges to which only the pure ones of their party have a right. As far as the nations are concerned, they entertain a sophism. Either the relationships of God with the nations are compassionate, and the oracle of destruction of Nineveh is without object; or they are strictly according to justice, and Nineveh will be irrevocably destroyed—in which case it is not even worthwhile to proclaim it in advance. Furthermore, if God intends, conditionally, to forgive and save the wicked city, why did he not show the same compassion for his own people whom he submitted successively to the Assyrians, the Babylonians, the Persians, the Macedonians, thus chastising Israel and Judah without measure? The problem is without solution.[49]

In a certain sense, whatever God would do with the nations appears as nothing less than capricious injustice.

The response of Jonah's author is a narrative fiction. The verisimilitude is quite secondary, as we saw above. But clearly, even fiction has its logic, which is not so strictly its own as it is commonsensical for the community it addresses; otherwise there would be no communication. If it is unusual in the Old Testament that a prophet be sent to a foreign nation, it is not, however, without precedent. Elijah constitutes an important parallel, which we shall develop later, and several prophets in Israel have uttered oracles against nations. Moreover, the word that Jonah is commissioned to deliver to Nineveh is a condemning one, as expected.

But, in the tale, the situation grows more complex. Jonah's word, against all expectation including his own, changes the hearts of the Ninevites, who convert and live. The bourgeois dogmatism as reflected in the prophet's attitude falls into its own trap. According to it, Israel's worth is greater than Nineveh's. Israel has trusted God's word while the nations reject it. Why should anyone preach to them a message that they will not understand? The chips are down; some are elected, others exclude themselves from the election. That is the satire of Jonah: the central character philosophically opts for a stance that the author rules out. Paradoxically, the party that was open to Hellenism missed the fact that Jewish particularism could not resist Western universalism.

The book of Jonah is one more evidence that the Hellenization of Palestine did not occur wholesale in some milieus and not at all in others. There were at least two faces to Hellenism, something like modern "Americanism" servilely imitated in its licentious aspects by many, understood in its generosity and pluralism by very few. At any rate, Jonah evidences the pervasive influence of the Hellenized *polis* like Gadara.

Jonah is a satire of the theocratic party and of its complacent isolationism. But, if the author has recourse to irony, he refrains from caricaturing his opponents.[50] He knows that their theological position is far from being stupid or even petty. He presents his hero as holding firm the promise of God to his people. Jonah is so far from being a narrow-minded bigot without breadth that he dares oppose God when he thinks that God's designs are wrong or unjust. That God is all that Jonah says he is (4:2), as far as Israel is concerned, does not raise any question in his (Jonah's) mind. The irony and the scandal are that God is also all these things vis-à-vis barbarian killers of Israel's children.[51]

In an equally subtle way, another aspect of the ambiguous attitude of the ideologists vis-à-vis foreign nations is also criticized.[52] If the character Jonah is none else but an orthodox Jew upset by an extravagant divine command, then the "Ninevites" of the third century B.C.E. are the Hellenists, kept at bay but also envied by the party of the Temple. The satire of Jonah proceeds first to their reduction to the status of Ninevites, the arch-enemy of Israel. They deserve one thing: total destruction within forty days. The only redeeming factor is not their superior culture, their philosophical humanism, or their religious tolerance, but their capacity to repent, that is, in fact, to *stop being what they used to be.* In response to the modernists, the author of Jonah suggests that if there were Hellenists to be imitated in Jerusalem, they would be those who repented. No criticism of the Hellenization of Jewish mores in the third century could be more subversive than this. The roles are inverted, as becomes the Menippean; the prophet becomes an antiprophet, the hero an antihero, the just God has a strange conception of justice, the masters of thinking of the post-Alexandrian world do indeed teach what they eschew, namely, only those who are ready to die deserve to live.

This is the extreme difficulty and also the extreme fascination of the book of Jonah. It must be read with the living consciousness that the problem it traces is theological/philosophical, psychological, and political. That is why our essay tries to approach it from all directions at the same time, as a theological pamphlet and a social-political critique, as a popular narrative whose bearing upon the human soul is direct and universal. The third century author has a deep knowledge of the inner struggle in everyone to discover the meaning of life and of destiny. The social, political, and theological context of the time was conducive to the stance one finds in Jonah. The book was written in reaction against the intellectual provincialism and the religious fanaticism of some in Judah. It affirms that to be Jewish means to be

44

fully human in one's relationship with life under all forms, something that cannot be fulfilled by belonging to a sect or to a coterie. The universal and the particular are in dialectical mutual relation; one must remember this in reading this biblical book written on two different levels: it is a Jewish book addressed to Israel within a particular historical and geographical context; it is also a universal message addressed to all people at all times. The satire is a popular literary genre with universal claim. Behind the unique personality of the hero it is not difficult to understand that the whole of humanity is put on stage and questioned.[53]

That is why the external influences upon the composition of Jonah are not limited to the Menippean satire. Jonah is also a popular tale drawing many of its resources from the funds of universal folklore. In the next chapter, we shall review some of the parallel myths and legends putting on stage a hero in search of himself through confronting and superseding external obstacles, clear symbols of his own inhibitions. Because of this, precisely, psychology has found in those stories an inexhaustible source of depth symbolism. Carl G. Jung in particular has attached his name to a specific psychoanalytical research in that direction. We intend in chapter 3 to present also a critique of Jung's conclusions.

NOTES

1. See, for example, "Paul Ricoeur on Biblical Hermeneutics," *Semeia* 4, ed. J. D. Crossan (Missoula, Mont.: Scholars Press, 1975); or P. Ricoeur, *Interpretation Theory: Discourse and the Surplus of Meaning* (Fort Worth: Texas University Press, 1976).

2. J. D. Crossan, *The Dark Interval* (Niles, Ill.: Argus, 1975), p. 66. He writes, "the most magnificent parable in the Hebrew Bible is the book of Jonah which is the precursor for the parables of Jesus and the distant ancestor of the contemporary parabolic genre" ("Parable, Allegory, and Paradox," in *Semiology and Parables*, ed. D. Patte [Pittsburgh: Pickwick Press, 1976], p. 251). Jonah is considered as a parable by Bewer, Smith, Bentzen, Smart, Good, and others. E. Haller calls it a *"Beispielerzählung"* ("Die Erzählung von dem Prophet Jona," p. 50).

3. Ricoeur, *Temps et Récit*, vol. 3 (Paris: Seuil, 1985), pt. 3, chap. 2. (our trans.).

4. *Poetics*, 1451b.15–18: for the narrative to be convincing, it must be "verisimilar."

5. What is at stake is more what happens than what happened.

6. See B. Uspenski, *A Poetics of Composition: The Structure of the Artistic Text and Typology of a Compositional Form* (Berkeley: University of California Press, 1973). The book entirely focuses on the notion of "point of view."

7. E. Rohde, *Der griechische Roman und seine Vorläufer* (4th ed.; Hildesheim: Georg Olms, 1960), p. 267, speaks of the presence of the "picaresque" novel in the Satires of Petronius. Such "cameos," he says (note 1) were widespread at the beginning of the so-called Hellenistic time. Particularly remarkable was Menippos the Cynic (middle of third century B.C.E.). He mixed poetry and prose and appeared humorous and sarcastic as it fitted a Cynic.

8. See Barthes, *S/Z* (Paris: Seuil, 1970), p. 47.

9. But, here again, the ambiguity of the book of Jonah would accommodate the definition of myth as proposed by N. Frye (*The Great Code: The Bible and Literature* (New York & London: Harcourt Brace Jovanovich, 1982), p. 47: "There are and remain two aspects of myth: one is its story-structure, which attaches it to literature, the other is its social function as concerned knowledge, what it is important for a society to know."

10. R. Scholes and R. Kellogg, *The Nature of Narrative* (London: Oxford University Press, 1966), p. 229.

11. Cf. W. Booth, *A Rhetoric of Irony* (Chicago: University of Chicago Press, 1974), p. 73. There is irony "whenever we notice an unmistakable conflict between the beliefs expressed and the beliefs we hold *and suspect the author of holding*." Jonah belongs, I think, to what Booth calls "ironies of event or nature" (p. 241n7). Such ironies are "unstable," for they do not tell us "with any confidence how far or in what direction the poem takes us beyond these openly asserted local ironies [in Jonah, the events and the natural phenomena]" (p. 248).

12. See B. Uspenski, *Poetics of Composition* (see n. 6, above).

13. F. K. Stanzel, *Theorie des Erzählens* (2nd ed.; Göttingen: Vandenhoeck u. Ruprecht, 1982).

14. Uspenski, *Poetics of Composition*, p. 103.

15. Ibid., p. 126.

16. Dorrit Cohn, *Transparent Minds* (Princeton: Princeton University Press, 1978).

17. As when the author writes, "he seemed to be happy with it" or "he evidently enjoyed the scene," and so forth.

18. Uspenski, *Poetics of Composition*, p. 87.

19. Ricoeur, *Temps et Récit*, vol. 3, chap. 2.

20. M. Bakhtin, *Problems of Dostoevsky's Poetics* (Ann Arbor, Mich.: Ardis, 1973).

21. Bakhtin, *Rabelais and His Work* (Cambridge, Eng.: Cambridge University Press, 1968).

22. Bakhtin, *Dostoevsky*, pp. 100ff.

23. Ibid., pp. 165ff.

24. Ibid., p. 89.

25. The extent to which irony differs from a hero cult is stressed by A. von Schlegel (nineteenth century). He opposes irony and tragedy. See R. Wellek, *A History of Modern Criticism, the Romantic Age* (New Haven: Yale University Press, 1955), p. 300. Irony is the antipode of epics.

26. See E. M. Good, *Irony in the Old Testament* (Sheffield: Almond Press, 1981); J. C. Holbert, " 'Deliverance Belongs to YHWH' : Satire in the Book of Jonah," *JSOT* 21 (1981): 59–81.

27. "Dans le texte," says Barthes in *S/Z*, p. 157, "seul parle le lecteur."

28. Bakhtin, *Dostoevsky*, chap. 1.

29. Ibid., p. 76.

JONAH, A MENIPPEAN SATIRE?

30. Ricoeur, *Temps*, vol. 3, *in fine*.

31. Barthes, *S/Z* p. 23; quotation from p. 82. Cf. E. Staiger, *Die Kunst der Interpretation* (2nd ed.; Zurich: Atlantic Vlg., 1955), p. 33: "All authentic and living artistic work is, within its genuine limits, left uncompleted." Other works, ancient and modern, are similarly incomplete, including the Gospel of Mark, or the above-mentioned "Der Zauberberg." Iris Murdoch writes, "Since reality is incomplete, art must not be too afraid of incompleteness" ("Against Dryness," *Encounter*, January 1961). About Mark, J. L. Magness says that Mark's "sense of absence" encourages his readers to make sense of that absence for themselves in a positive and powerful way (*Sense and Absence* [Chico, Calif.: Scholars Press, 1986]). One will remember the "end" of F. Kafka's *The Trial* (1915): "From that moment, K. forgot the tribunal."

32. Barthes, *S/Z*, p. 82.

33. R. Alter, *The Art of Biblical Narrative* (New York: Basic Books, 1981). pp. 125–26.

34. Ibid., p. 154.

35. See R. Reitzenstein, *Hellenistische Wundererzählungen* (Darmstadt: Wissenschaftliche Buchgesellschaft, 1963), p. 35. The book of Jonah is the first example of that literary genre in the Bible, but it is not the last; it is striking to find traces of it in the Gospels, but the genre is there, it is true, largely molded by other ideological imperatives. See, e.g., U. Simon, *Story and Faith* (London: SPCK, 1975), p. 55. It is thus remarkable that Jonah's story, to which Jesus refers as a "sign" of his own destiny (Matt. 12:38ff.), is from a literary point of view as well *praeparatio evangelica*.

36. A Hellenistic dating of Jonah has been advocated by several critics: (1) O. Eissfeldt, *Einleitung in das A. T.* (Tübingen: J. C. B. Mohr, 1934), p. 451: "unter 200 v. Chr. dürfen wir mit der Ansetzung des Buches keinesfalls hinuntergehen." (2) M. Hadas, *Hellenistic Culture, Fusion and Diffusion* (New York: Columbia University Press, 1959), p. 174: ". . . there can be no doubt that [Jonah] belongs to the Hellenistic age." (3) H. W. Wolff, *Studien zum Jonabuch* (Neukirchen-Vluyn: Neukirchener Vlg., 1965), pp. 68–69: excludes a date before the first half of the fourth century. (4) M. Hengel, *Judentum und Hellenismus* (Tübingen: J. C. B. Mohr, 1973f), p. 205: ". . . rather towards the end of the Persian empire than the beginning of the Hellenistic era." (5) Attila Fáj, "The Stoic Features of the Book of Jonah," *Instituto Orientale di Napoli Annali* (Rome, 1972), pp. 309–45.

37. For example, Qoheleth probably imitates the Greek diatribe invented by Bion of Borysthenes, another Cynic of the fourth-third centuries. The diatribe was adopted as such by Menippos and Meleager. See esp. 12:1–7.

38. O. Loretz, "Herkunft und Sinn der Jona-Erzählung," in *BZ*, n.s. vol. 5, no. 1 (1961): 24.

39. So on coins from Tyre. See M. Pohlenz, *Die Stoa* (Göttingen: Vandenhoeck & Ruprecht, 1948–49), vol. 1, p. 22.

40. See Epictetus, II.10; M. Aurelius, VIII.52; Seneca, *Ep.* 41.7f.; 82.6; Persius, III.67.

41. See below in this chapter.

42. See Hans von Arnim, *Stoicorum Veterum Fragmenta*, 4 vols. (Leipzig: G. B. Teubner Veg., 1903–24; new ed., Stuttgart: G. B. Teubner, 1968), vol. 3, pp. 78f. (fragments 316–323).

43. Cf. M. Hadas, *Hellenistic Culture*, p. 111. Menippos was imitated by Seneca (*Apokolokyntosis*) and Petronius (*Satyricon*), both Menippean satires. But the

clearer example is provided by Lucian, our main source of information on the Menippean satire.

44. See Isa. 66:1–2, where one can read: "Thus says the Lord, The heaven is my throne and the earth my footstool. What is this house that you would build unto me and what is this place of my rest? All beings my hand made them, all are mine, oracle of the Lord. The one I do look to is this one: the humble whose spirit is down and who trembles at my word."

45. See A. LaCocque, "Date et milieu du livre de Ruth," *RHPR* 3–4 (1979): 583–93. Ruth reinterprets the Deuteronomic laws, as do Isa. 56:3–8 on the presence of strangers and eunuchs in the community, and Zech. 14 who broadens the narrow frame of the Levitic laws of purity.

46. See n. 35 above.

47. M. Hadas, *Hellenistic Culture*, pp. 173f.

48. There is "ideology," says P. Ricoeur, when the rhetoric is subservient to a process of legitimation of authority. Of "utopia," he says that one is unable to define it from its contents. "The consistence of the phenomenon of utopia is not due to its contents, but to its function that always consists in proposing a social alternative" (Personal communication to the authors).

49. It is still the problem in focus in the apocalypses of 100 C.E. (2 Baruch, 4 Esdras, Apocalypse of Abraham).

50. Wilhelm Rudolph, *Joel-Amos-Obadja-Jona* (Gütersloh: Mohn 1971), p. 369, has correctly seen that the author's adversaries are the disciples of Ezra and Nehemiah. In opposition to their opinion, he sees the foreign rule over Israel as an obstacle on the way to the restoration and the *eschaton*. Rudolph's stance is rejected by G. von Rad (*Theology*, vol. 2, ad loc.), O. Loretz ("Herkunft und Sinn der Jona-Erzählung," p. 28), O. Eissfeldt (*The Old Testament, An Introduction* [New York: Harper & Row, 1965], p. 405, or *Einleitung*, p. 547), P. Trible (*Studies*, pp. 262–63), and others. In point of fact, the author of Jonah deals with his adversaries with the same tact as Cervantes deals with Don Quixote, with respect and empathy.

51. See chap. 7, below.

52. See chap. 7, below. As B. Childs says, the eighth-century fictional setting gives credence to the interpretation that in question are the relations between Israel and the nations (*Introduction to the Old Testament as Scripture* [Philadelphia: Fortress Press, 1979], pp. 425–26).

53. See Ricoeur, *The Conflict of Interpretations*, ed. Don Ihde (Evanston: Northwestern University Press, 1974), pp. 349–50: ". . . a *textual* exegesis is abstract and remains meaningless for us so long as the 'figuratives' it comments on are not inserted into the affective and representative dynamics. . . . The symbol is a phantasm disavowed and overcome but not at all abolished."

THREE

HEROES, MONSTERS, AND INITIATORY ORDEALS: A Response to Carl G. Jung

> Symbolic language is language in which the world outside is a symbol of the world inside, a symbol for our souls and our minds. . . . The story [of Jonah] is told as if these events had actually happened. However, it is written in symbolic language and all the realistic events described are symbols for the inner experiences of the hero.
>
> Erich Fromm, *The Forgotten Language*
> (New York: Grove Press, 1951), pp. 12, 22.

As is well known, Greek and Roman myths and tales have deeply inspired human disciplines and particularly depth psychology. The latter found a well of symbols for the needs, the goals and means, the fantasy and the dreams, which are fundamental to humankind (Oedipus, Thanatos, Electra, Narcissus . . .). It is our contention that the book of Jonah lends itself no less than does Greek tragedy to psychological and psychoanalytical interpretation. Moreover, as the vision of Jerusalem is profoundly different from that of Athens, one can expect the symbolic patterns of the Israelites to reveal *other* human dimensions and images. Athens and Jerusalem are speaking of and to humanity. This simple fact bridges their respective conceptions. It is considerably strengthened by the fact that the book of Jonah

---

Part of this chapter was published by Pierre-E. Lacocque in the *Journal of Religion and Health* 23 (1984): 218–28, under the title "Fear of Engulfment and the Problem of Identity." It is here reprinted with the permission of Human Sciences Press.

belongs to a literary genre close to the Menippean satire. This does not mean that the Greek and Hebrew worlds have become homogenous. One is heroic and tragic, that is, marked by a certain sense of determinism. The other, as it expresses itself in the book of Jonah, presents an antihero whose "tragic destiny" is transcended by a dialogue with God, creator of life. In it Jonah is fully involved, and to it he decisively contributes by the very course of his existence. From such a perspective, the issue with Jonah is not would he succeed in becoming what he can be, but rather, will he become what he actually is by vocation.

Donald G. Miller is reported to have called Jonah "the high point of the Old Testament . . . the peak of Old Testament revelation."[1] The statement is striking and it may well represent the truth. It is all the more interesting that such a profound theological achievement adopted the form of a tale. Its brevity and unassumingness did not prevent it from becoming very famous. Although "one of the smallest strands in the mighty cable of the Scriptures" —as Father Mapple says in Herman Melville's famous work[2]— the narrative of Jonah, told in the language and with the ideas of the time, has easily triumphed over centuries and remains today one of the most intriguing stories of the universal repertoire.

Perhaps the fact that the biblical tale ends with such a striking lack of resolution sparked the exceptional imaginations. Psychology knows of the "Zeigarnik Effect," according to which completed tasks tend to be more easily forgotten than uncompleted ones,[3] because in the former case the motivation to perform is satisfied "while the drive persists and enhances memory when [the tasks] are uncompleted."[4] We all feel the urge to take over Jonah's uncompleted task. The art of the narrator is such that when we allow the narrative to grasp us, we *become* Jonah. His unfitness in life painfully reminds us of our own daily struggle with meaning.

No wonder, therefore, that the book has received various psychological interpretations. Bruno Bettelheim, for one, has shown that different personal meanings are found in the same story, depending upon the emotional maturity of the reader.[5] These symbolic stories, we feel, reflect universal, unresolved conflicts deeply rooted within the human psyche, so that they must be dealt with ever anew and at every stage of a person's emotional growth. Bettelheim sees Jonah's struggle from a psychoanalytic point of view. For him the key to the narrative lies in Jonah 2 where the prophet discovers his "higher morality" and is "wondrously reborn." The acknowledgment of his "higher self" helps him to go to Nineveh. This he was able to do only when he reached "full humanity" (i.e., when he was able no longer to depend on his id or pleasure principle, which had urged him to run away to Tarshish).

It is, however, to Hyman Fingert that we owe the first detailed Freudian analysis of the prophet's inner anguish.[6] Fingert sees Jonah's character and behavior as revealing an emotionally disturbed person who actually lived centuries ago. The main theme of this historical parable is that Jonah is angry at his mother for preferring his father over him. This injustice "could be the wickedness of Nineveh that Jonah feels called upon to denounce."[7] At this point, the "prophet" of the story receives from his ego the command to rebel against his parents' preference for each other. The saving of Nineveh symbolizes his renunciation of his sexual longing "and wishes for the mother and her destruction."[8]

Besides seeing mother symbols in practically all events in the story (e.g., Tarshish, the ship, the fish, Nineveh, even the king), Fingert comes up with interpretations still more difficult to follow. For example, with regard to the worm that ate the gourd (Jon. 4:7), he had this to say:

> It seems indicated that the worm responsible for the gourd's destruction represents Jonah's fantasy of the destructiveness of the penis in intercourse. . . . Preoccupation with pregnancy or birth is also indicated. . . . It would appear possible to surmise that Jonah's wife may have died following, or during, pregnancy or from a disorder of the female organs he could relate to intercourse.[9]

The analyst did not take into consideration any of the historical, conceptual, or existential issues facing Israel at the time the narrative was written. The result is a farfetched, unwarranted interpretation. Jonah's fantasies are less apparent than are Fingert's.[10]

Another psychoanalytic study of the Jonah narrative is proposed by Joseph More.[11] For him the tale has no connection with a real person, contrary to Fingert's opinion. More understands the book as a "myth of biblical man, his character and his vicissitudes."[12] He sees the prophet Jonah experiencing resentment and jealousy toward the Ninevites: "God, Jonah's father figure is the God of Nineveh too, and thus the father of the people of Nineveh, who thereby become Jonah's brothers."[13] In biblical times, the author argues, large families and strong sibling rivalries were not uncommon. The stories of Cain and Abel or of Joseph and his brothers depict well such situations. What Jonah wants is to get the love of God all for himself. Nineveh represents "the bad mother whom [he] wants to destroy because she mothers others."[14] The issue for Jonah is not, however, Oedipal. He does not want to get rid of his father in order to get his mother's undivided love and attention, as Fingert believed. Rather, More argues, he is jealous of his siblings because of the love they also receive from his parents. That is why, afraid of his death fantasy as regards his brothers in Nineveh, the prophet decides to run away to Tarshish. Moved by his fear to destroy those he loves in Nineveh, he runs away lest his murderous wishes (id impulses) be fulfilled should he go eastward to the Assyrians.[15]

So goes More's psychological abstraction. No more than Fingert does he take into consideration the historical context of the book of Jonah. This omission entails the oversight of crucial points of the tale and consequently is a tendentious reading.

Of particular relevance to our study are the contributions of Carl G. Jung and Erich Fromm. Unlike Fingert or More, who saw Jonah struggling with his incest taboos, Oedipal complex, or sibling rivalry, Fromm's approach is more psycho-social in orientation. All the events in the narrative, he explains, are symbols of the prophet's inner experiences (e.g., going aboard the ship and down to its inner parts, falling asleep, being in the ocean or inside the fish). These guaranteed him a condition of "safe withdrawal from communication with other human beings. They represent what could be represented in another symbol, the fetus in the mother's womb."[16] Jonah runs away from God because he is afraid that the people in Nineveh will repent and be forgiven.

The prophet differs from other prophets in the Hebrew Bible in that he is not prompted by love of and solidarity with fellow human beings.[17] In fact, Fromm argues, "he wanted 'justice' to be done, not mercy."[18]

Carl G. Jung was among the first to hold that all in all, we are not different from our ancestors, even the most distant ones.[19] It is because of these similarities, he continued, that we can learn about ourselves through their legacies (i.e., their myths, legends, and recorded reflections). One motif in particular must be emphasized in conjunction with the Jonah book: the motif of engulfment. It is found in myths and legends from all over the world and will serve here as a heuristic means to realize the universality of the archetype and the revelatory dimension of the symbol, veritable gold mine of psychological truths about ourselves. It will also serve as background to Carl G. Jung's contribution to the symbolism of the Jonah tale. As we shall see, for him the theme of engulfment is of paramount import and symbolizes the potential dangers associated with introspection and the search for a cohesive sense of self. We thus start with an exploration of some hero myths that illustrate the fear of engulfment.

HERO MYTHS WITH ENGULFMENT MOTIFS

From time immemorial, humans have understood that inner peace is unequivocally tied up with the taming of our most primitive fear, namely, the fear of death. The image of being swallowed by a monster and the ensuing "resurrection" from it was typically used to portray such connection. What is striking about most hero myths is the gruesome and frightening dimensions of their ordeals. The image or archetype of a hero battling a monster can be found in myths and legends from the earliest civilizations. The theme is found in New Zealand, Japan, China, Africa, Mexico, among other places.[20] Already at the time of Sumer, over 4,000 years ago, we find the creation myth with the divine hero Marduk and the wicked goddess Tiamat. Marduk kills Tiamat in a duel by entering her mouth with seven winds. He cuts her insides into pieces and makes mincemeat with her heart. By eating a vital part of a monster, archaic man believed a hero acquired wisdom.

He won magical powers and strengths previously held by the slain creature; and as a result he became invulnerable and immortal.[21]

Leo Frobenius, in a book entitled *Das Zeitalter des Sonnengottes* ("The Age of the Sun-God"), gives numerous examples of heroes from all civilizations fighting a giant monster, for instance a great octopus, entering its belly, going through a terrible ordeal ("The Night Sea Journey"), and finally emerging victorious (like the sun at dawn) after killing it (see fig. 1).[22] In many such stories, the hero is swallowed by a water monster while on a journey going East (symbol of consciousness).[23] The engulfment typically takes place in the West (symbol of unconsciousness), at the antipode of the planned destination. The hero's trip resumes toward the East while he is in the monster's belly. The hero loses his hair—symbol of power of thought[24]—because of the intense heat within the monster. He then experiences hunger pangs. He finds, however, a way to light a fire and eats the monster's heart. Finally, he cuts the animal's belly and slips out bald, that is, he is reborn, renewed yet branded by his confrontation with the monster.

Frobenius tells also of a Polynesian hero named Nganaoa being swallowed by a huge clam, then by an octopus with giant tentacles, followed by a final engulfment in a great whale with jaws. To liberate himself, Nganaoa makes a fire inside the monster. The latter dies and the hero frees himself by his own courage and cleverness. The "whale-dragons" that are killed, Frobenius continues, sometimes contain not only people or the hero's parents, but plants, animals, even an entire country longing to be delivered.

There is also an Indian tale that tells of a hero, Saktideva, who, while searching for the "Golden City of Legend," finds his ship capsized and is swallowed by a "great fish." The hero is saved by a king who slits open the monster's belly. Similar stories are found in Ceylon, New Guinea, and other places.

The theme of Jonah and fish is also found, with the psychological and emotional dynamism that characterizes it, in many a modern tale. Jules Verne's Captain Nemo (1877) in his submarine, the *Nautilus,* lives in the depth of the seas away from all civilization; Collodi's Pinocchio (1883) is swallowed by a "dog-fish" after disobeying the fairy and his "father"; Herman Melville's Captain Ahab (1851) strives for vengeance against the whale

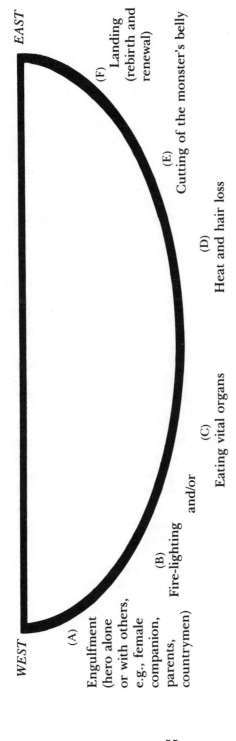

WEST

(A)

Engulfment
(hero alone
or with others,
e.g., female
companion,
parents,
countrymen)

(B)

Fire-lighting

and/or

(C)

Eating vital organs

(D)

Heat and hair loss

(E)

Cutting of the monster's belly

(F)

Landing
(rebirth and
renewal)

EAST

Figure 1. The Night Sea Journey.

(Adapted from Frobenius, *Das Zeitalter des Sonnengottes*, Berlin, 1904, p. 421; Jacobi, *Complex, Archetype, Symbol*, Princeton, 1959, pp. 108f.; and Jung, *Symbols of Transformation*, 2nd ed., Princeton, 1956, pp. 210f.)

Moby Dick; Daniel Defoe's Robinson Crusoe (1719) displays a real kinship with the traveler Jonah.

Typically, we find the hero alone, wandering and searching for a (hidden) treasure of some kind.[25] A voyage across the seas is often called for. Gilgamesh wanders throughout the world in search of a marsh plant named "dittu" supposedly having miraculous powers to restore youth and prolong life indefinitely.[26] A Norse myth tells a similar story about magic apples that keep people young forever. Hercules must also travel to the end of the world to find the golden apples of the Hesperides.

In most tales involving a hidden treasure, dragons, sharks, or other monsters roam around it. In the modern tale *The Pearl* of John Steinbeck, the pearl divers must watch for poison fish, the spotted botete, which lie on the bottom of the eel-grass beds.[27] The danger depicted in symbolic narratives of this sort was not altogether unrealistic. In Polynesia, pearl divers risk their lives to get at the gem.

The mythical motif of engulfment is also present in the initiation rites of many cultures.[28] Mircea Eliade, for instance, tells us of a secret African society named Ngakola.[29] The initiation of its candidates calls for the reenactment of the deeds of a mythical hero battling the monster Ngakola. It is told to them how Ngakola swallows people and spews them out renewed. To initiate the candidates, they are put through extreme pain and ordeals to help them experience what it must have felt like by their predecessor in the monster's belly. Eliade describes the process:

> The candidate is put in a hut which symbolizes the monster's body. There, he hears Ngakola's eerie voice, there he is whipped and tortured, for he is told that he is now in Ngakola's belly and is being digested. More ordeals follow; then the master of initiation proclaims that Ngakola, who has devoured the candidate, has disgorged him.[30]

This type of rite of passage in rebirth ceremonies can be seen in practically all civilizations. In some Hindu rites, the sinner or penitent must go through an artificial cow to be purified. The Shamans of Lapland are supposed to enter the intestines of a big fish or whale.[31] These hero-myths, Jung asserted, reveal deep psychological truths about ourselves. To his reflections we now turn.

CARL G. JUNG ON THE BIRTH OF THE HERO

[The hero] is first and foremost a self-representation of the longing of the unconscious of its unquenched and unquenchable desire for the light of consciousness . . . the purpose of the descent as universally exemplified in the myth of the hero is to show that only in the region of danger (watery abyss, cavern, forest, island, castle, etc.) can one find the "treasure hard to attain" (jewel, virgin, life-potion, victory over death). . . . [the fear of introspection is] at bottom, the fear of the journey to Hades. . . . The psychic substratum, that dark realm of the unknown, exercises a fascinating attraction that threatens to become the more overpowering the further [the hero] penetrates into it. The psychological danger that arises here is the disintegration of personality . . . a form of *mortificatio*.[32]

The appealing element in those myths and related tales, for Jung, is that the heroes' search for the Pearl of the World or the Grail, really symbolizes our own search for meaning.[33] The "treasure hard to find," as he calls it, is in fact the knowledge of and mastery over the unconscious processes and desires. The wish for immortality so commonly shared by mythical heroes must be viewed *symbolically*. Growing old with less and less awareness of the self means slowly losing grip on life. And this psychological awareness is what heroes seem to intuit. Their "immortality" is already within themselves but not yet fully detected. The search of the hero, Jung concludes, is really for *himself*, "newborn from the dark maternal cave of the unconscious where he was stranded. . . ."[34]

In opposition to Freud, who believed that mythical heroes' deepest longings were for incest, Jung saw such desires as generally and purely *symbolical*.[35] The deepest wish is not so much for sexual contact with the mother, he claimed, as it is to regress to an anxiety-free state reminiscent of how it must have felt to be in her womb: nurtured, protected, and held. The longing, in short, is for the fantasy she triggers in us all: for "a paradisiacal state of unconsciousness."[36]

This particular longing is often witnessed in clinical practice. Mrs. N, for instance, is a middle-aged woman whom the second author of this book has seen in therapy for some time. For over twenty years now she has complained of depression, tiredness, and low self-esteem. Though never found to be psychotically depressed, she has been in many psychiatric hospitals. It soon became obvious that Mrs. N's basic mode of relating to the outside world, including therapy, is by seeking anyone she can merge with in the hope to be held and taken care of. When anxious or fearing insanity (i.e., ego-dissolution), she typically numbs herself by taking pills. These she often takes over the recommended dosage. Furthermore, when the going gets especially rough for her, she withdraws to her bedroom and covers herself with blankets. This regression-to-the-womb symbolism is here unmistakably clear, especially since in addition to covering herself, she reports holding her body in a fetal position. Behind the *desire* to merge or regress also lies the *fear* of the loss of self.[37] For Jung, this wish to return to the "mother" by far transcends the alleged incestuous desires in the Oedipal complex. He writes: "The regressing libido apparently desexualizes itself by retreating back step by step to the *pre-sexual* stage of earliest infancy. Even there, it does not make a halt, but in a manner of speaking, continues right back to the intra-uterine, pre-natal condition."[38]

In the dynamics of the unconscious, Jung saw many similarities with the image we have of the mother. Like her, the unconscious contains, holds, nourishes. As the mother stands for the foundation of life, so does the unconscious stand for the foundation of consciousness. But there is more to that image. As Erich Neumann clearly demonstrated in *The Great Mother*, she has ever symbolized not only the good and loving mother, but also the Terrible Mother: the one who holds back to herself, the one who suffocates and destroys the child.[39] Thus the unconscious is not only "all the nourishing and creative energies that are at the root of life," but represents also the "*maw of death.*"[40]

This ambivalence of the mother-unconscious explains why to plunge into one's depth could be a perilous voyage. No one can predict whether one will come out unscathed. The battle for deliverance over the unconscious is an ongoing life-long process. To reach "individuation," Jung concludes, one has to conquer daily the unconscious forces lurking in the depth of one's psyche.

But the question remains: What is there to be gained by risking the plunge into one's depth? What do heroes find in the underworld or at bottoms of oceans? Eliade responds: "One goes down into the belly of a giant or monster in order to learn *science* or *wisdom*."[41] The hero is now a person who *knows*. He has learned the mysteries surrounding life and is one who has been given revelations that are metaphysical in nature. To face one's demons and to succeed in taming them implies that one no longer fears the disintegration of the self. Such initiation is tantamount to transcending the death anxiety.[42]

But, according to Jung, heroes long for more than inner cohesion. Since the self is directly linked and influenced by the unconscious, and since the latter, for Jung, has collective and spiritual dimensions, it ensues that the self sought after by heroes is not just an "inner self" but also a "world self," that is, a self in interconnection with other selfs. Jung defined such self as an ideal image we all long for. It is the image of the divine, of God within us.[43] Self-seeking is therefore tantamount to aspiring to be Godlike.

In summary then, for Jung, heroism has two basic components: first, it means risking being alone with oneself and accepting the need to be severed from the biological mother.[44] It means relinquishing the great temptation to have someone fully caring or protecting one. Second, a hero is one who is not afraid of the messages of the unconscious and one who allows them to shape consciousness. But ultimately, it means longing for a better, more peaceful world to live in, both for oneself and for humankind as a whole. Heroes aim toward such a goal by assuming the roles of models and teachers. Through these, they point the way to how to live life while in relationship with the divine.

CARL JUNG: A CRITIQUE

In our opinion, Jung did not emphasize enough the importance of the "world self" in defining psychic health. As opposed to Alfred Adler, for instance, who stressed the social orientation and the cooperation among members of humankind as *sine qua non* to being mentally healthy,[45] Jung seems to pay much more attention to the roles the personal and collective unconscious play in shaping the self. In spite of acknowledging such shaping to include also directing the self toward communal and altruistic goals, Jung is much more preoccupied with how to decipher and tame the inner demons and forces lurking at the depths of the psyche.[46] In reading his memoirs, for instance, one cannot avoid noticing Jung's main preoccupation, perhaps even obsession, with the dynamics of the unconscious. What makes his theoretical framework difficult to accept is his assertion that the ego is weak and basically unable to cope with the unconscious forces underlying it. He says:

> We are a psychic process which does not control, or only partly direct[s]. . . .[47] Man, that is to say his conscious ego, is a mere bagatelle, a feather whirled hither and thither with every gust of wind. . . .[48] Furthermore, since the Will is rooted in consciousness, and specifically within the Ego, it is also weak and unimportant in shaping the Self. In fact, being at the mercy of the Ego, the Will is a mere "wish-dream."[49]

And on freedom:

> We have gotten accustomed to saying apotropaically, "I *have* such and such a desire or habit or feeling of resentment," instead of the more veracious "such and such a desire or habit or feeling of resentment *has me*." The latter formulation would certainly rob us of even the illusion of freedom. But I ask myself whether this would not be better in the end than fuddling ourselves with words.[50]

So, if the ego is so weak an entity, where does freedom of choice and social responsibility fit in Jung's system? Are we to believe ethical choices are a waste of time, since the unconscious controls us at all times? Surely Jung is correct in advising us to look deep within for a better understanding of who we are ("the treasure hard to find"), but he loses sight that because we are born *through* and *by* communication (first, the parental union), our ontological root *is* encounter. Indeed, our ontological need is encounter. At the deepest fibers of ourselves, we are called to become beings-for-the-world.[51] Only when actively involved in genuine I-Thou relationships and *healthy* communal life can we discover our true self.[52]

Finally, we believe Jung did not emphasize enough that more often than not, the obstacle to healthy growth lies in the avoidance of something we *already know* but refuse to acknowledge, let alone integrate, within consciousness. We shall return to these points in chapters 8 and 9, below.

JONAH, MIRROR OF OUR SOUL

The story of Jonah also depicts an engulfed hero. But in contradistinction with those heroes who by sheer force, snatch treasures jealously protected by dragons or monsters, Jonah here has no recourse to heroic acts. There are no indications that he wants to kill the fish or that he wants to be liberated from its womb!

Also, inasmuch as the engulfment motif looks similar to other hero-myths, the resemblance really stops there. Jonah is saved not by wit or superhuman strength, but after a prayer of thanksgiving! Even though he is at the antipode of Jerusalem, Jona's salvation lies in the *remembrance* of God's presence. The story could be called "heroic" only through a semantic broadening of the term. Actually, what Jonah is struggling with is not so much his own unconscious—though one is never exempt from such struggle—as with *something he already knows but refuses to accept*. As Jonah says, "Now, Lord, is not this what I thought while yet on my own turf? That's why I fled in the first place to Tarshish, *for I knew all along that you are a merciful God, slow to anger, rich in kindness, and forgiving of evil intention*" (Jon. 4:2, italics added).

Thus Jonah knew. He is not a hero questing for the Grail or his own unconscious. Jonah is a man who, like most of us, runs away from his vocation. The biblical tale is the antipode of an epic. Its message to everyone is that true heroism is not where one customarily finds it, as suggested by popular tales, myths, or legends à la Jung. True heroism—which Jonah at first refuses to envision for himself—lies in the confrontation with one's destiny, one's raison d'être, one's vocation. The new proposed "initiation rite" is, here, not to go and fight supernatural monsters in mythical lands. For the enemy is in us: a rejection of the commandment that only is capable of letting us find our authenticity (see chap. 8, below).

Before we proceed, however, it is of particular interest that the author of Jonah presents an episode on the model of an initiation rite. Below, in chapter 7, we shall discuss another such initiatic model apropos the gourd-tree that grows above Jonah's head in Jonah 4. In both cases, the author is satirical. Jonah's "initiation" is as remote from history-of-religion paradigms as can be. The choice by the author of a material so marked by mystery religions is, however, a precious indication of the time of the narrative composition.[53]

NOTES

1. Quoted by H. M. Crawford, *A Reluctant Missionary* (Chicago: U.P.C. Board of Education, 1965), p. 34.

2. H. Melville, *Moby Dick* (New York: Holt, Rinehart & Winston, 1957), pp. 40–41.

3. B. Zeigarnik, "Über das Behalten von erledigten Handlungen," *Psychologie Forschung* 9 (1927): 1–85. See also H. Cason, "The Learning and Retention of Pleasant and Unpleasant Activities," *Archives of Psychology* 21 (1932): 5–10.

4. R. M. Goldenson, *The Encyclopedia of Human Behavior*, 2 vols. (Garden City, N.Y.: Doubleday, 1970), see p. 1382.

5. B. Bettelheim, *The Uses of Enchantment* (New York: Alfred A. Knopf, 1976).

6. H. Fingert, "The Psychoanalytic Study of the Minor Prophet Jonah," *Psychoanalytic Review* 41 (1954): 55–65.

7. Ibid., p. 58.

8. Ibid., p. 61.

9. Ibid., p. 62. Otto Fenichel heralds Fingert's Freudianism in "The Dread of Being Eaten" (1928), in *The Collected Papers of Otto Fenichel* (New York: W. W. Norton, 1953), pp. 158–59.

10. Psychoanalysis views the nature and function of the Bible as the expression of Oedipal struggles; e.g., see D. F. Zeligs, "A Psychoanalytic Note on the Function of the Bible," *American Imago* 14 (1957): 57–60.

11. J. More (Muggia), "The Prophet Jonah: The Story of an Intrapsychic Process," *American Imago* 27 (1970): 3–11.

12. Ibid., p. 6.

13. Ibid., p. 7.

14. Ibid.

15. Ibid., pp. 7–8.

16. E. Fromm, *The Forgotten Language* (New York: Grove Press, 1937), p. 22.

17. E. Fromm and R. I. Evans, *Dialogue with Erich Fromm* (New York: Harper & Row, 1966), p. 119.

18. E. Fromm, *Man for Himself* (Greenwich, Conn.: Fawcett, 1947), p. 105. Cf. the conclusion of Robert Frost's poem, "The Mast of Mercy": "Nothing can make injustice just, but mercy."

19. See esp. C. G. Jung, *Symbols of Transformation* (2nd ed.; Princeton: Princeton University Press, 1956); *Memories, Dreams, Reflections* (New York: Random House, 1961); *Analytical Psychology: Its Theory and Practice* (1935) (New York: Vintage Books, 1968); and *The Archetypes and the Collective Unconscious* (Princeton: Princeton University Press, 1968).

20. The list of authors having demonstrated the universality of this theme is too long to be given here. Among the best-known sources are J. Campbell, *The Hero with a Thousand Faces* (1949) (New York: Pantheon Books, 1968), esp. "The Belly of the Whale," pp. 9ff., and "Rescue from Without," pp. 107ff., 347ff., etc.; M. Eliade, *Patterns in Comparative Religions* (New York: Sheed & Ward, 1958); *Birth and Rebirth* (New York: Harper & Row, 1958), e.g., pp. 35ff., 57ff.; *The Sacred and the Profane* (New York: Harcourt, Brace & World, 1959), esp. chap. 4, "Human Existence and Sanctified Life," pp. 162–213; *Myths, Dreams and Mysteries* (New York: Harper & Row, 1960), e.g., pp. 220ff.; J. Frazer, *The Golden Bough* (2nd ed.; London: Macmillan and Co., 1967); L. Frobenius, *Das Zeitalter des Sonnengottes* (The Age of the Sun-God) (Berlin: G. Reimer, 1904); C. G. Jung, *Symbols of Transformation* (Princeton: Princeton University Press, 1956), e.g., pt. 2, chap. 4, "The Origin of the Hero," pp. 171–206; O. Rank, *The Myth of the Birth of the Hero* (Vienna: F. Denticke, 1909); and G. E. Smith, *The Evolution of the Dragon* (Manchester, Eng.: Longmans, Green and Co., 1919).

21. C. G. Jung, *Symbols of Transformation*, e.g., pp. 261, 322, 367. Many authors have asserted that origins of tales of heroes battling whale-dragons first appeared in India. Indeed, in these stories, it is not uncommon to follow the heroes through sequences of events similar to Jonah. Indian tales often include heroes running away from danger and going to sea, facing strong winds and tempests, the casting of lots to discover sinners, the fate of being thrown overboard and swallowed by a sea monster, and finally killing it out of sheer courage and cleverness. See T. Gaster, *Myth, Legend and Custom in the Old Testament*, vol. 2 (New York: Harper & Row, 1975); O. Komlos, "Jonah Legends," in *Études Orientales: À la Mémoire de Paul Hirschler* (Budapest, 1950), pp. 41–61; and Rank, *The Myth of the Birth of the Hero*. In *The Evolution of the Dragon*, Smith held all these hero myths as first originating from Sumer with the creation myth of Marduk and Tiamat (see esp. his chap. 2, "Dragons and Rain Gods," pp. 76–139). For Smith, the latter myth spread to all corners of the earth as the trading of foods and goods became necessary for Sumer's survival. Jung disagreed with all the interpretations above. For him, myths and fairy tales *spontaneously* come to the fore in each and everyone's psyche. He explains in *Symbols of Transformation* that, should all civilizations with their traditions and literary records be forgotten or destroyed, with the exception of a few scattered groups of people, these survivors would recreate on their own similar myths, tales, and stories to explain how the world was created, the meaning of life, heroism, and so forth.

22. Frobenius, *Das Zeitalter*, pp. 84ff.

23. Almost invariably we find the dragon lives deep in water. The water plays a very important symbolic role in the tales, for it represents the maternal

depths and the place of (re)birth. It also symbolizes the unconscious. This is why the descent into the belly of a monster or the underworld is always an *ambivalent venture*. On the symbolism of water, see Eliade, *Patterns in Comparative Religion*, pp. 188ff.; *The Sacred and the Profane*, pp. 130ff.; and Erich Fromm, *The Forgotten Language* (New York: Grove Press, 1951), pp. 16ff.

24. Cf. J. Jacobi, *Complex, Archetype, Symbol* (Princeton: Princeton University Press, 1959), p. 177. The story of Samson and Delilah is also a case in point. In *Psychology and Alchemy* (Princeton: Princeton University Press, 1968), Jung connects the hero's loss of hair as symbol of rebirth and renewal: "he is reborn bald as a babe" (p. 339). The heat in the monster-unconscious, for Jung, is tantamount to a state of incubation, a state in which transformation and rebirth is possible (ibid.).

25. Jung (e.g., *Symbols of Transformation* and *Psychology and Alchemy*) brings the interesting interpretation that, symbolically, wandering means *longing for* something or someone heroes know they need to feel integrated (cf. Gilgamesh, Herakles, Dionysus . . . Jonah). Gautama Sakyamuni, the future Buddha, is said to have wandered for years before his way to Enlightenment. See also Campbell, *The Hero with a Thousand Faces*, pp. 31ff.

26. See Smith, *The Evolution of the Dragon*, "The Mandrake," pp. 192–206. See also Campbell, *The Hero with a Thousand Faces*, pp. 185ff., and Mircea Eliade, "La mandragore et les mythes de la naissance miraculeuse," *Cahiers Zalmoxis* 3 (1942): 1–48; *Patterns in Comparative Religion;* and "The Cult of the Mandragora," chap. 7, in M. Eliade, *Zalmoxis: The Vanishing God* (Chicago: University of Chicago Press, 1972), pp. 204–25.

27. John Steinbeck, *The Pearl* (New York: Bantam Books, 1945). On monsters jealously guarding the treasure hard to find, see Campbell, *The Hero with a Thousand Faces;* Eliade, *Patterns in Comparative Religion,* e.g., pp. 168ff., 193ff., 288ff.; *The Myth of the Eternal Return* (New York: Harper & Row, 1959), e.g., pp. 17ff.; *Images and Symbols,* esp. chap. 4; Jung, *Symbols of Transformation,* e.g., pp. 171ff., 274ff., 394ff.; *Psychology and Alchemy,* pp. 333ff., 340ff.; Smith, *The Evolution of the Dragon,* among numerous references.

28. See, e.g., Eliade, *Birth and Rebirth*.

29. Eliade, *The Sacred and the Profane*, p. 192.

30. *Ibid.*

31. Eliade, *Myths, Dreams and Mysteries*, p. 221; and Jung, *Symbols of Transformation*, p. 268n. On the symbolism of rebirth ceremonies in initiation rites, see also Eliade, *Birth and Rebirth;* and Frazer, *The Golden Bough*, esp. "The Ritual of Death and Resurrection," pp. 905–17.

32. Jung, *Symbols of Transformation*, p. 205; and *Psychology and Alchemy*, pp. 335, 336–37.

33. Jung's most thorough account on the symbolism of the hero is found in *Symbols of Transformation;* see also his *Psychology and Alchemy,* pp. 334–44.

34. Jung, *Symbols of Transformation*, p. 374. In the seventh book of the *Republic*, Plato also saw the uninitiated or "unenlightened" as prisoners in a dark cave, i.e., as prisoners of their unconscious. On the hero symbolizing an urge toward individuation, see, e.g., Edward F. Edinger, "The Tragic Hero: An Image of Individuation," *Parabola* (1976): 66–75; and P. L. Travers, "The World of the Hero," *Parabola* 1 (1976): 42–51.

35. Jung, *Symbols of Transformation;* see also *The Psychology of Transference* (Princeton: Princeton University Press, 1966).

36. In the words of Jacobi, *Complex, Archetype, Symbol,* p. 90.

37. On this particular point, see Otto Rank on "Life Fear" and "Death Fear" in *Will Therapy* (1936; New York: W. W. Norton, 1964), pp. 119–33.

38. *Symbols of Transformation*, p. 420, italics his. Sandor Ferenczi held a similar position to Jung's. Though he did not refer to mythology to demonstrate his viewpoint, Ferenczi asserted the deepest longing to be the return to the mysterious waters where all life originated. However, in interpreting such a regressive wish, he kept a strict Freudian stance (S. Ferenczi, *Thalassa, Versuch einer Genitaltheorie* (Vienna: Internationale Psychoanalytisches Vlg., 1922).

39. Neumann, *The Great Mother* (New York: Pantheon Books, 1963).

40. Jacobi, *Complex, Archetype, Symbol*, p. 183, italics ours. See also Campbell, *Hero with a Thousand Faces*, p. 8.

41. Eliade, *Myths, Dreams, and Mysteries*, p. 225, italics his.

42. Cf. Eliade, *Birth and Rebirth*, p. 64. There is agreement among most depth psychologists that the fear of engulfment or of being suffocated by the mother or the unconscious is indeed tantamount to experiencing the most dreadful and primitive of all anxieties: death anxiety. Cf. M. Klein, "On the Termination of a Psychoanalysis" (1950), in M. Klein, *Envy and Gratitude and Others Works* (New York: Dell Publishing Co., 1975), pp. 43–47, esp. p. 43; Ronald D. Laing, *The Divided Self* (Baltimore: Penguin Books, 1965), pp. 43ff.; and D. W. Winnicott, "The Theory of the Parent-Infant Relationship" (1960), in D. W. Winnicott, *The Maturational Processes and the Facilitating Environment* (London: Hogarth Press, 1965), pp. 37–55, esp. p. 41.

43. Cf. C. G. Jung, *Aion* (2nd ed.; Princeton: Princeton University Press, 1957), e.g., pp. 22, 30f., 40ff., etc.

44. Jung called this process an "act of sacrifice." It is the deliberate choice to resist or fight off the longing to regress to anxiety-free states. See *Symbols of Transformation*, esp. "The Sacrifice," pp. 394–440; and *Psychology and Alchemy*, pp. 333–44.

45. A. Adler, *Social Interest: A Challenge to Mankind* (New York: G. P. Putnam's Sons, 1964).

46. See, e.g., Jung's *The Undiscovered Self* (New York: New American Library, 1958), pp. 34, 117; *Memories, Dreams, Reflections*, p. 354; *Two Essays on Analytical Psychology* (2nd ed.; Princeton: Princeton University Press, 1966), p. 178; *Psychological Reflections*, ed. J. Jacobi (Princeton: Princeton University Press, 1970), pp. 99, 163; among other references. In spite of referring to mental-health-heroism in those altruistic terms, Jung rarely expanded upon such interpretation. Typical quotations would more likely fall in the same category with the following remarks: "As far as we can discern, the sole purpose of human existence is to kindle a light in the darkness of mere being" (Jung, *Memories, Dreams, Reflections*, p. 326).

47. Jung, *Memories, Dreams, Reflections*, p. 4.

48. Jung, *Symbols of Transformation*, p. 56. On the powerlessness of the ego or the will, see also Jung, *Two Essays on Analytical Psychology*, chap. 4, "The Problem of the Attitude Type," pp. 41–63; his Tavistock Lectures in *Analytical Psychology: Its Theory and Practice*, e.g., p. 193; *Aion*, p. 5.

49. Jung, *Analytical Psychology: Its Theory and Practice*, p. 81.

50. Ibid., p. 213, italics his.

51. See P.-E. Lacocque's development of these ideas in "On the Search for Meaning," *Journal of Religion and Health* 21 (1982): 219–27, and here our chap. 7, below. Maurice Friedman also criticizes Jung for deifying the self. See *To Deny Our Nothingness: Contemporary Images of Man* (Chicago: University of Chicago Press, 1978), pp. 146–67. See also Martin Buber's response to Jung, which essentially

criticized him for being a Gnostic; *Eclipse of God* (New York: Harper & Row, 1952), esp. pp. 84ff. However, in all fairness, Jung also spoke of God from a Judeo-Christian perspective; see *Modern Man in Search of a Soul* (New York: Harcourt, Brace & World, 1933), e.g. pp. 101–2.

52. We emphasize *healthy* here because dedicating one's life to a community can also be rooted in pathogenic realms. Hitler, the Reverend Jim Jones (Jonestown), and Julius Caesar, for instance, had a deeply felt sense of "community" and were also actively involved in converting such ideal image into concrete reality. Universal ethics cannot be ignored in defining "mental health." For more on the points above, see Lacocque, "On the Search for Meaning."

53. With regard to initiatory themes in literature, see M. Eliade, *Myth and Reality* (New York: Harper & Row, 1963), esp. Appendix 1, "Myths and Fairy Tales," pp. 195–202. To recall, Philo is indignant about the participation of Jews in Mysteries (*On the Special Laws* I. 391f.).

PART II

PSYCHO-THEOLOGICAL CHARACTER ANALYSIS

FOUR

ANONYMITY AND VOCATION
(Jonah 1)

Why does man accept to live a trivial life? Because of the danger of
a full horizon of experience, of course . . . freedom is dangerous.
Ernest Becker, *The Denial of Death*
(New York: Free Press, 1973), p. 74.

The book of Jonah opens with a commandment. In its individual and collective dimensions the commandment is a call to go
"beyond," that is, an exhortation to have the courage to be sepa-
rated from the crowd. Ultimately, however, this is not a divorce
from society but, on the contrary, the true contribution to society,
for a person's wholeness in the world consists not in protecting
the status quo but in the choice to go further in the quest for
truth. We shall deal with this issue more fully later (see chap. 8,
below), but it should be made clear from the outset that the problematic of Jonah is not one of "happiness" but of liberation. This
is why Jonah starts to be Jonah the very moment he hears God's
call. Before, he is anonymous and his life is not "oriented." Afterward, his name is Jonah and his raison d'être is to go toward the
ultimate, toward that which is both impossible and necessary. Viktor Frankl writes: ". . . it is my conviction that man should not,
indeed cannot, struggle for identity in a direct way; he rather
finds identity to the extent to which he commits himself to something beyond himself, to a cause greater than himself."[1]

The construction of verse 1 appears frequently in the Bible
("The word of the Lord came to so and so," see 2 Sam. 7:4; 1
Kings 17:2, 8; Jer. 1:4, 11; etc.), even at the beginning of a book

69

(Hos. 1:1; Joel 1:1; Mic. 1:1; Zeph. 1:1; Hag. 1:1; Zech. 1:1). The conjunctive "and" at the start of the narrative indicates that the beginning is not absolute. Jonah is not yet Jonah before the call is heard, but he is already living in expectation of what will happen to him. When it occurs, however, the irrevocability of the phenomenon is threatening.

Intuition tells Jonah that no matter what he is going to do about his situation, something is changing within him. From now on everything in his life depends upon how he will handle this existential conflict. What he assuredly cannot do is to ignore the call. He has become the living illustration of a psychological complex singularly exemplified in his destiny. Abraham Maslow spoke of the "Jonah syndrome," that is, the fear of standing alone, the escape from greatness, and the unwillingness to face the necessary obstacle on the way to one's fulfillment:

> . . . to discover in oneself a great talent can certainly bring exhilaration but it also brings a fear of the dangers and responsibilities and duties of being a leader and of being all alone. Responsibility can be seen as a heavy burden and evaded as long as possible.[2]
>
> . . . [The Jonah syndrome] is partly a justified fear of being torn apart, of losing control, of being shattered and disintegrated, even of being killed by the experience.[3]

It is therefore normal that Jonah should react to such a situation with the wish that the commandment had not been given in the first place. Without the commandment, there is no feeling of guilt.[4] As Paul says in the New Testament, there is no sin without commandment. Jonah experiences the commandment of God as the imposition of the impossible upon him and he develops a feeling of culpability that will eventually bring him to flee to Tarshish, in the direction opposite to the one given in his orders. Jonah revolts in the name of an idea; it is inconceivable, objectively speaking, that he be called to do the impossible. No "God" would logically make such a demand. The commission to go to Nineveh and to proclaim the doom of the city is simply not reasonable. If there is any "God" capable of such insane calling, one must flee as quickly as possible. In the name of sanity Jonah sails west instead of riding east; and any sensible person must approve of Jonah's decision. The whole of international wisdom literature agrees with Jonah, for it abhors above all the lack of moderation.

But what is required of Jonah (and of humanity in general) is to go *beyond* one's own limits (Abraham is said to go "towards the land I shall show you"), because he has been chosen (like all other humans) by One who is beyond all limits. While the calling does not make Jonah an epic hero, one could say that it makes him leave his condition of subhumanity to become—in the image of his commissioner—bondless, liberated, free. The paradox is that Jonah, before he receives God's commandment and while he flees from the commandment, is *not* free. Only when one assumes responsibility for the commandment is one free, for the simple reason that it enunciates for the first time the *project* of a person, one's raison d'être, one's ultimate meaning. Of course, Jonah, son of Amittai, faced an unlimited number of existential possibilities throughout his life. Once the commandment is uttered, however, only *one* choice is capable of making Jonah the man he actually is: the decision to fulfill his vocation by going to Nineveh and there proclaim his message. That is why the story of chapter 1 of the book, which seems self-contained, is in fact open-ended. As long as Jonah refuses to go to Nineveh—indeed, as long as he refuses to be Jonah—the story of Jonah cannot end.

One can say without stretching the evidence that Jonah himself brings about the sea storm; he is at the same time its author and its victim. He *cannot* have a safe trip because the turmoil of his soul needs finds an echo in the turmoil of his environment. He cannot contain the whirlwind of excitement, passion, or remorse within his chest. Jonah is guilt-stricken and, contrary to the statements of simplistic psychological schools, guilt in itself is no flaw of the personality. As Maslow said:

> . . . it is good, even *necessary*, for a person's development to have intrinsic guilt when he deserves to. It is not just a symptom to be avoided at any cost but is rather an inner guide for growth toward actualization of the real self, and of its potentialities.[5]

Martin Buber offers the following insight: "True guilt does not reside in the human person but in his failure to respond to the legitimate claims and address of the world."[6]

Similarly, the sea tempest, mirror of Jonah's soul, has more than a one-sided value. It is not just a punishment of Jonah's stubbornness but also an appeal, an opportunity offered him to respond to the call (as Jon. 2 makes clear).

Verse 3 introduces the first escape of Jonah (for there is more than one in the tale). Jonah is conscious of the fact that he is about to discover something about himself that scares him. Hence he returns to anonymity or to a substitute identity by delving into the commonplace (a defense mechanism we shall study in chapter 9, below). He denies what has been revealed about himself. But, paradoxically, his running away demonstrates how relevant is his vocation. Had the call been hollow and meaningless, Jonah would have simply remained untouched and unconcerned. But ". . . it is well known that we are susceptible only to those suggestions with which we are already secretly in accord."[7]

Jonah delves into the crowd and leaves behind his particularity in the wake of general indifference. Furthermore, being the only Jew on the ship, it is interesting to note that it is no light matter for him to leave Israel and go abroad, whether to Tarshish or to Nineveh. As it happens when someone is put off balance or has to leave behind the source of his being, thus erring in the marginal area called alterity, there are various degrees in the alienation of the self. The lands of the *golah* ("exile," "dispersion") are not uniform. Only Zion, the point of departure, the center, remains identical to itself; the concentric circles around it either are more or they are less in the image of their *omphalos*.

As strange as it may appear, this has nothing to do with geographical distance or proximity, not even with the relative goodness or wickedness of the foreign peoples involved. It is clear that Tarshish is not any less "worthwhile" than Nineveh. If anything, that city of Spain is to be preferred at the time of Jonah to the capital of the Assyrians at whose hands Israel was historically to suffer so much. But Jonah must go to Nineveh and not to Tarshish. There is now a message to be delivered to the Ninevites; tomorrow, perhaps, there will be a message also for the people of

Tarshish. Thus, in turning his back on Nineveh, Jonah "profanes," so to speak, the *galut* ("exile"); he empties it of its content and reduces it to a mere escape. Jonah's geography has lost all character of sacredness. It has become an object he uses for his own gratification. That is what psychology knows as manipulation of the milieu. Jonah has perfectly understood that the vocation he has received will make him face the unknown—and maybe even death, nothingness. He therefore resorts to a sheer instinct of survival. Who could blame him for doing so? Ironically, however, he does not know that his choice is deadly.

In short, part of the struggle of Jonah lies in his realization that his vocation is so extraordinary that it defies the common stance of any human being. He feels threatened by an appeal that singles him out so completely that it makes him a being of exception in the world. As a matter of fact, one must realize that Nineveh constitutes the very opposite of all that Israel held as valuable and worthy of praise. To go to Nineveh means, for Jonah, to go to hell. No one, he thinks, can demand this from him, nor for that matter from anyone in the world.[8]

As R. E. Clements, among others, has noticed, there is in the book no presentation of the Ninevites "as arch-enemies and oppressors of Israel,"[9] but such a characterization would have been totally superfluous. (No one would expect an explication of the term "Auschwitz" when used by a contemporary author.) More serious is the question, Why Nineveh? Why not Babylon, for example? We must remember that the tale brings us back to the eighth century, at a time when Assyria was the threatening power in the Middle East. Babylon will succeed it only in the sixth century. Moreover, in the Hebrew literature of the Second Temple period, "Assur" is the symbolic name for the Persian empire, which, when the Jonah tale was written, had just been overthrown by the Macedonians. Nineveh, it is true, had been destroyed since 612, more than three centuries before the composition of Jonah, but its name, for centuries to come remained a well-known allegory for evil. We still find it so in the seventh and eighth centuries of our era! In the background is the whole problem of Persian prosperity representing the nations' welfare in contrast to Jerusalem's destitution. Jonah brings us

right to the middle of the postexilic problem with the nonfulfillment of exilic prophetic oracles.[10]

The topology of vocation is completed by the nonillustrious
identity of Jonah, son of Amittai. Jonah is an inconspicuous
member of his people, not a Moses or a David—a fact that gives
more credibility to Jonah's incapacity to live up to the grandeur of
his task. This, however, is the result of his choice, not a character
flaw, and one can readily recognize the antideterminism that is so
characteristic of Hebrew thinking. Jonah, as we saw, has every
reason not to become heroic, and he exercises his freedom ac-
cordingly. It is precisely this human trait that allows readers to
feel at home with the story, never overwhelmed by heroic actions
with which they cannot identify. In this way, the author under-
lines the universal character of the vocation to self-transcendence,
while keeping intact the universal character of the human condition. People hardly feel called to imitate a Greek hero, but all
know they are unique and consequently irreplaceable in the fulfillment of their destinies. Besides, the Greek epos is severely limited. No document has shown better than the *Iliad* the
impossibility of immortality through heroism.[11] But Jonah precisely is not looking for immortality. He does not seek a Holy
Grail, because he knows that the treasure is *given*. All he has to
do is to open his hands to receive it, or, using another metaphor,
all he has to do is place himself in the presence of God in his
Temple (Jon. 2). The secret of life is not granted to those who
run and tire, but to those who accept their vocation to become
alive. If there is, therefore, a quest proper to Jonah, it must be
quest for life—his and others', even the Ninevites! *The Hebrew
Scripture posits that human vocation involves a certain quality of life, a
becoming that brings humans to be themselves by means of an ongoing
dialogue with the source of life, namely, God.*

The problem is therefore not how to become divine, as in the
Gilgamesh Epic[12] or in the *Iliad*, but how to become fully human.
The "heroes" try to steal liberty from those who, by their divine
nature, are the sole possessors of freedom, but Jonah is not after
divine prerogatives, not even after natural human liberty. As Maimonides once wrote, "Man has not been created free, he has received the commandment to be free." Divine vocation requires

that the human choose to be free, that is, to transcend the self and reach out to the impossible. Were Jonah a Greek tale, for example, the author would take aesthetic delight in showing that his main character chooses the ideal. Jonah, from that perspective, would jump into the extraordinary, and his story would become for us entertainment, that is, a device offered to the populace to escape temporarily the daily routine. On the contrary, Jonah's reaction is purely prosaic—as anyone else would do in his position, he unlocks a defense mechanism to protect his threatened self. He actually is our "alter ego."

Like Jonah of old, we also entertain the illusion of an existence exempt of concern for death, clear of obstacles, perpetual reminders of our limitations. With all the strength he can muster, Jonah flees afar from failure and from death that he intuits at the end of the road indicated to him by the commandment. It behooves the narrative to go on with the highly ironical demonstration that the prophet was wrong: in attempting to save his head, he put his life on the spot. The shipwreck, the "drowning," the engulfment in the monster are the paradoxical responses of life to his fatal choices. That is why those increasingly staggering events lose some of their negativity and become ambivalent.[13] They are not purely terrible, for they also carry a message. They reflect the chaos in Jonah's heart, objectification, so to speak, of what the prophet must discover within himself. But the lesson is disquieting; the fleeing Jonah is evolving from one state of alienation to another. He empties, as we saw, the past of his people and his own of all vocation, and the future of all project. Clearly, the present time cannot emerge intact from such a "burned-earth" tactic. The choice not to die (in the figurative and also perhaps nonfigurative sense) at Nineveh happens not to be the choice to live! The Greek philosopher Democritus (fifth century) says so with vigor: "it is not really living poorly, it is slowly dying" (frag. 160).[14] It is, according to Jung, "a partial suicide."[15]

The biblical text makes sure that we do not miss that point. It does not shy from extremes. Tarshish marks the western boundary of the inhabited world (Isa. 60:9; Ps. 72:10). One thinks of Spain or of Sardinia. Josephus prefers Cilicia (*Ant.* 9:10.2). It is in any case the symbol of the *ultima Thule*, which does not know the word of God, and this is, according to the Bible, the apex of ignorance (see Isa. 66:19).[16] "YHWH, the God of heaven, has made the sea and the dry land" (Jon. 1:9), the whole of the universe is God's, but symbolically the more remote one is from the center, the less directly is God's presence felt. There is thus on the part of Jonah no naïve belief that he can escape God anywhere in the world. In the words of George M. Landes, it is an escape from "Yahweh's *cultic* presence where the prophetic oracle is vouchsafed."[17] The expression used here, "to flee from the face of YHWH," is the very opposite of the formula "to stand before the Face of YHWH," sign of prophetic receptivity (I Kings 17:1; 18:15; 2 Kings 3:14; 5:16; Jer. 15:19). Paradoxically, in response to Jonah's attempt to run away as far as possible from YHWH's presence, God will take him even further than he himself imagined: to hell—and there precisely is God waiting for Jonah!

Wilhelm Rudolph labels Jonah's reaction to the call a "desertion."[18] The term is well chosen if we recall that the reason for the flight to Tarshish is clearly expressed in Jonah 4:2 and that one should not therefore look for other motives such as the fear of pagans, the dangers of the journey, and similar excuses.[19] Jonah flees from his mission, and we have emphasized how much of human weakness is involved in his move. But things are never so one-sided as they appear to be. Jewish literature, as we noticed earlier, empathizes with his attitude! Jonah is credited for not putting Israel to shame with the repentance of Gentiles (cf. *Jer. Sanhedrin* 11, 30b, 45; *Mekilta on Exodus* 12:1 [2a]; *Pirqe de Rabbi Eliezer* 10 [beg.].[20]

The rabbinic interpretation is attractive. It does not lack depth, for what is indeed intimated here is that God's command is unethical. Jonah is right to resist. In order to obey God, Jonah would have to violate an ethical principle. The alternatives are clearly delineated: either Jonah restricts himself to a well-defined ethical realm (a realm rabbinic legalism firmly upholds), or he chooses the risky solution that Søren Kierkegaard, in his homily on the "Aqedah" (the "binding" of Isaac in Gen. 22) labels the "teleological suspension of the ethical." With the first option, according to the Danish thinker, Jonah is a "general," a "husband," with the other, he becomes a "hero," a "lover," and he seizes the

occasion offered to him to become great. In this fashion precisely
Abraham transcended theological and ethical standards. Jonah
then confronts—much like Abraham's grandson, Jacob—the
Other strangely similar to himself, who extravagantly demands
from him to go beyond his love for his people, for himself, and to
love even his enemy. But in the Jacobian or Pascalian night, one
never knows who does the hitting or the receiving, who wins or
loses, who is the "Angel" or whether he is but a ghost. Is it really
clear that the demanding voice expresses all there is to be said?
In the midst of the fracas at the brook of Jabbok where Jacob's
fight takes place, or in the tempest where the hull of the ship
squeals and breaks all around Jonah, is it certain that the voice is
clearly heard? The alternative is unexpressed. Reality or fiction?
Vocation or illusion? Jonah chooses to go to Tarshish, not to Nineveh. This can be an easy way out. Yet considering Jonah's response in the context of his demand for justice toward Israel, an
exigency that goes to the point of heroically opposing divine designs that he feels unable to condone, he may retrospectively raise
daringly a question as to whether Abraham's willingness to sacrifice Isaac was really opportune. Perhaps, secretly, God wanted the
patriarch to resort to holy disobedience, to sublime revolt?

Anyway, according to the rabbis, Jonah saw a sign of approval
for his decision to flee to Tarshish in the fact that he found a ship
ready to go from Joppa. This made him so glad that he paid in
advance for the trip rather than afterward, as was customary!
(*Pirqe de Rabbi Eliezer* 10). He thus decided to face the most terrible danger for a Jew, namely, the ocean—the abyss of Genesis
1:2. In Psalm 48:8 "the ships of Tarshish" are those that dare to
face the deep seas (cf. 1 Kings 10:22). The emphasis is surely not
on Jonah's cowardice. If anything, Jonah is ready to die for his
convictions. One can therefore speak of a death wish "with the
intention of ending decisively and irrevocably any possibility of
God's renewing his commission."[21] But, as the narrative will ironically show, if one flees from the place of theophany where God
expresses his exigencies, the theophanic exigencies will then be
manifested in the belly of a big fish!

In concluding this analysis of verse 3, let us note (along with
other exegetes) its impressive structure.[22]

a. Jonah rose . . . from YHWH's presence
b. and he went down to Joppa
c. and he found a ship
d. going to Tarshish
c'. and he paid the fare thereof
b'. and he went down into it
a'. to go . . . from YHWH's presence.

(In vss. 4–16 the structure also revolves around a nucleus, vss. 9–10a.)

Raphael Weiss[23] has shown that the sea is here the central theme, as if everything pertaining to the commission of God would lead there. God's action within nature is somewhat surprising. Hebrew literature is generally more interested in history, in *Heilsgeschichte*. Among the exceptions, wisdom literature comes first. There are in Jonah strong wisdom trends,[24] which, it is interesting to note, are also present in the postexilic protest literature such as Job and Ruth. Both of these, we recall, also introduce foreigners to Israel's concern. It was therefore appropriate to explore the realm of "natural theology" and to send the reader back to the "Noachian covenant" between God and the whole universe, as mentioned in Genesis 8 and signified by the rainbow. However, in doing so, the postexilic works were at least implicitly relativizing Israel's exclusive election. Consistently, they stepped onto the ground of universal folklore, finding there the fitting tone for their mode of discourse. That is why there is nothing wrong in seeing sea and fish as symbols of death and rebirth—the tale itself supplies the proof as it continues. Although wind, sea, fish, and sun are, for Israel, "neutral" creations, totally dependent upon God's orders, in contradistinction to heroic legends in which the natural elements are powerful adversaries of the divinity of the cosmic order, there is a remnant of mythological conceptions in the synonymity of sea and monster in Israel.[25] The sea is a symbol of darkness, of violence and destructive power (Ps. 88:7). In Jonah, besides, it loses nothing of its literal meaning, as the context demonstrates. As for the whale, it has nothing to do, needless to say, with a "sea taxi" appointed by God to save the prophet, as an ill-inspired reader once wrote. It is a chaotic monster, on the model of Leviathan.

Jonah's engulfment in this shark is synonymous to entering a state of disintegration. All these sea motifs find a typically Israelite expression here, but we must praise Gabriel Cohn for displaying prudence in attempting to locate the origin of these archetypal images. More important, he says, is the question of how those motifs are experienced in the book of Jonah.[26]

Similarly, Jonah's flight to the west is probably to be interpreted in parallel with many popular legends as a plunging into darkness. One can find confirmation of this in the awakening of Jonah's conscience at *dawn* (4:7), while he sits to the *east* of Nineveh (4:5) under the blowing of an *east* wind (4:8).[27]

As we have seen in chapter 1, above, the ship—and later the giant shark—may represent the exile of the Judeans to Babylon (see Jer. 51:34, 44). In accordance with a general prophetic stance about the catastrophe that befell Jerusalem in 587 B.C.E., the book of Jonah intimates that Jonah-Israel have themselves provoked their own exile. The victory of the Babylonian monster (cf. Dan. 7:4) did not result from an arbitrary decision of God and was certainly no accidental. The prophets canceled all shreds of historical determinism and affirmed the people's full responsibility for their destiny. Hence, Israel could have avoided the exile to Babylon, and Jonah the sea storm and his subsequent "death" in "the belly of the netherworld" (2:3). How? By fulfilling their call. It is important to realize that in revealing Israel's shortcomings and bringing to the level of conscience its repressed feelings of culpability, the prophets made clear to their fellow Jews, however paradoxically, that they could bring about their own salvation just as they had provoked their own condemnation. The same principle applies here; Jonah is no toy in the hands of fate. Nor is the sea storm in Jonah 1:4ff. a purely natural phenomenon. Nothing happens by chance or according to mechanistic cause-and-effect relations.[28] The storm does not remain on a meaningless level, independent of human existential problems. Although it could be a senseless cataclysm, Jonah has gathered all the requisite elements for making the event meaningful, and now he is living it through as such. This is so clear that nobody on the ship is fooled by the "anonymity" of the phenomenon. On the contrary, all try to say its name, to discover its veiled sense, to translate its message into an intelligible language. Their intuition proves entirely correct, for as soon as the message is received the storm recedes.

We cannot insist strongly enough on the fact that Jonah has by now reached the point of no return. He has symbolically retrieved the fetuslike condition within the motherly womb. In the words of Fromm:

> The story is told as if these events had actually happened. However, it is written in symbolic language and all the realistic events described are symbols for the inner experiences of the hero. We find a sequence of symbols which follow one another: going into the ship, going into the ship's belly, falling asleep, being in the ocean, and being in the the fish's belly. All these symbols stand for the same inner experience: for a condition of being protected and isolated, of safe withdrawal from communication with other human beings. They represent what could be represented in another symbol, the fetus in the mother's womb. Different as the ship's belly, deep sleep, the ocean, and a fish's belly are realistically, they are expressive of the same inner experience, of the blending between protection and isolation.[29]

That Fromm is right is shown, for example, by parallel passages in the Bible where a storm gives expression to an inner experience of a hero (2 Kings 2:1, 11 [Elijah]; Job 38:1; Jer. 23:19; 30:23). It is also demonstrated by the use of the same verb *twl* in Jonah 1 for the stirring up of the wind (vs. 4) and the casting forth of the freight (vs. 5) *or of the prophet* (vss. 12, 15).

Jonah's new flight—into the "uterus"[30]—is, at the same time, the very condition for his "rebirth." One thinks of the words of the Nazarene to Nicodemus in John 3:3: "Unless a man has been born over again he cannot see the kingdom of God."

Parallel to the inner transformation of the hero, the sailors "clean up" the boat and thereby open the place to new possibilities. The situation is clearly one of transition, already beyond the former condition but not yet yielding the new. That is why the action of the sailors is itself ambiguous; one might understand it as a repression of the awareness of reality. Not having resolved the problem of the storm on the spiritual level, they face that unusual obstacle in a state of unpreparedness. They are fearful because the tempest demands an approach different from the usual, and hence they must themselves be different. They are thus on an equal footing with Jonah. But with a difference, for they put their trust in the untrustworthy. The gods do not answer, either because they themselves are paralyzed by the storm or because they were but illusory human self-projections in the first place. Between Jonah and the sailors is a yawning chasm in terms of their respective religious beliefs, intellectual formations, sophistications, professions, and so on. But the human predicament is the same, be it in Israel or on a cosmopolitan sea vessel. The only difference is on the cognitive level. What Jonah has identified as God's calling, the sailors intuit and unconsciously detect as potentially transforming power that compels their choice. Paradoxically, however, the sailors who are unable to pinpoint the source of their anxiety are closer to the truth than the sleeping Jonah! At least they are awake and searching. We must remember that the book of Jonah is a third-century polemical work confronting the Middle Eastern wisdom traditions, in the first place those of Israel, but also those of the new Hellenistic culture with its claim to universalism and humanism. As here the mariners, and later on in the tale the Ninevites, symbolize the "Greeks", they are portrayed as open to the Truth. And yet, as we have already noted, they become wise only at the moment they convert to the God of Israel and leave behind their former convictions. Along these lines a very interesting, even ironic, phenomenon arises: wherever the prophet goes, everyone repents and converts. Were this unbelievable feat, becoming a fiction narrative, not known to the reader to be God's will, we would have to look at Jonah as a man blessed with a kind of charisma never seen before or after in human history.

Crisis demands relief. Jonah tries to obtain it by sleeping. Sure, Jonah may be physically and emotionally exhausted after an experience fraught with anxiety. But as the story unfolds it becomes obvious that his sleep is but a mere attempt to run away from his conscience, and his refuge in the boat's womb a symbol for his regressive longings. Did he dream while he was sleeping? If he did, it yielded no salutary effect, for he closed himself to any interpretation that would have made all the difference. Freud, however, called dream analysis the "royal road" to the unconscious, that is, the best method available to apprehend who we truly are. Maimonides associated sleep with moral unconsciousness (or "sin" as he called it), while the state of being awake, hence of consciousness, he associated with repentance.

Jonah's "sleep" is not itself a sign of unusual faith and serenity, as is Jesus' sleep in the boat during the storm on the lake of Galilee (Luke 8:22ff.). The term used in Jonah indicates a catalepsy rather than a sleep. That is why R. B. Y. Scott translates "in a stupor," and refers to Psalm 76 where the term can be rendered "to be stunned."[31] Similarly, W. Vischer speaks here of the "auto-hypnose de l'église."[32] It is a numbness but not an unprovoked one (cf. vs. 6: "how can you sleep?"). Once again, the rabbis were not at fault; Jonah slept, they said, "because of the anguish of his soul."[33]

It would be a mistake to reduce Jonah's numbness to the dimension of a mere episode. In fact, the Jew who fled the center of creation is now presented as paralyzed in the midst of an endangered universe.[34] The scene of verse 5 is unmistakably parallel to 1 Kings 18, the confrontation of Elijah with the prophets of Baal on Mount Carmel (see vss. 26–29). This connection is also made by Rabbi Hananiah in *Pirqe de Rabbi Eliezer*. On the ship, he says pointedly, there were seventy languages (= the whole world), and each one, with his idol in his hand, was calling to his god with the idea that the god who would save them is the true God. So much for R. Hananiah. Contrary to the scene on Carmel, it seems that here the prophet is not in the picture, for to be is also to be seen, to be exposed to the others' "look," as Jean-Paul Sartre puts it. Thus the pessimistic reading of Hananiah regarding the sailors is counterbalanced by the remark of Fromm to the effect that by now the mariners are showing an unexpected sense of humanity in trying everything to avoid the irreparable.[35] They invite Jonah to join them in their quest (vs. 6). The skipper even uses the same words as those of God in 1:2: "arise . . . call." Allen compares this repetition to what happens during a nightmare.[36]

It is not one of the least surprising features of the book that the narrative constantly deals first with the effects of the events on the Gentiles and only afterward on Jonah himself. One finds the same phenomenon in chapters 3 and 4, where the order is as follows: (1) the population of Nineveh, (2) the king (3:5, 6–9), and (3) Jonah (4:1–4).[37] The text is already preparing for the second part of the tale. To the "perhaps" of the skipper will correspond the "who knows?" of the king in 3:9. This way of keeping the future open to the divine grace is deeply moving.

We do not know what Jonah answered the mariners, for verse 7 brings us to a situation comparable to that of verse 5. In fact, the sailors have concluded in the meantime that someone on the boat is causing the common evil. Will that person become a scapegoat? It does not seem so, since Jonah is considered equal to all others in the casting of lots. There is no plot against the Jew here. We, however, had the optimal conditions gathered for the eruption of anti-Semitism in all its ugliness. Most of the pogroms in history occurred under circumstances more tentative than this one. It is thus again made clear that the author of the book of Jonah had the definite purpose of portraying the non-Jews in a favorable light. At the outset the sailors are ignorant of Jonah's origins (vs. 8), but even when they find out, they do not jump to conclusions, nor do they plot against his life despite the tie they have discovered between his "crime" and their destiny. On the contrary, they try to save him even when he has told them to throw him into the sea. Their moderation is exemplary, their humanity is a model. They take it upon themselves to increase their efforts and they row even harder (vs. 13). Only as a last resort do they appeal to Jonah's God and beg that the responsibility for Jonah's death rest not upon them but upon God, since God and only God demands the capital punishment of the reluctant servant. In short, there is a remarkable absence among the sailors of bigotry and ethnocentricity. If the lot "fell upon Jonah," it is not owing to any prejudice. It is forthwith understood as God's acting because Jonah effectively *is* responsible for the storm.

We shall expand upon this political dimension of the book when we study the prophet's encounter with the Ninevites. For now, we must remember that the polemical aim of the Jonah tale goes against national or ethnic pride, which the author sees rampant in the ruling class of Jerusalem. It is rare to find in the Bible such an open-mindedness toward the "nations," especially because Israel suffered so much and so often from their conquering appetites and—later—from their anti-Semitism. Let us cite, however, texts like Isaiah 51:5; 45:20, 22; 60:11; 56:7; Zechariah 8:23; 14; Isaiah 19:25. (Also in the so-called "intertestamental" literature, cf. 1 Enoch 10:21, where all pagans become righteous; or Sib. Or. III: 716ff., where they bring gifts and incense to the Temple of Jerusalem, cf. Test. XII Patr., esp. Test. Levi 14:4ff., etc.) We must not see in the foregoing texts, including the Jonah story, a sign of Jewish assimilation to the surrounding milieu. It even goes without saying, at a deeper level, that the Jewishness of Jonah is in no way downplayed.

The mariners' discovery is of greater import than they themselves imagine. All Jewish readers of the tale understand immediately that the real issue is Jonah's unwillingness to perform his priestly vocation in the world. This is precisely what endangers the whole world, for the whole of humanity has embarked on the same boat. The very first to acknowledge this is Jonah himself, so when the lot falls upon him, it does not come at all as a surprise. He had expected it all along; he was looking for it like a magnet attracting iron filings. He is the only one in touch with the real issue and the only one able to make sense of it. However, the others are not sidetracked, for in the end, when Jonah-Israel is sacrificed and "all is accomplished" as far as he is concerned, the "nations" gathered on the ship realize that God was present with them in the person of the Jew. They fear YHWH, offer a sacrifice, and make vows (vs. 16).

The sailors have recourse to casting lots, a process with which the modern reader feels uncomfortable because of its strong flavor of superstition. In a sense, this feeling is not without ground, and there is a definite irony in the fact that the mariners, having a prophet of God in their midst, think that they must resort to lot-casting! This is not, however, the first time that the practice appears in the Bible (see Josh. 7:14; 1 Sam. 10:20f.; Prov. 16:33). The focus of Jonah 1:7 is not on the *ex opere operato* power of the lot, although the Bible does not generally shrink from giving credit to numinous manifestations even when they are wrought by pagan magicians or sorcerers. What is at stake here is something similar to what we described when discussing the meaning of the sea storm. As the tempest was Jonah's tempest, the casting of lots is the external manifestation of an "inner experience." The "magnetic" Jonah attracts to himself his own condemnation. It is not—let us emphasize the point again—that Jonah is a tragic hero comparable with the fateful Atrides. Though at times life takes on aspects resembling those depicted in Greek tragedy, the book of Jonah as a whole makes clear that determinism does not ultimately prevail. According to determinism, "yet forty days and Nineveh shall be overthrown." According to God's graciousness and long-suffering, however (cf. 4:2), Nineveh shall be spared. According to determinism, Jonah would die for his disobedience to the divine will, but he emerges alive from the fish's belly. The mariners, however, never knew. Not any more than Greek philosophers envisioned the necessary transcending of Necessity. In short, Jonah appears as a tragic hero only to those who do not go beyond chapter 1 of the book. To those who continue reading, he is a man who encountered tragedy but transformed it into a human drama.

We anticipate. For now, the narrative artfully lets Jonah come out of his incognito condition. The process by which others recognize the exceptional man as described in the text—here, the Jew Jonah—is strikingly realistic. At first he appeared inconspicuous; he was one of their group and nothing distinguished him from the average. Then Jonah's attitude caught their attention, and soon enough provoked their suspicion. Eventually they concluded that Jonah was different.[38] Now this pattern is so significant in its universal recurrence that one can wonder whether the former inconspicuousness of Jonah was not owing to the others' deliberate refusal to see, *Jonah wanted to hide, and it pleased everyone,* at least until it is realized that all energies available must be actuated (see 1:6). If exceptional beings, if free persons, if Jews remain anonymous, no one is sorry. On the contrary, their "assimilation" means the disappearance of the threat they represent to the mediocre others (see below, chap. 8).

Jonah intuits that this is indeed the universal norm. He is therefore confident that his presence on the ship "to flee unto Tarshish from the presence of the Lord" will remain unnoticed. His will for anonymity corresponds to the unwillingness of others to confront the problem that Jonah poses—giving a face, as it were, to the faceless. This is why the "miracle" in this instance lies not necessarily where it seems to be found. It is not so much in the sea being stirred by the storm as it is in the event of human consciousness being compelled to acknowledge reality instead of fleeing from it. At exactly this point, Jonah's flight is stopped and with it the human impulse to self-imposed blindness. Jonah, it must be noted, goes far beyond what was demanded of him. He not only answers the mariners' question but adds a response of his own that reveals his full identity; he confesses: "I am a Hebrew and I fear the Lord, the God of heaven, *who has made the sea and the dry land*" (vs. 9).[39] He is thus stamped with a mark of identity as a creature of the God of heaven. Conformity, "the great destroyer of selfhood,"[40] is defeated. Jonah is forced to emerge from the crowd. He is "Hebrew and he fears the Lord."[41]

Whether the mariners indeed understand the whole of Jonah's confession or not, this much they know: the diffuse causes of their general troubles have been condensed into one particular man with his particular problems. Such a discovery inspires fear in them, but surprisingly no one of them wonders why one culprit among them effects such a collective chastisement. Modern readers, however, feel less inclined to accept this fact. They cannot but find somewhat revolting the fact that a whole ship is threatened with destruction because of the sin of one passenger. The historian of religion responds to this problem with the concept of the so-called "corporate personality." According to this idea, the individual is inconceivable apart from a group, whose "personality" transcends individual limits. Clearly, this refers primarily to kinships, and beyond, to covenantal communities. But there is also a more general category to which all people belong, that is, to which they are properly responsible, namely, humankind.[42] Such a unity of all humans has been emphasized in both the heathen origin-myths and in Israel's concept of a common human ancestor. "We are all responsible for all," Dostoevsky wrote. What this implies is that everyone has a particular vocation to fulfill within the collective unit for the betterment of the latter. The refusal by one to answer the call brings a threat to the whole group. In the words of Ernest Becker, "This . . . is the only real problem of life, the only worthwhile preoccupation of man: What is one's true talent, his secret gift, his authentic vocation? . . . How can the person take . . . the great mystery that he feels at the heart of himself, . . . to enrich both himself and mankind with the peculiar quality of his talent?"[43]

Here, the lot falls upon Jonah just as in Joshua 7 it fell upon Akhan. And, as Akhan was stoned to death by the community as a sign of dissociation from his crime, so also must Jonah eventually be rejected lest he be taken as representative of the collective personality of the ship, and so draw the whole group along with him into death. The attitude of the sailors here is particularly interesting insofar as it involves not hatred but, rather, fear and paralysis before the unknown. Fear and the absence of hatred: let us reflect on these elements.

As far as the mariners are concerned, something has occurred that has displaced the dramatic center. The mariners' cosmic anxiety has become fear directed toward a specific object, Jonah. From this point the sea storm bears a name; it has a cause and a project.[44] We recall here Maslow's analysis of the need to know and the fear of knowing.[45] The sailors realize that some step must be taken (for the sea grows more and more tempestuous), but at that point they focus on Jonah alone. Allegedly, the culpability of the one absolves the many. As Rollo May wrote, ". . . the reason we do not see truth is . . . that we do not have enough courage. . . . For to seek truth is always to run the risk of discovering what one would hate to see."[46]

The sailors, after attempting everything else, eventually find relief by throwing Jonah into the sea, "bundled" with their fears. But what do the mariners so carefully avoid? Why do they display such "selective inattention," as Harry S. Sullivan says?[47] The answer lies in the numinous aspect that accompanies Jonah and which makes of him an unusual human being. His difference, as we saw, is the threat. It evokes a feeling of anxiety in the crowd because it demonstrates that there are other games that are played by other rules, while we had thought all along that our game was the only possible one. No system, no highly structured society can afford the presence of the unique in its midst. When Nebuchadnezzar erects the statue, the symbol of his regime, it becomes intolerable that one man in the vast empire might go to his room and pray to the God of Israel. Similarly, the sailors at first are those "one-dimensional men," of whom Becker speaks, who are "totally immersed in the fictional games being played in their society, unable to transcend their social conditioning."[48]

Verse 12 shifts our attention from the sailors to Jonah. Strikingly, Jonah displays here the full depth of his desperation. Against all expectation, he does not intercede for God's forgiveness; such a prayer would have implied a radical change in himself, and he knows that the tempest is "the reflection of [his] own turmoil and anger."[49] Instead, he prefers to die. We have already said that it is wrong to speak of Jonah in terms of cowardice. Here again the rabbis interpret the episode in the most favorable light. For R. Johanan (ca. 140 C.E.) Jonah fled precisely in order to be sent to the netherworld in the train of the patriarchs and prophets who gave themselves up as oblations on behalf of their people; so Moses (Exod. 32:32; Num. 11:15), David (2 Sam. 24:17). (See *Mekilta on Exodus* 12:1 [2a]). For *Pirqe de Rabbi Eliezer*, "the ship is a type of the world which only can find its salvation through the willing martyrdom of the Hebrew, who, although inoffensive in his conduct with his fellow-men of all nationalities, is nevertheless quite willing to allow himself to be doomed to destruction in order to relieve his fellow-men of their threatened ruin."[50]

Jerome calls the sea storm here "the storms of this world" (*tempestas mundi*), and he sees in Jonah the one "who slew thee [death]" (*ille te vincit*), for he "surrendered his dear life into the hands of those that sought it" (*dedit dilectam animam suam in manus quaerentium eam*).[51]

Be that as it may,[52] from a psychological vantage point Jonah behaves like an acutely depressed person—hopeless, helpless, and feeling as if he were carrying a contagious disease. His injunction to the sailors to dispose of him is a gesture of suicide. "Despair expresses the feeling that time is short, too short for the attempt to start another life and to try alternate roads to integrity."[53]

Ultimately, the mariners have to throw Jonah overboard, and so put an end to what has been, after all, just an episode in history. Or so it seems, but reality does not espouse the form of a reductionist fiction. As soon as the sailors work the irreparable, not only does Jonah disappear from their sight, but they themselves fall into oblivion. They never come back into the story; they pursue a purposeless voyage on an anonymous ship. For all, both writer and readers, they have fulfilled their role. For a while, they had emerged from darkness and had been in the spotlight. They now return to their former obscurity. We cannot but feel that they have missed a golden opportunity. For a short time they were making history; now they are swallowed up in the mist. Their sacrifice to YHWH has been no doubt a grand event, but it has no far-reaching effect. In short, in throwing Jonah into the ocean, did not the sailors also throw themselves? Are they not also sinking with him to the bottom of the "shapeless and void"? In this sense it could be said that, all things considered, Jonah has been their scapegoat, the vicarious victim of their collective culpability. To the extent that René Girard[54] is right to identify the sacrifice of substitution as the central element of all religion and of all depth psychology, Jonah epitomizes our sentiment of guilt, our death wish, as well as the amphibological resolution of a situation become unbearable. On the one hand occurs a substitutive transfer of atonement upon the head of a chosen victim, but on the other hand, that victim is none other than the projection of ourselves. That is why, by implication, the sailors follow Jonah, whom they delegate, so to speak, into the infernal depths; and they also are present in the transfiguration that follows. Indeed, Jonah's tragic exhortation to the mariners to rid themselves of him may have had another motive than suicide. We must underline the feature, twice expressed in verse 12, of altruism. Literally the text reads, "the sea will calm down upon you . . . this great storm is upon you." Not a suicide perhaps, but an oblative act of generosity; this is at least one plausible interpretation left carefully open by the author.[55]

But then the question arises, where, in the remainder of the tale, are the sailors "raised from the dead" with Jonah? It must be said that they are in the midst of the non-Jews to whom the prophet is sent. Ever since the beginning, their function with regard to Jonah has been to represent the outside world. Jonah must meet them, talk to them (even when he would rather sleep), and he must save them, even at the price of his own life. After all, the mariners are not lost adrift on a *Flying Dutchman*. They are now found again at Nineveh, unaware of whom they really expect although this one will be both known and unknown, carrier of a message both unfamiliar and recognized.

Jonah continues to represent more than just himself. He is "loaded" with the cowardice and the treason of all. His descent into the netherworld is a sign of condemnation for the general human failure to comply with the divine entreaty. His "death" is significant because humanity sinks with him as a result of similar panic in the face of vocation, responsibility, and authenticity. That is also why the story must follow him in his fall. To stay indifferent, at this point, would mean that one shuns humanity in general. To remain on the deck of the boat means, paradoxically, to leave history and adopt the phantasms of a ghost ship.

We must follow Jonah into the sea because he is all of us. True, we are unable to imagine how it is that history continues beyond the hero's drowning, beyond the seemingly final fact of death. But *it is not necessary to imagine an impossible future in order to question the finitude of the present.* Jonah cannot be simply blotted out or annihilated. The return to *Urzeit* ("primeval ages") is also the condition for the coming of the *Endzeit* ("ultimate ages"). That is why Daniel 7 and 4 Esdras 13 in particular describe the enthronement of the human (*Homo*) emerging from the ocean, as if these mystics were rewriting the story of Jonah after chapter 1!

NOTES

1. Viktor Frankl, *Psychotherapy and Existentialism* (New York: Washington Square Press, 1967), p. 9.

2. Abraham Maslow, *Toward a Psychology of Being* (New York: D. Van Nostrand, 1968), p. 61.

3. Maslow, "Neurosis as a Failure of Personal Growth," *Humanitas* 3 (1967): 165–66.

4. For *Jer. Sukka* 5, 55a, 54, Jonah's (call) occurred on the second day of Succoth when his heart was rejoicing (cf. Strack-Billerbeck, vol. 1, p. 643).

5. Maslow, *Toward a Psychology of Being*, p. 195.

6. Martin Buber, *Knowledge of Man* (New York: Harper Colophon Books, 1965), p. 47.

7. C. G. Jung, *Modern Man in Search of a Soul* (New York: Harcourt, Brace & World, 1933), p. 65.

8. Suffice it here to refer to Zeph. 2:13 or to the book of Nahum. Nineveh was the capital of Assyria when Sennacherib conquered the kingdom of Judah (702 B.C.E.). The city was destroyed in 612 by the Medes. It is curious that, according to a popular etymology, "Nin-naveh" would mean the "place of the fish." The cuneiform pictogram for the city shows "Nina, a sign representing an enclosure with a fish inside" (E. A. Speiser, *IDB*, vol. 3, p. 552). Moreover, in Hellenistic times, a parallel was drawn with the Greek god Ninos, who was a god-fish.

9. R. E. Clements, "The Purpose of the Book of Jonah," *VTSup.* 28 (Leiden: Brill, 1975), p. 18. This leads Clements to minimize the element of Nineveh so that it all but disappears from the picture (p. 21: ". . . it makes no difference to the point that is being made" [*sic*]). For a similar point of view, see Trible, "Studies in the Book of Jonah."

10. On the generic sense of "Nineveh" as symbolizing evil, cf. the Demotic papyrus "The Lamb" (*Peḥib*), ca. seventh-eighth centuries C.E. but representing a tradition going back probably to the Ptolemies. It announces the conquest of Egypt by "Nineveh"! On the nonfulfillment of exilic prophetic oracles, see O. Plöger, *Theocracy and Eschatology* (Richmond: John Knox Press, 1968); P. Hanson, *The Dawn of Apocalyptic* (Philadelphia: Fortress Press, 1975); J. L. Crenshaw, *Prophetic Conflict: Its Effect upon Israelite Religion*, BZAW 124 (Berlin, 1971); and the works of R. P. Carroll, esp. *When Prophecy Failed* (New York: Crossroad, 1979).

11. See J. M. Redfield, *Nature and Culture in the Iliad: The Tragedy of Hector* (Chicago: University of Chicago Press, 1975).

12. When we compare, for instance, the deluge story as told in Babylon and in the Bible, it appears clearly that in Israel the flood does not interrupt history; here, rather, *mythos* is complemented by *ethos*. Noah is a righteous man. Similarly, the vocation of Jonah is to be righteous.

13. See Rollo May, *Existential Psychology* (New York: Random House, 1960), p. 81: "Anxiety is the state of the human being in the struggle against that which would destroy his being. . . . One wing of this struggle will always be against something outside the self. But even more portentous and significant for psychotherapy is the inner battle, . . . namely, the conflict within the person as he confronts the choice of whether and how far he will stand against his own being, his own potentialities."

14. See M. Solovine, *Démocrite, Doctrines philosophiques et réflexions morales* (Paris: Alcan, 1928).

15. C. G. Jung, *Symbols of Transformation* (New York: Pantheon Books, 1967), p. 110.

16. One will notice the *centrifugal* character of the book of Jonah. The myth of the center is broken. See *Myths and Symbols: Studies in Honor of Mircea Eliade*, ed. J. M. Kitagawa and C. H. Long (Chicago: University of Chicago Press, 1969).

17. Landes, "The Kerygma of the Book of Jonah," *Interp.* 21 (1967): 19. The same opinion is present in the Targum, Ibn Ezra, and Redaq on this verse.

18. Wilhelm Rudolph, *Joel-Amos-Obadja-Jona* (Gütersloh: Mohn, 1971), p. 337. "See ye not then, shipmates, that Jonah sought to flee world-wide from God?" (Melville, *Moby Dick* (New York; Holt, Rinehart & Winston, 1957), p. 41).

19. Rudolph, *Joel-Amos-Obadja-Jona*, ad loc. 4:2; contra Ellul, Vischer, Keller, et al.

20. Jonah was like an escaped servant of a priest, who decides to go into a cemetery to escape his master—illustration of the unrighteous judge of Jesus' parable, cf. Luke 18—for the priest cannot follow him there for purity reasons. But

the master said: "I have your peers who can go after you!" So God "sent out a great wind into the sea, etc." (Jon. 1:4) (*Mekilta on Exodus* 12:1 [1b]).

21. Landes, "The Kerygma of the Book of Jonah," p. 4.

22. So N. Lohfink, "Und Jona ging zur Stadt hinaus (Jon 4, 5)" *BZ* 5 (1961): 200; P. Trible, "Studies in the Book of Jonah" (unpublished) p. 206; Allen, *The Books of Joel, Obadiah, Jonah, and Micah*, p. 204.

23. " 'Al Sepher Yonah,' " *Mahanayim* 47 (1961): 45–48, quoted by G. Cohn, *Das Buch Jona* (Assen: Van Gorcum, 1969), p. 67 n2.

24. H. W. Wolff speaks of "weisheitliche Lehrerzählung" and of "Weisheit-dichtung" (*RGG*, vol. 3, cols. 853–56).

25. See Isa. 51:9–10; Ps. 74:13–15; 89:10–11; Job 26:12.

26. Cohn, *Das Buch Jona*, p.78 n1.

27. Cohn, *Das Buch Jona*, p.88 n3. The symbolism of "east" and "west" is interpreted everywhere, it seems, as representing birth and old age, respectively. For the Zohar, "east" symbolizes childhood, dawn, spring, and "west" implies middleage, evening, autumn. See J. E. Cirlot, *A Dictionary of Symbols* (New York: Philosophical Library, 1962), p. 269. For Islamic thinking, "east" is an allegory for intentionality, fountain of youth, illumination. "To turn westwards," explains Cirlot, "is to prepare to die, because it is in the watery depths of the west that the sun ends its journey" (ibid., p. 245).

28. Cf. A. LaCocque, "A Return to a God of Nature? A Reply to R. Rubenstein," in *Sources of Vitality in American Church Life*, ed. R. L. Moore (Chicago: Exploration Press, 1978), pp. 108–19.

29. Fromm, *The Forgotten Language*, p. 22.

30. The Hebrew word for "fish" is usually masculine. In Jon. 2:2 it is given in a feminine form.

31. R. B. Y. Scott, "The Sign of Jonah," *Interp.* 19 (1965): 16–25.

32. W. Vischer, "Jonas," *EThR* 24 (1949): 117.

33. *Pirqe de Rabbi Eliezer*, trans. with notes by G. Friedlander (New York: Hermon Press, 1965), chap. 10, "The Story of Jonah."

34. See below our reflections on vs. 7 and anti-Semitism.

35. Fromm, *The Forgotten Language* (New York: Grove Press, 1951), p. 21. See also More (Muggia), "Prophet Jonah," *American Imago* 27 (1970): 3.

36. Allen, *Joel, Obadiah, Jonah, and Micah* (Grand Rapids: Eerdmans, 1976), p. 207.

37. This has been noticed also by Cohn, *Das Buch Jona*, p. 57.

38. This progression corresponds to the "stair style" of which Cohen speaks. So, e.g., as Jonah increases the gap with God, the sailors come even closer to him: *vs. 5*, "they feared the divine"; *vs. 10*, "these men feared of a great fear"; *vs. 16*, "these men feared of a great fear YHWH." We see the same thing regarding the story: *vs. 4*, "and there was a great storm on the sea"; *vs. 11*, "for the sea continued to rage"; *vs. 13*, "for the sea continued to rage against them" (Cohn, *Das Buch Jona*, p. 53.)

39. See Melville, *Moby Dick*, p. 45. On God, creator of sea and dry land, see Ps. 95:5.

40. Rollo May, *Man's Search for Himself* (New York: W. W. Norton, 1953), p. 88.

41. May writes: ". . . [modern man] has a significance only if he gives up his own significance. . . . [He] maintains a protective coloring so that he won't be singled out from the others and shot at. To this extent you are said to be significant,

but it is a significance that is bought precisely at the price of giving up one's significance" ("Modern Man's Image of Himself," *Chicago Theological Seminary Register* 52 [October 1962]: 2).

42. Cf. A. Adler, *Social Interest: A Challenge to Mankind* (New York: G. P. Putnam's Sons, 1964); and *What Life Should Mean to You* (New York: Capricorn Books, 1958), passim.

43. E. Becker, *The Denial of Death* (New York: Free Press, 1973), p. 82.

44. In the words of Paul Tillich, "Anxiety strives to become fear.... It is impossible for a finite being to stand naked anxiety for more than a flash of time. People who have experienced these moments . . . have told of the unimaginable horror of it [naked anxiety]. This horror is ordinarily avoided by the transformation of anxiety into fear of something, no matter what" (*The Courage to Be* [New Haven: Yale University Press, 1952], p. 39).

And as May writes, "In fear we know what threatens us.... In anxiety, however, we are threatened without knowing what steps to take to meet the danger. Anxiety is the feeling of being 'caught,' 'overwhelmed' and instead of becoming sharper, our perceptions generally become blurred or vague" (*Man's Search for Himself*, p. 39).

45. Maslow, *Toward a Psychology of Being* (Princeton: D. Van Nostrand, 1968), pp. 60–67.

46. May, *Man's Search for Himself*, pp. 247, 250.

47. Harry S. Sullivan, *The Psychiatric Interview* (New York: W. W. Norton, 1954), p. 218.

48. Becker, *The Denial of Death*, p. 73. Following Sullivan, one could say that the real characteristics of Jonah as perceived by the sailors are distorted for their convenience, a process called "parataxic distortion."

49. More (Muggia), "The Prophet Jonah," p. 8.

50. G. Friedlander, ed., *Pirqe de Rabbi Eliezer* (New York: Hermon Press, 1965), p. 67 n10.

51. Jerome, Letter LX (Jerome's approach is, of course, Christocentric). See *Select Letters of St. Jerome*, with an English translation by F. A. Wright, Loeb Classical Library (Cambridge, Mass.: Harvard University Press, 1933), pp. 267–69.

52. For Haller and Trible, vs. 12 is the final attempt to evade his mission. For Smart, Brockington, Keller, and Ellul, on the contrary, it is a gallant bid for vicarious sacrifice.

53. Erik Erikson, *Identity, Youth, and Crisis* (New York: W. W. Norton, 1968), p. 140.

54. René Girard, *La Violence et le Sacré* (Paris: Bernard Grasset, 1972).

55. Cf. Elie Wiesel, *Five Biblical Portraits* (Notre Dame: University of Notre Dame Press, 1981), pp. 129–55. "Beaten by life, humbled by God, this antihero, though he chooses despair for himself and others, thinks of others before he thinks of himself. He opts for life, however filled with anguish, in order to prevent others from dying" (p. 153).

FIVE

FROM NOTHINGNESS TO BEING
(Jonah 2)

... Initiation lies at the core of any genuine human life. And this is
true for two reasons. The first is that any genuine human life implies profound crises, ordeals, suffering, loss and reconquest of
self, "death and resurrection." The second is that, whatever degree
of fulfillment it may have brought him, at a certain moment every
man sees his life as a failure. This vision does not arise from a
moral judgment made on his past, but from an obscure feeling that
he has missed his vocation; that he has betrayed the best that was
in him. In such moments of total crisis, only one hope seems to
offer any issue—the hope of beginning life over again. This means,
in short, that the man undergoing such a crisis dreams of new, regenerated life, fully realized and significant. This is something
other and far more than the obscure desire of every human soul to
renew itself periodically, as the cosmos is renewed. The hope and
dream of these moments of total crisis are to obtain a definitive
and total renovatio, a renewal capable of transmuting life. Such a
renewal is the result of every genuine religious conversion. . . .
Death prepares the new, purely spiritual birth, access to a mode of
being not subject to the destroying action of Time.

Mircea Eliade, *Birth and Rebirth*
(New York: Harper & Row, 1958), pp. 135–36.

"Salvation lies in Remembrance," said the Baal Shem Tov,
father of eighteenth-century Eastern European Hasidism. In this
context, it is interesting to note that one of the most striking features of Jonah 2 is the use of the past tense. Jonah remembers,

94

that is, he rewrites the past,[1] creating it anew all along, so to speak. He reorganizes a material for which he had previously surrendered responsibility. This he does through *interpretation*, through deciphering its *meaning*, "taking the story of a life which was experienced as shaped by circumstances and which was recounted as such, and retelling it in terms of choice and responsibility."[2]

In this process of reminiscence, we regain the present. Jonah's ultimate goal is to find meaning in his present condition, which, in and of itself, is a radical negation of sense and of life. Invariably, any human being caught in the absurd dimension of existence must come to terms with the past. When the Judeans were exiled to Babylon and their holy Temple in Jerusalem was destroyed, their existential problem surpassed their present circumstances of being in a foreign country and of having to adapt to conditions that were totally alien to them. In fact, the most profound question had to do with the validity or invalidity of their past. Had the foundation of their history so far resisted the new crisis? Had they lived, had they believed, suffered, hoped, only to come to this emptiness? Had it been worth living up until now by the values of yesterday?

We draw this parallel between Jonah's plight in chapter 2 and the exile of the nation to Babylon not only on account of similarities in the two situations but also because, as we noticed earlier, scholars have seen in the story of Jonah being swallowed by the fish a typology of the exile on the model of Jeremiah 51:34, 44. So, for example, James D. Smart writes that we have here "a symbolic representation of the Exile and the return."[3] Perhaps we should not stress this point. We may have here merely a discreet allusion to rather than a "symbolic representation" of that traumatic event in the history of the people. But this much remains: it raises the fundamental question of the values of yesterday. It is a mistake to believe that there are substitute values available when the former ones are questioned. Only the inexperienced and the gullible can be persuaded by demagogues that a new world order will spring from the vacuum left by the rejection of the old order. On the contrary, the wise and the prophets know that a society or an individual does not change values as one changes clothes. As the talmudic story goes, in order that Rabbi

Eliezer and his family will not suffer hunger anymore, God must re-create the world, another world. But is it certain that Eliezer will not be hungry in the new world? "Perhaps!" says God. Eliezer then exclaims: "All that for a 'perhaps'!" (*Ta'anit* 28a). Yes, perhaps. For another raison d'être means another history, another past. What is now offered to Jonah is not a past from which the call to go to Nineveh is absent. Rather, Jonah is offered the possibility of a transfigured existence. In some way, it remains the same existence, but it is endowed now with meaning; it is integrated rather than disoriented; the present, up until now characterized by emptiness, takes on profound significance. Life prevails over death, resurrection over decay and rot.

That is why chapter 2 of Jonah dwells upon the different elements of a prayer, which critics often reject as later accretions. This questioning of the psalm's authenticity probably reflects, however, a deep misunderstanding of biblical characterization. We must, rather, follow Erich Auerbach, in the famous first chapter of his book *Mimesis,* and distinguish between that which is credible in a "Greek" tale and a Hebrew text. Auerbach has shown that the "Greek" heroes lack background; in the course of the story, changes affect attitude, not character. Not so in a biblical narrative; it is entirely underpinned by human freedom (confronted by the divine will). Here the mystery inherent to the person is fully respected, so that the personages can indeed undergo deep changes. Abram, the idolater in Ur of Chaldea, becomes Abraham, the father of faith in the One Living God. Jacob, the trickster by birth, becomes Israel, "the one who fought with God and triumphed." Here the person is envisaged in its unpredictability, as has judiciously been emphasized by Robert Alter.[4] Thus, even if those who question the authenticity of the psalm were correct (but they are not; see below), the insertion of the prayer into the book at this point would be a stroke of genius on the part of the final redactor. It allows us to follow Jonah's movement from numbness to meaningfulness. Integral to this movement, paradoxically, is the deliberate suspension of the plot. At last, Jonah takes time to reflect upon his experience.[5]

It is a kind of musical counterpoint, so that the preceding cacophony becomes a polyphonic psalm. If the psalm were not present at this point in the narrative, the tempo of the story as well as its configuration and meaning would be transformed. We would be left with the wrong impression that the swallowing of Jonah by the fish was only an episodic accident, an almost casual obstacle on the road to success. Jonah would then be a toy in the hands of God, tossed hither and thither by the capricious waves and billows of the divine mood. The proper accent, on the contrary, falls upon the decisive importance of Jonah's sense of failure. There is no element here to minimize it. The prayer of Jonah, that is, the sense-giving, creative, celebrative "name" by which the prophet speaks of his experience and by which he transfigures chaos into meaning (and thus "Good Friday" into "Easter"), is uttered in the fish's belly, not after Jonah finds the security of dry land.

The following quotation from Rollo May seems to have been written with Jonah in mind:

> A dynamic struggle goes on within a person between what he or she consciously thinks on the one hand and, on the other, some insight, some perspective that is struggling to be born. The insight is then born with anxiety, guilt, and the joy and gratification that is inseparable from the actualizing of a new idea or vision. . . . the insight must destroy something.[6]

In biblical language this experience is called resurrection. And does not the whole message of the book of Jonah lie in the fact that when everything seems to be lost (in the case of Jonah, of the sailors, of the Ninevites), everything becomes possible? For life is an endless start; a continuous creation of meaning; a leap of faith, says Kierkegaard; a passage from darkness to light, from nonbeing to being. What this means is that a new world can be shaped from the netherworld; from nonbeing (in exile or in the heart of the seas) being can emerge. In the midst of confusion, despair, and death, Jonah mysteriously chooses to let an insight be born and to give it substance.[7] He turns to the "source of life" (Ps. 36.10) and, as the Jonah text puts it, "prays unto the Lord" (2:2); he restores the channel of communication with the Other.

When the circumstances are so terribly overwhelming that it would seem most natural for Jonah to think only of himself and of the incomprehensible arbitrariness of his fate, precisely then Jonah breaks through the wall and reaches out toward another One.[8] He passes from a state of complacency to one of generosity, from the narcissistic sentiment of feeling sorry for himself to self-oblation.[9] This, according to Israelite understanding, is indeed the passage from death to life, a fact that verse 11 confirms.

Of course the psalm has a cultic origin.[10] It is even a kind of psalmic potpourri of themes that are present in the biblical Psalms (vs. 3, cf Pss. 120:1; 18:6; vs. 4, cf. Ps. 42:7; vs. 6, cf. Ps. 69:2; vs. 7, cf. Pss. 18:16; 30:3; vs. 8, cf. Pss. 142:3; 143:4). The psalm is either an editing of these motifs or has been borrowed by the author and inserted into the place it now occupies in the tale. It carries, besides, the same title as a "Thanksgiving Psalm" like Psalm 100:1 (cf. 50:14, 23; 107:22). Its structure is typical: (1) short introduction expressing the intent of showing gratitude; (2) exposition of the psalmist's experience ("here," cf. vss. 4–7a); (3) prayer (vss. 3, 8); (4) deliverance (vs. 7b); (5) vow to offer thanksgiving sacrifices (vs. 10).

As Theodor Gaster says:

> To keep his audience awake and interested, a storyteller often punctuates his narrative, at appropriate places, with popular songs, in which all may join. . . . A good example in the Old Testament is the song put into the mouth of the Israelites after crossing the Sea of Reed dryshod (Exod. 15). So too, when the prophet Jonah is ensconced in the belly of the "great fish," and the story comes to a logical and dramatic standstill until he is disgorged'.[11]

Thus those who deny the "authenticity" of the psalm on the ground that Jonah "is not a creature of gratitude and thanksgiving" are mistaken.[12] Theodore Robinson says that the psalm is "sicher nicht ursprünglich,"[13] but he makes this assumption primarily on the false ground that the fish is a saving device and does not properly belong to the awfulness of the sea (see below).[14]

A much more potent argument, although unused so far to our knowledge, would be that the Jonah psalm's style recalls the parlance of the conservative party in Jerusalem at the time. It mentions the Temple, its sacrifices, vows, localized theophany. It could echo in general the bourgeois complacency and triumphalism of those for whom the return from exile and, above all, the rebuilding of the Zion shrine constituted a resurrection from the dead.

It is within the range of possibility that the Jonah author satirically identifies his hero, even swallowed up by the waters of the sea, with the conservative party in Jerusalem. Then the psalm would be a sample of complacent pietism. The biting irony, met earlier, would go on here: even at the moment of confronting his Judge, the "Sadducee" does not relent from his insipid religious hymns. Even the terrible sea-dragon is so disgusted that it feels nauseous.

Such an interpretation is all the more attractive as it perfectly becomes the Menippean satire (see chap. 2, above). The psalm, then, is a parody, and so is also the confession of faith in Jonah 4:2. The prophet Jonah is but a Tartuffe displaying external signs of piety but deeply callous to the fate of others, whether these be Ninevites or sailors.

It is not, however, the direction that we shall take. For we hold that the reader witnesses here the dynamic transformation that takes place within Jonah, namely, his repentance, a theme that would be absent were it not for the prayer. Jonah is here going through that "crisis" of selection which is judgment upon one's history.

Repentance, says Paul Tillich, "is the act of the whole person in which he separates himself from elements of his being, discarding them into the past as something that no longer has any power over the present."[15] And we quote also this statement from a rich article by Max Scheler: "Repenting is equivalent to reappraising part of one's past life and shaping for it a mint-new worth and significance."[16]

Repentance is in reference to the present as it is to the past. It is a leap from the mediocrity of an absurd history. Prior to the incidence of the psalm in the tale, Jonah is that average man (of whom Kierkegaard speaks) who is shaping his own inauthentic universe where he may forget his nothingness. Repentance, then, requires that one transform the meaning of one's nothingness, in order that it be no longer provocation of God but invocation of God. Before, the human being was nothing; but in the course of the dialogue, the nothingness is filled by the creative love of the discovered Thou. Eliade writes: "One goes down into the belly of a giant or a monster in order to learn *science* or *wisdom*. . . . No initiation is possible without the ritual of an agony, a death, and a resurrection."[17]

Jonah can now look at his resurrection in the past tense—as St. Paul will later do (1 Cor. 15)—and address his prayer to God as if all were already accomplished for him. The whole of Jonah's previous existence is transformed by the very fact that he is understood, that someone else shares the same perspective and sympathizes. Hope is born while facing the unknown and discovering that one is not alone, for surely enough, Jonah has Company in the fish's belly! All the difference lies here. He is the same man with the same existence and the same commission, but he is filled now with hope instead of despair. Nothing magical has occurred, no *deus ex machina* has come down from heaven, no angelic trumpet has resounded, no lightning has rent the skies. Jonah experiences not triumph but, if anything, the ultimate worsening of his predicament. All the conditions are set for Jonah's disappearance, and the prayer shows that indeed he could die now, for, from a spiritual point of view, he has gained the insight, he has reached the peak. What must follow can only be a commentary upon the event he has witnessed. Hence Jonah's death would not be the sterile end of a worthless existence, a "death by accident" in the words of Sartre. Jonah's death would be a death *for something*. The waves and the billows that surround him are not simply what they appear to be; rather, they are *"Your* billows and *Your* waves"! Jonah faces not nothingness but God, not death but life. This happens mysteriously enough through Jonah's gestation in the womb of a new "mother." He discovers his father and mother. The Nazarene asks, "Who is my mother, who are my brothers? . . . Whoever does God's will, this one is my brother, my sister, and my mother" (Mark 3:33, 35).

In the history of religion, as we saw in chapter 3, above, the hero, swallowed by a monster or by a giant, experiences both death and a "re-entry into a pre-formal, embryonic state of being . . . which precedes all forms and every temporal existence. Upon the cosmological plane, this double symbolism refers to the *Urzeit* and the *Endzeit*."[18]

In the story of Jonah, the myth is compounded by the highly symbolic element of the sea. The symbolism of water, recalls Eliade, has to do with the pre-formal.[19] It is first and foremost the water inside the womb, yet simultaneously it is a sign of nondevelopment and to a certain extent of nonbeing. Nevertheless, it is also the primordial milieu full of promise where life begins. The ambiguity of type becomes particularly clear once again: in the fish's belly at the bottom of the sea, while a man is singing a hymn to life enduring, life and death neighbor one another. Moreover, the fish with its symbolic connotation of life and fecundity adds to the analogy in representing the motherly womb and it takes on a significance that is rooted in the mysterious origins of life. Thrown into the ocean by the sailors, Jonah returns to the very source of his existence.

Although G. Campbell Morgan is right when he says, "Men have been looking so hard at the great fish, that they have failed to see the great God,"[20] we cannot neglect to say a few words about the "whale." Some scholars have insisted that it has a wholly positive and providential aspect. Someone even made of it a "sea-taxi" apppointed as a means of salvation for the prophet.[21] Jonah therefore finds a harbor in its entrails, and the psalm of thanksgiving makes sense, coming as it does from a man who realizes that he is alive and well after all. There is some confirmation of this understanding in Jewish tradition. For instance, R. Tarphon, in *Pirqe de Rabbi Eliezer* on Jonah 2:1, says that the fish had been prepared by God "from the six days of creation." Jonah entered the fish's mouth "just as a man enters the great synagogue. . . . The two eyes of the fish were like windows of glass giving light to Jonah."[22] Furthermore, the fish carrying Jonah inside is itself about to be devoured by Leviathan. It is thus clearly distinguished from the latter, with the motive of presenting Jonah as a savior (even a messiah[23]); for Jonah saves the fish, which takes the prophet to the bottom of the abyss. Jonah says, "On thy account have I descended to see thy abode in the sea." He then witnesses the bottom of all waters (including the primordial ones, the Reed Sea, the Sheol; see *Pirqe de Rabbi Eliezer* 10).[24]

But the rabbis are not unanimous on this point. For R. Judan (ca. 350 C.E.), God has saved Jonah *from* the guts of the fish (*Jer. Berakot* 9, 13a, 42). In parallel with this, the use of the image provided by Jonah 2:1 in Matthew 12:40 ("three days and three nights at the heart of the earth") shows that the fish is not to be construed as "a salt-water taxi," but as a primeval chaos-monster "tamed" for particular purposes. Landes is right when he writes: "It is to be noted that Jonah's being devoured by the sea monster was not a providential intervention to save him from drowning but was the penultimate act of his destruction. This seems clear from Amos 9:3 and Jeremiah 51:34."[25] Besides, does not Jonah say that much in verse 3 ("From the belly of Sheol, I cried for help")?

According to the narrative, "God appoints" four things: a fish (1:17), a plant (4:6), a worm (4:7), an east wind (4:8). The distribution of those motifs follows the pattern 2 + 2. One could thus consider the pair number one as positive and the pair number two as negative. But, in fact, the first things are ambiguous. The fish is first the sea dragon, but it is unexpectedly changed into a shelter for the prophet by God. In the reverse order of the signs, the plant is first positive, then becomes negative. It is "appointed"—this device of demythologizing the material borrowed by the author must be noted with E. Haller—"for saving [him] from his discomfort,"[26] but it becomes also an occasion of fall. Because of the *qîqāyôn*, the gourd tree in Jonah 4, Jonah, in contradistinction to Elijah on Mount Horeb, misses the rendezvous with God.

The problem of the fish is thus more important than meets the eye. If one were to follow the parallelism that exists between chapters 1 and 2, on the one hand, and chapters 3 and 4, on the other, then a "friendly" fish in chapter 2 would correspond to a "friendly" Nineveh in chaps. 3–4. Nothing is further from the truth. The whole parable pivots around the wickedness of the pagan city and also the terrible nature of the sea monster in chapter 2. Nineveh is the nest of cruelty, inhumanity, and bloodthirstiness (cf. Nah. 3:1 and passim). Hence, to present Jonah as a "reluctant missionary" is to resort to a false cliché, insensitive to the real purpose of the tale. The truth of the matter is that Jonah's theology cannot reconcile a God who stands in covenant with Israel with a God who stands on the side of the Nazi SS. For Nineveh is as *gemütlich* (nice and cute) as a Gestapo torture-chamber, and the fish of Jonah 2 can be dubbed a "sea-taxi" only by a wishful-thinking *eisegete*. The fish is a monster, just as Nineveh is a monster. In the one case as in the other, salvation occurs at the very heart of chaos.[27] To miss this point is to miss the very "apocalyptic" kind of thinking that gives to the tale its highly dramatic dimension (see below, appendix).[28] Clearly, Jonah could not have been made to cut his way through the flesh of the fish, as did Herakles and so many other heroes in the fairy tales (see chap. 3, above). Similarly, Nineveh shall not be destroyed. Nineveh is spared, although it does not deserve to live, and the sea monster lives because it did not annihilate its prey. Jonah's psalm itself is the substitute motif for the hacking through from inside. Jonah "cuts" away from darkness and thus becomes a foreign body inside the fish. The monster becomes sick with the prophet and vomits him out. The dramatic liberation of Jonah is on a par with Daniel spared by the lions or the psalmist saved from the horns of bulls and the fangs of lions (Ps. 22:14, 22). In all of these cases, survival (or resurrection) is the manifestation of the inner victory of the faithful. Indeed, one could say that the events in reality did not occur in the belly of a fish; they happened inside Jonah himself. He is the one who, in remembering that the grace of God endures forever (cf. 4:2), gave courageously a decisive twist to the complaint, making it a cry of victory.

On the contemporary scene, one thinks of a Maslow, surviving a severe heart attack and discovering life as it were afresh. He said, "One very important aspect of the post-mortem life is that everything gets doubly precious, gets piercingly important. . . . If you're reconciled with death or even if you are pretty well assured that you will have a good death, a dignified one, then every single moment of every single day is transformed because the pervasive undercurrent—the fear of death—is removed."[29]

It is paradoxical that Jonah, swallowed as he is by natural elements, realizes that the problem is not one of nature. He does not bow before its alleged unswerving laws. His obedience is not to its dictates but to Someone who dominates over it. That is why his prayer is properly "impossible" and its outcome (not its recompense) unbelievable. But it is no more impossible and unbelievable than the moral transformation of Jonah. In the depth of the abyss, swallowed by the fish, he has torn himself away from introversion and has turned toward *another*. It is *how* he is an extraordinary man, not through what occurred from outside him, but through what he worked upon himself.[30] Many in his stead would indeed succumb to the abyss of nothingness and oblivion, but Jonah, on the contrary, transcends the abyss in a move toward life. Jonah has overcome meaninglessness and absurdity. Through his existential choice, he stands on the "dry land" (cf. Jon. 2:11 with Gen. 1:9; 2:7–8) instead of lying forever in the entrails of the chaos-monster. "[Man] can exercise selectivity toward his history," says Rollo May; "[he] can adapt himself to parts of it, can change other parts, and, within limits, can mold history in self-chosen directions."[31]

What this last quotation fails to convey, however, is the dialogical character of Jonah's redemption. The history that the prophet "molds" is an I-Thou relationship in which he, Jonah, reaches out to another. The storyteller skillfully expresses this in several ways, one of which is to draw a contrast to Jonah's attempt (in 1:5) to regress, and to repress reality by sleeping "in the innermost parts of the ship." Now, *mirabile dictu,* Jonah is led not only to the innermost parts of the fish, but also to the innermost parts of his being, where, paradoxically, he hears the Voice from Without. Now he does not sleep—a Jewish metaphor for death (Gen. 47:30; Jer. 51:39; John 11:11); rather, he is fully awake and searching, an attitude that in Jonah 1 was proper to the mariners.

The dialogue in which he engages with the One who called him proves an important corrective to our growing feeling that the hero was totally alone throughout.[32] We now learn that his focal situation is also mediational. For Jonah is a kind of third term between God and the sailors, God and the Ninevites, God and natural elements. Even his message, according to the Greek text, is that in *three* days all will be over for Nineveh. He himself spent three days in the fish's belly. Jonah is third party wherever he goes. How could he not feel alone? Even the temporality that fits his stance seems to be the swaying "midnight," when it is no longer yesterday but not yet today. He always seems to be out of tune. Is he really on his way when he boards the ship for Tarshish? It is a move, but in the wrong direction; it takes him anywhere in the world but to Nineveh! Is he entombed or sheltered in the monstrous belly? Is he alive or dead? What is that limbo of three days and three nights for that new kind of speleologist? Again his ministry in Nineveh finds him wavering between two parties. Is he a prophet? Does he want the sinner's death, or does he warn him before it is too late? Is he still in Nineveh in chapter 4? Has he really ever been there, in spirit as well as in the flesh? Where is his shelter, under a *sukkah* or under a tree?

True, one could think that the author felt free to leave unexplicated certain details, but precisely his use of the number 3 prevents us from falling prey to this facile solution.[33] The triad always makes a problem. It puts in tension the first and the last terms.

The resolution of the tension comes not when one of the terms swallows the others. For yesterday remains integrally yesterday, no today can really take its place. Both must meet in the "between" that binds them, the middle term, the "midnight," the eschaton that is simultaneously end of time and beginning of beyond-time.[34]

It remains that for the personage Jonah; it is highly uncomfortable to be always an extra wheel of the cart. Besides, it is to be noted that in this satirical work, irony is found in the *situations* described rather than at the level of discourse. In the midst of funny or ironic circumstances, the characters, such as the sailors or the Ninevites, or even the city's animals, keep their dignity. Jonah himself loses his balance only through external situations. He ridicules himself, only to the very extent that he is not without responsibility for what happens to him. But it is an indirect responsibility, and he acts in the name of respectable principles. At any rate, when he addresses to God the prayer of chapter 2, he reaches a summit that no irony minimizes. At that moment, there are again three personages on the stage: God, the fish, and the prophet. But now Jonah has become the terrain on which converge past and future, and he transcends both in an attitude that Buber calls "acceptance, affirmation and confirmation"[35] of the purposefulness of existence. *This he does precisely in addressing himself to Someone who was present from the first.* Jonah breaks out of his isolation. He painfully gives birth to himself, which is another way of saying that he passes from death to life.[36]

Typical of Israel's way of thinking is the attempt to capture a movement in its very process.[37] Jonah's movement from zero to the infinite takes place in the "in-between" field where simultaneously the point of arrival is *already* reached while the point of departure is *not yet* fully left! Jonah is in the belly of the chaos-monster, in the depth of the abyss, in the valley of death and absurdity, yet he holds a dialogue with the Ground of Being and Meaning. In the words of Emil Fackenheim, he puts "sanity in the midst of insanity, hope in the midst of death."[38] Jonah's action "in the midst of" is the cathartic collapse of the negative into the positive; it is the climactic point of the dialogue with God. Therein lies the full meaning of the prayer of Jonah. In the grave of his lost illusions, Jonah "remembers" (vs. 8), and the grave is emptied by his decision to transform absurdity and death into meaning and life.

For the victory that really counts does not come once the battle is over and when there is no danger of relapse, but *in* the battle itself when one confronts the enemies face to face and fully recognizes them for what they are and the nature of the danger they pose. When such enemies are effectively changed into friends,[39] when Jonah's phantasms are tamed and integrated, when the suicidal drives are transformed into the humble love of God, then the chaos-monster becomes a fish-belly that truly harbors Jonah for his protection and survival.

We now have Jonah and his God in full view, but what about humanity? The author makes community as present as possible without destroying the verisimilitude of the situation into which he placed the hero, in the entrails of the fish. Jonah's fellow humans are indirectly included in his prayer. As a matter of fact, at "the bottoms of the mountains," he still finds himself in God's "holy temple" (2:8). The very mention by the prophet of this surprising element in such circumstances means that Jonah does not face his God in a private I-Thou dialogue. He rediscovers the "cloud of witnesses" who bridge all the generations of his people in a historic and cultic community.

We now come close to one of those taut paradoxes that only Israel could maintain. In the abyss, in the belly of the chaos-monster, Jonah prays face to face with the living God. For this he did not have to become a Guru, abstracting himself from the prison of his flesh. Nor did he have to become somehow ubiquitous. The Temple itself has come to him and stands exactly where the holy man stands. In Israel, the sacred is not tied with topography, but with revelational events. There is properly speaking no privileged place for the theophany. At no time does Sinai become a place of pilgrimage.[40] This statement can appear paradoxical at the very moment when the text mentions the Jerusalem Temple as if it were the only place of worship. But the question raised by the exclusive sanctuary at Jerusalem is complex. It requires a dialectical response. True, a mystique of the Temple, on the model of the sacred Canaanite shrines, developed in Israel's populace, encouraged by a functionary clergy. But it stirred strong protest among the prophets. For the latter, guardians of the covenantal terms with God, it was no less than an idolatry. In the postexilic subversive literature, the "Temple" is but the poor, the humble, the one who fears the word of God. The "Temple" is thus not, as such, the sacred in opposition to the secular, but it is the sacrament of God's universal presence. The "Temple" is as much in the fish's belly as it is in Zion. God and his host meet Jonah in his "exile."

But if God's presence is there, then surely it is also in Nineveh! For nothing is by nature or creation more "foreign" to God's celestial abode than the *tehom*, the abyss (Gen. 1:2) where Jonah now finds himself. Nothing is more "deprived" of the divine presence. Nothing speaks more clearly of death and emptiness. Even Nineveh cannot compete with *tehom*. Jonah relives the age-old experience of his people in history. He has now gained the ultimate human capacity to envision the divine where it is least logical, least imaginable.

The immediate context makes clear that Jonah is unable to *hold* the mystery of life; the vision of God cannot be anything but a flash in the darkness. Besides, it would be too much for one to integrate, were it not caught in a gracious glimpse as, for instance, Moses was allowed to see God's back, while God's "face shall not be seen" (Exod. 33:23). Precarious as it is, however, the vision of God in Jewish tradition is the very meaning of life. Paradoxically noncontemplative in its essence, "vision" here means participation in God's doing.[41] Truth here is a *way*, in contradistinction to static ideals. Existence is a perpetual beginning from the ashes of the past. It is so because life consists of the ceaseless attempt to have the vision of the invisible God or, after the profound intuition of Tennessee Williams (in *Suddenly Last Summer*), to utter the ineffable Name.

The vision, therefore, is here also a hearing![42] Jonah finds the answer to his search only in dialoguing with someone else. Only in the direct relation with a particular and unique "Thou" can his plight be transcended. For only in singling out one partner can Jonah truly reach out to all other partners, including the Ninevites. As Fromm writes, "If I can say to somebody else 'I love you,' I must be able to say 'I love in you everybody, I love through you the world.' "[43]

The parallel with modern psychotherapies is striking. The aim of nearly all psychological schools is precisely to help patients discover the roots of their sufferings. The "patients" find out, often to their own amazement, that in reaching out to other human beings by sharing their concerns, they are able to break the cyclical patterns from which any escape was previously impossible. This is not to say that there is a radical break in the personality (or in the narrative). Jonah does not leave a sinful condition to adopt a saintly one. There is here no "metamorphosis" from a formerly stiff-necked, stubborn, and hardhearted sinner, into a broadminded, radiant, and successful "P.R. person." For it is the same Jonah of chapter 1 who now prays in chapter 2. The "reborn" Jonah has in no way discarded his human nature and temperament. He is the Jonah of always, replete with both flaws and virtues, who shows occasional good will and frequent short temper and is capable of untold courage and some all-too-specific acts of cowardice. This Jonah, the story tells us, went to Nineveh and delivered his unbelievable message, but he also expressed anger at the sparing of the city. Thus in a way the "resurrected" Jonah "accepts, affirms, and confirms . . . the work which [the soul] is destined to perform upon the world,"[44] but Jonah's "core" remains identical to itself.[45]

From Nothingness to Being

All the same, whatever the throngs of others do to deceive themselves "regarding lying vanities" (vs. 9), Jonah now affirms and confirms his uniqueness and vocation (vs. 10). This offers a stark contrast to his former attitude (in chap. 1) when he wished to remain anonymous. He displays a concrete sign of self-abnegation: he offers a sacrifice and says his vows (vs. 10), thus opposing this new image of himself to the preceding one when he narcissistically used others as mirrors of himself. Sacrifice in Israel has a highly symbolic bearing upon which the Scriptures insist. It is a totally gratuitous and disinterested act. It is not a bargain. Verse 11 here emphasizes that Jonah's salvation is no *quid pro quo* offered in recompense for the gift of the sacrificer. Jonah's move toward God finds a response, but not a recompense. Jonah is restored to life at the very moment when all seems to be over for the prophet, at the moment that he accepts death, not as a supreme act of injustice and absurdity but as an act of God, and he greets it with thanksgiving.[46] "Real sacrifice occurs only when we run the risk of having sacrificed in vain" says Viktor Frankl.[47] He adds: ". . . only insofar as a person is capable of ignoring and forgetting himself is he able to recognize anything in and of the world."[48]

Jonah does not remain in the grave; he discovers his own self. But such a "Jonah" sees no change in his vocation: he must go to Nineveh. He must accept what he earlier refused. True, as we said above, when one breaks the monologue with the self and acknowledges a "Thou," one passes from "death" to "life" (see below, chap. 8), but as the sequel of the tale shows "the worst is not death, but the rebirth itself. . . . It means *for the first time to be subjected* to the terrifying paradox of the human condition, since one must be born not as a god, but as a man."[49] Of this, the following chapter of Jonah (chap. 3) is an illustration.

Notes

1. A. Wheelis, "How People Change," *Commentary* 47 (May 1969): 65.
2. Ibid.
3. Smart, "Jonah," *IB*, vol. 6, p. 874. So C. H. H. Wright, "The Book of Jonah Considered from an Allegorical Point of View," *Biblical Essays* (1886): 34–98, quoted by Trible, "Studies in the Book of Jonah" (unpublished) p. 155 n3.

4. Robert Alter, *The Art of Biblical Narrative* (New York: Basic Books, 1981), p. 129.

5. St. Jerome writes: "Jonah, that headstrong prophet, once fled from me, yet in the depths of the sea he was still mine" (Letter XXIX, 3 in *The Principal Works of St. Jerome*, trans. Fremantle, Lewis, and Martley, Nicene and Post-Nicene Fathers, Series 2 [Grand Rapids: Eerdmans, n.d.], p. 51).

6. Rollo May, *The Courage to Create* (New York: W. W. Norton, 1975), p. 59.

7. "When this breakthrough of a creative insight into consciousness occurs, we have the subjective conviction that the form should be this way and no other way. It is characteristic of the creative experience that it strikes us as true. . . . And we think, nothing else could have been true in that situation, and we wonder why we were so stupid as not to have seen it earlier" (May, *The Courage to Create*, p. 68).

8. "But observe his prayer, and learn a weighty lesson. For sinful as he is, Jonah does not weep and wail for direct deliverance. He feels that his dreadful punishment is just. . . . And here, shipmates, is true and faithful repentance . . ." (Melville, *Moby Dick*, [New York: Holt, Rinehart & Winston, 1957], p. 46).

9. From "prior-self" to "authentic self"; see our discussion of these categories, below, in chap. 8, on the "outer voice."

10. See Y. Kaufmann, *Toldot ha-emunah ha-yisraelit* (Tel Aviv: Bialik Institute, 1963), vol. 4 (it has been inserted by the author himself from an extant Psalm collection); so also Allen (*The Books of Joel, Obadiah, Jonah, and Micah* [Grand Rapids: Eerdmans, 1976], p. 183): "The motifs and metaphors of this Psalm are stereotyped vehicles of devotion used by spiritual folk in many a situation of distress." See also A. R. Johnson, "Jonah 2:3–10: A Study in Cultic Fantasy," in *Studies in Old Testament Prophecy*, ed. H. H. Rowley and T. H. Robinson (New York: Scribners, 1950), pp. 87–100; Eissfeldt, *The Old Testament: An Introduction* (New York: Harper & Row, 1965), pp. 121–24; and especially Landes, "The Kerygma of the Book of Jonah," *Interp.* 21 (1967): 3–31.

11. Gaster, *Myth, Legend and Custom in the Old Testament*, vol. 1 (New York: Harper & Row, 1969), p. xlvii.

12. Trible, "Studies in the Book of Jonah", p. 80; cf. Wolff, *Studien zum Jonabuch* (Neukirchen-Vluyn: Neukirchener Vlg., 1947).

13. T. H. Robinson and F. Horst, *Die Zwölf Kleinen Propheten*, HAT 1/14 (Tübingen: Mohr-Siebeck, 1964), p. 117.

14. W. M. L. DeWette appears to have been the first to contend for the inauthenticity of the psalm here, in *Lehrbuch der historisch-kritischen Einleitung in kanonischen und apokryphen Bücher des A.T.* (Berlin: G. Reiner, 1917), p. 298. See Landes, "The Kerygma of the Book of Jonah," pp. 3–31.

15. Paul Tillich, *The Eternal Now* (New York: Charles Scribner's Sons, 1963), p. 128. For Martin Heidegger, the way to freedom is the conversion to Being. The inauthentic existence is a negative sign of its reference to Being; its sense can always be reversed.

16. Max Scheler, "Repentance and Rebirth," in *On the Eternal in Man* (Garden City, N.Y.: Doubleday Anchor Books, 1972), pp. 41–42. See also n. 8, above.

17. Mircea Eliade, *Myths, Dreams and Mysteries* (New York: Harper & Row, 1960), pp. 225, 237.

18. Eliade, *Myths, Dreams and Mysteries*, p. 223. In the Greek parallels of the Jonah story, the fish is a dolphin. C. G. Jung and K. Kerenyi see in it a delphuterus, an etymology that we have been unable to verify. See *Einführung in das Wesen der Mythologie* (Zurich: Rascher, 1951), pp. 73ff. We refer the reader to the

myth of Herakles who is swallowed by a sea monster before he is saved. Arion (ca. 625 B.C.E.) is said to have been carried to land on a dophin's back after a shipwreck. Significantly, Abrabanel defends the historicity of the miracle through analogy with the living embryo, living for nine months in the mother's womb.

19. Cf. M. Eliade, *Patterns in Comparative Religion* (New York: Sheed & Ward, 1958); Eliade and J. Kitagawa, eds., *The History of Religions* (Chicago: University of Chicago Press, 1959), chap. 5. See also Eliade, *Myths, Dreams, and Mysteries*, p. 223, and *The Sacred and the Profane* (New York: Harper & Row, 1961), pp. 130f.

20. G. C. Morgan, *The Minor Prophets* (London: Pickering, 1960), p. 69.

21. G. B. Stanton, "The Prophet Jonah and His Message," *Bibl. Sacra* 108 (1951): 371.

22. Friedlander, ed., *Pirqe de Rabbi Eliezer* (New York: Hermon Press, 1965), p. 69.

23. Ibid., p. 73 n1.

24. Cf. J. Steinmann's statement: "It was necessary that the prophet know the trial of going down into hell in order that he have the courage to preach salvation to the heathens" (J. Steinmann, *Le Livre de la consolation d'Israël et les prophètes du retour de l'exil* [Paris: Cerf, 1960], p. 290; our English trans.).

25. Landes, "The Kerygma of the Book of Jonah," pp. 12–13. So also Rudolph, *Joel-Amos-Obadja-Jona* (Gütersloh: Mohn, 1971), ad loc. 2:1; P. Reymond, "L'eau, sa vie et sa signification dans l'Ancien Testament," *VTSup.* 6 (Leiden: Brill, 1958), p. 198; et. al. For the opposite view, see Cheyne, van Hoonacker, Bewer, Feuillet, Weiser, Trible, etc.

26. E. Haller, "Die Erzählung von dem Prophet Jona," *ThEH.* (1958): 28 n36.

27. Despite the affirmation of Trible ("Studies in the Book of Jonah," pp. 139, 141) that the fish is "an instrument of salvation," not at all a "chaos-dragon monster," one must realize that in Judaism and in Christianity, as soon as there is descent into water, the symbol is uniformly a catabasis into the shapeless death realm where the dragon dwells. Even the baptism of Jesus in the little-threatening Jordan was so interpreted by a unanimous Christian tradition. See H. Riesenfeld, "La Signification sacramentelle du baptême johannique," *Dieu Vivant* 13 (1949): 29–37; cf. *Odes of Solomon* 24:1–3, and the study by R. Harris, *The Odes and Psalms of Solomon* (Cambridge, Eng.: Cambridge University Press, 1909), p. 123. It is possible to go even further. The descent of Jesus into the river has been seen as a messianic process of purification of the waters. *So also was the catabasis of Jonah* viewed by the rabbis, who see in Jonah the Messiah ben Joseph. See Ignatius of Antioch, *Letter to the Ephesians* XVIII. 2; in Jewish tradition, see *Exodus Rabbah* 18, 97–98. For Jonah as a type of Christ, see Matt. 12:39, Luke 11:29.

28. The Greek text has the word *kētos*, which means "monster." It is the term used by the Septuagint for Rahab (see Job 26:12), Leviathan (see Job 3:8), or the "dragon" of Add. to Daniel (vs. 79) whose parallel text, Ps. 148:7, has "dragon." See also Gen. 1:21 (for the Hebrew *thaninim*).

29. Quoted in J. L. Christian, *Philosophy* (San Francisco: Rinehart Press, 1973), p. 11.

30. There is a contrasted parallel between Jon. 1 and certain stories composed during the Hellenistic time. There then happened a blossoming of voyage-legends, more or less inspired by the Eastern conquests of Alexander the Great. The name of Lucian must again be mentioned here in this connection (see chap. 2, above), for his *True Stories* are a parody of those legends. The hero, after he went on the moon and on other planets, is swallowed by a monstrous fish that

takes him to the island of the saints and to the place of the atheists. Finally he is brought to a country beyond the ocean, of which many of the Greek voyage-legends speak. See E. Rohde, *Der Griechische Roman and seine Vorläufer* (4th ed.; Hildesheim: Georg Olms, 1960), pp. 183ff., esp. 204ff.

31. R. May, "Modern Man's Image of Himself," *Chicago Theological Seminary Register* 52 (October 1962): 14. Cf. Tillich, "Remembrance of the past preserves the identity of a human being with himself" (*The Eternal Now*, p. 29), and H. Feifel, "The past is an image that changes with our image of ourselves" ("Death-relevant Variable in Psychology," in *Existential Psychology*, ed. Rollo May [New York: Random House, 1960], p. 59).

32. For Fromm, e.g., the fish symbolizes "the state of isolation and imprisonment which his lack of love and solidarity has brought upon him" (*Man for Himself*, p. 105). See also *Dialogue with Erich Fromm* (New York: Harper & Row, 1966), p. 119.

33. On the psychological symbolism of number 3, see Cirlot, *A Dictionary of Symbols*: "Three symbolizes spiritual synthesis; it is associated with the concept of heaven."

34. The great sixteenth-century rabbi, the Maharal of Prague, has eloquently shown that, in the number 3, the focus is on the middle term; the middle term simultaneously separates and binds, distances and approximates, differentiates and homogenizes, rends by hatred and mends by love. "Three" is the in-between, the "no-man's land," which is open to any and every possibility, both the most rewarding and the most painful. A. Neher refers to Hos. 6:2, which shows, he says, that the number of three days is symbolic of the maintenance of the "life of time." (See n. 36, below.) "Whether time is crossed by illness and death, within three days it shall not be exhausted: wait for healing or resurrection at the end in certainty. Beyond, there is the hazard of a fatal accident" (*L'exil de la parole* [Paris: Seuil, 1970], pp. 28–29; our English trans.).

35. M. Buber, *The Way of Man* (New York: Citadel Press, 1967), p. 34.

36. It is interesting to note with Landes ("Jonah," *IDB Sup.*, p. 490; "The Kerygma of the Book of Jonah," pp. 11–12; or again in *JBL* 86 [1967]: 446–50), that three days are necessary for covering the distance from here to the nether-world, according to the Sumerian myth of the Descent of Inanna to the Nether-world (*ANET*, p. 55, cf. pt. II, lines 169–73). The theme has been reversed here; it takes three days to bring Jonah back to the world of living. On the basis of Hos. 6:2 and Gen. 42:18, the rabbis concluded that God does not leave his righteous ones in need more than three days (*Genesis Rabbah*, 56, 57; *Yalquṭ* to Josh. 2:16). Jon. 4:2 here uses a term like "billows," which is elsewhere in the Bible a synonym of "abyss" (cf. Exod. 15:5; Neh. 9:11; Mic. 7:19; Pss. 68:23; 69:3, 16; etc.). In the Gilgamesh Epic, Siduri, the goddess of life, has her throne in the sea (*ANET*, p. 90).

37. Cf. Frankl: "What man actually needs is not a tensionless state but rather the striving and struggling for some goal worthy of him" (*Man's Search for Meaning* [Boston: Beacon Press, 1962], p. 107), or again, ". . . meaning must not coincide with being, meaning must be ahead of being" (*Psychotherapy and Existentialism* [New York: Washington Square Press, 1967], p. 12).

38. Address delivered at Temple Emanuel, Chicago, Illinois, 1971.

39. "Thank you for what my eyes have seen, and for the deeper insight I was granted when I became blind" (reconstruction by memory of Old Lodge Skins' parting words in Arthur Penn's film, *Little Big Man*).

40. Particularly the text of 1 Kings 19 has been taken by some critics as an indication that "pilgrimages like that of Elijah were a frequent occurrence during the early days of the nation's history" (G. E. Wright in *IDB*, vol. 4, p. 376 B, s.v. "Sinai, Mount"). This, however, is pure speculation. More impressive is that there is in the Scriptures no mention of such collective or individual pilgrimage (apart from Elijah's; the accent of the narrative is elsewhere), and no overt or covert invitation to go to Horeb/Sinai.

41. Mere contemplation implies that the visionary remains somewhat uninvolved. The visionary stands, as it were, on an aesthetic level. What ravishes the visionary is an *object*, always unreachable, as in a dream.

42. See A. Neher, *Amos, contribution à l'étude du prophétisme* (Paris: J. Vrin, 1950), particularly his development on Amos' visions, chaps. 7ff.

43. E. Fromm, *The Art of Loving* (New York: Harper & Row, 1956), p. 39.

44. Cf. n. 35, above.

45. The same idea is found in Haller, *Die Erzählung.*

46. Cf. Jerome: "You will note that where you would think should be the end of Jonah, there was his safety" (quoted by Bickerman, *Four Strange Books of the Bible* [New York: Schocken Books, 1967], p. 12).

47. Frankl, *The Doctor and the Soul* (New York: Knopf, 1955), p. 122.

48. Frankl, *Psychotherapy and Existentialism*, p. 50.

49. Becker, *The Denial of Death* (New York: Free Press, 1973), p. 58.

SIX

FAITH AND DOUBT
The Ambiguity of Commitment
(Jonah 3)

Man's struggle for his self and his identity is doomed to failure unless it is enacted as dedication and devotion to something beyond his self, to something above his self.

Viktor Frankl, *Psychotherapy and Existentialism*
(New York: Washington Square Press, 1967), p. 82.

The book of Jonah could have ended with chapter 2.[1] Its content would then approximate that of a Greek myth or a Sophocles tragedy, and its message would concern a rigid uncompassionate God, to whom a person has no choice but to surrender. Or, the book could have begun with chapter 3 in epic fashion à la Homer. We would then have something like the following: as soon as he receives God's commission, the prophet, like a Greek hero, shows his readiness to fulfill it. Triumphantly he proclaims the message to the Ninevites and brings them to their knees. But his victory is no more than a Pyrrhic one, and he addresses a complaint to the gods about their radical reversal of intentions.

But the book of Jonah does not end with chapter 2, nor does it begin with chapter 3. Once again, God calls the antihero, Jonah, despite his unwillingness to go. This receives considerable stress at this point of the story by the repetition of the very commandment that appeared in chapter 1. That is why the text says that God spoke to Jonah "a second time," a statement that raises a problem of verisimilitude, for is there really a second chance in a person's life? Life does not go in circles; an opportunity missed is an opportunity lost. We never swim twice in the same river, Heraclitus said. Then does Jonah actually receive the word of his calling a second time? Not necessarily. But he finds himself confronted once again with the same vocation after his "death" in the fish's belly. The content of Jonah 3:2 is exactly the same as that of Jonah 1:2. Jonah is the one who "hears" it "a second time." "The Lord" does not need to open his mouth a second time. We are not dealing here with a myth or a fairy tale, where a calling might well remain inconsequential and the hero unaltered, owing to the more or less oneiric relationship that exists between characters and events.[2]

"The word of the Lord came to Jonah," from within, we might say, after it had come from without. The choice that he made in the fish's belly implies that from then on he would not allow the events to remain voiceless. Were the tale a myth, the second divine order issued to the hero might be construed as blackmail; something like "Now that you know God's will is inescapable and how fatal it is for one to resist it, hear once more the call, but this time don't be stubborn!"[3] But in the case of Jonah nothing of the kind happens. Jonah remains totally free; free to say Yes or No, free to obey, but also to give vent to his anger and disappointment (see Jon. 4). Again, Jonah's personality is not crushed by what has happened at sea.[4] One must bear in mind the dialectic that we stressed in the preceding chapter between the change that occurs in Jonah and the integrity of his person. Too often modern readers of the tale short-change this tension. Wilhelm Rudolph, for example, projects elements of chapter 4 onto Jonah 3 in order to show that Jonah has not changed his mind in the fish's belly. This way, Rudolph unwillingly makes the psalm of chapter 2 look like a hoax, and he belittles Jonah's compliance with God's order in chapter 3. He even uses the term "sabotage" to describe the prophet's restricting himself to the letter of his commission so as to be blameless before God (see the discussion below on this point). Such a stance becomes all the more suspect when the German critic falls into the trap of equating the narrow-minded Jew Jonah with the whole of his people.[5]

At the basis of this misunderstanding is a "static" conception of liberty in which revolt would be a state of mind and freedom its opposite. Between liberty and automatism, no shades of nuance. Either a vibrant *guerrillero* or a complacent bourgeois. Thus the existential choice would not be inserted in the dynamism of historical mobility. But the text here does not give room to such a reductionist conception. On the contrary, verse 3 here states: "so Jonah arose and went to Nineveh according to the word of the Lord." In passing, let us note the stark opposition between this up-going and the down-going that was descriptive of the actions of Jonah in chapter 1. Here is the dynamic freedom of Jonah: a historical move—not a natural virtue. For Rudolph, Jonah's obedience comes only out of panic, while the text makes clear that the prophet does not crawl at the feet of a tyrant. Rather, he "stands up (arises)," as a free man and responds in obedience to the call of the liberator. He realizes that he misconceived freedom when he pretended to take his destiny into his own hands and to be responsible only to himself. That led nowhere but to chaos, to the shark's jaws, to "closed bars" (2.7). For liberty is not solipsistic. It cannot be achieved through self-alienation or through navel-gazing isolation. Humanness is a gerundive; it is not free; rather, it becomes free. The bipolar character of the word *šenit* ("a second time") suggests that no one becomes a person without first going into the entrails of "hades." Abraham must leave Ur in Chaldea and raise a murderous arm against his son. Isaac must live through the unforgettable and perhaps unforgivable trauma of becoming "the lamb for the burnt offering" of his own father (Gen. 22:7). Jacob must struggle the whole night with the angel and emerge crippled—but still standing. There is no escape from that crucible of liberty.

"A second time," therefore, is no mere repetition. It is the living rhythm of an act that is first thwarted by one's solipsistic instinct of survival (the "Jonah complex"), but which is followed by its fulfillment when the call is heard "a second time." This, then, is freedom, the liberation from the inhibitions that bog a person down in the quicksand of complacency.

When Jonah hears the word "a second time," he has in the interval (which might be either a split second or an eternity) passed from infancy to maturity, from inauthenticity to authenticity. To illustrate this, the tale uses a polyphony of sounds that deserves our attention. While Jonah is in the sea (chap. 2) sur-

rounded by the cruel elements, he realizes that the waves and billows are as deafening as the roars of the crowds at home would be
in response to his social success in conformism. Jonah discovers
that the way to his own sanity lies in rediscovering his own "voice"
(2:3). This is not to say that he would trust a response coming
from himself, for on the contrary he raises his voice in order to
beg for a response from someone else: "From the belly of Sheol, I
cried for help—You heard my voice." In the preceding chapter,
we stressed Jonah's reaching out, which breaks his cocoon and
makes him pass from "death" to "life." Now chapter 3 of Jonah
introduces a totally unexpected element to the concert of sounds
that takes place between God and the prophet. At first Jonah
hears nothing but the fracas of rolling water. No wonder, for the
response of God to Jonah's prayer is not what it should be. If we
were dealing with a myth, it would be easy to imagine a fitting
reaction to Jonah's discourse.[6] Surely the god or the fairy would
express a mixture of anger and benevolence. But here, instead of
speaking to Jonah, God speaks to the fish! "And it vomited out
Jonah upon the dry land." Moreover, when God speaks to Jonah,
it is neither anger nor benevolence that Jonah hears but the very
same commandment as in the beginning. The benevolence of the
fairy would obliterate past unsuccessful experiences with one
stroke. Time would be cyclical and the expression "a second time"
would not carry the tension it has here. In myth, the second time
would indicate mere repetition, and Jonah's voyage to the bottom
of the world would be only symbolical and without bearing on the
course of his history, as the "second time" would take him back
exactly to the point where he missed the target the first time.

Not so here. The commandment honors Jonah's experience
in its fullness. Jonah is addressed as a responsible man; hence he
is given an order, a call, a vocation. The one who speaks to him
does not see him as empty, worthless, and helpless, nor even as a
weakling exhausted by three days and three nights in the depths
of the sea. He is a command-able person. Moreover, the demands
of the caller have not lessened. If anything, they are even more
strict now. Obedience to the call remains today as foolish as before, for circumstances have not made the commandment more
reasonable. Jonah's decision to go to Nineveh does not level with

reason. Jonah does something *extravagant* in "going out of the usual path, . . . roving beyond just limits or prescribed methods."[7]

As if to emphasize the prophet's folly, the text presents Nineveh as having monstrous proportions. It is "an exceedingly great city of three days' journey." And not only is it an insurmountable obstacle before Jonah, but its magnitude is commensurate only with its deceptiveness. As Herman Melville's Father Mapple says in *Moby Dick:* "Jonah did the Almighty's bidding. And what was that, shipmates? To preach the Truth to the face of Falsehood! That was it!"[8] It is striking that the book of Jonah repeats no fewer than four times the phrase "that great city" (1:2; 3:2–3; 4:11). The number 4 is symbolic of the world. Nineveh is a microcosm of all the falsehood, the crime, the conformism, the solipsism, and the uniform anonymity of the human race. It deserves to be utterly destroyed within forty days because of its "evil way and the violence (*ḥāmās*) in their hands" (vs. 8). Now *ḥāmās* is precisely what was condemned by the prophets as regards Assyrian behavior toward the nations (Isa. 10:13–14; Nah. 2:11–12 and esp. 3:1; Joel 2:12–14; see also Job 16:17).

The text attempts so little to exonerate the Assyrian city that in verse 4 it implies that Nineveh is but another name for Sodom and Gomorrah.[9] True, the allusion is discreet, but it is unmistakable. The Hebrew verb used by Jonah is, as a matter of fact, *hapak* ("to overthrow"), a term that is specifically used by the Bible in connection with the total destruction of the two ancient cities along the shore of the Dead Sea (cf. Gen. 19:21, 25; Deut. 29:22; Amos 4:11; Jer. 20:16; Lam. 4:6). According to Jonah, Nineveh shall experience within forty days the same fate of annihilation, because its sin is similar. So the reader is left without illusion as regards the "virtues" of Nineveh. Jonah is sent to a nest of serpents. Noticeably, the course of events is the reverse from Lot's when he left behind the infamous cities to their doom: he left them without even looking back. Jonah's action, on the contrary, will eventually save Nineveh, and the prophet's initial refusal to go contrasts further with Lot, who was so much attracted to the riches of the valley's towns.

That comparability with the Genesis narratives about Abraham and Lot is no accident is confirmed by the wording of verse

5, where the Ninevites are credited with the same insight of faith as Abraham's (Gen. 15:6; or the people of Israel [Exod. 14:31]). In the three texts under consideration (Jonah, Genesis, and Exodus) we have the same verb "he/they believed" with the same syntactic construction. The main difference, and an important one, is that Abraham and Israel believe in YHWH, whereas the Ninevites believe in Elohim, a more general term to designate the divinity.[10]

One can also contrast Sodom, where not even ten righteous people could be found (Gen. 18:32), with Nineveh, where everyone "from the greatest to the least" (vs. 5) passes through repentance. Moreover, Sodom and Gomorrah had only the time from dawn to dusk to repent, while Nineveh had forty days. The swiftness of God's action, motivated by the enormity of Sodom's crime, had been sacrificed in Jonah to the "forty days" motif with the clear purpose of including Nineveh in Israelite destiny (see n. 8 above, this chap.). This twist evidently fits the subversive message of the third-century author.

The parallel between Jonah 3 and Genesis 19 is thus not without some ambiguity. Important elements of the model are given a reversed meaning in the book of Jonah. The readers recognize a familiar pattern, but they are all the more alerted by the differences in the new version. *Per contra,* it is without equivocation that the prophet fulfills his mission at Nineveh. The commandment of God is literally accomplished (see vss. 2 and 4). The prophet conveys the oracle exactly as God gave it—at least so it seems *prima facie.* Here, below, however, we shall express some doubt on this point, but by then we shall be in a position to attempt an exploration beyond the apparent meaning into a tropical one. To the extent thus that we stick to the obvious sense of the text, Jonah appears as a model of the scrupulous messenger that later the rabbis praise because of his literalism in transmitting the divine message. They call attention, for example, to how Adam abused his role as mediator by forbidding Eve to *touch* the tree of knowledge of good and evil, whereas God had laid injunction only against eating its fruit.[11] We can thus better appreciate Jonah's exactitude in complying with God's intent for the Ninevites.

But human acts are always open to more than one interpretation; they are never the result of one simple motivation.[12] Jonah, as is shown by 4:2, is not without his own understanding. The very transmission of the message in its seemingly unaltered form is already an interpretation in the sense of its unalterability. "Yet forty days and Nineveh shall be overthrown" is in fact how Jonah understands the divine commission. This is probably the reason why the text never says that God uttered that message (see vs. 2). It is on the basis of this personal interpretation that Jonah resolves to go to Mesopotamia. Though there is within him, in his innermost being, a devastating doubt as to the real bearing of the message (see 4:2), he readily smothers any other "translation" of the will of God. He does not even relate to the Ninevites the source of the wrath that hovers over them, nor does he suggest what attitude the Assyrians should take in response to the message. In brief, Jonah is really the representative—almost to a caricatural point—of his religious party. He sticks strictly to the letter. He is surely not incapable of grasping its spirit, for he shows that much in 4:2. He is also not of a sultry or mean character, so as to see in all things only their dark side. Rather, he realizes that the spirit is impervious, illogical, extravagant. But the letter kills—in forty days, or is it in three days, as the Greek version says? Only the spirit makes alive. Such is the aberration of dogmatic "orthodoxies" that they do not choose life in order to live, but death in order to let die all the "deviationists." For the "logic" of faith itself indicates that if there is a message for Nineveh it must be one of doom, as that cursed city has attempted to destroy Jerusalem and burn the Temple.[13] Any other alternative is insane. It is forbidden to add to Jerusalem's martyrdom by granting immunity to the chaos-monster.

Thus the only justification in Jonah's eyes for going to the arch-enemy of his people and for preaching there the word of God lies in the fact that it will seal the doom of Nineveh. Jonah has no inclination to play the role of a Cassandra whose words are never believed. Not only does Jonah want his words to be believed but also he is prepared to rejoice in the anticipated ruin of Nineveh. When the city burned in 612, Nahum the prophet exulted. It is in the same spirit that Jonah goes to Nineveh. True, the author of the Jonah narrative does not share the same convictions with Nahum, but at least he does not attribute to his ideological foes, whom he attacks in the person of Jonah, feelings that would be without traditional and respected moorings.

But the sequel of the tale shows that Jonah is wrong and that his interpretation of God's message is one-sided. Why this is so must be left unanswered for the moment, but at any rate it is clear that the ground collapses under Jonah's feet. God's repentance and his forgiving the Ninevites is the unexpected element that breaks logics, even religious logics.[14]

Jonah has intuited all along that God is too tender, too compassionate, too easily moved by his creatures. He is too quick to forget the crimes of the murderer, and how those crimes have crippled Israel. God's "justice" is equivalent to flagrant injustice. Who is God that he should be so prompt to overlook the infamy of his people's enemy—of his own enemy—but so slow and even reluctant to bind up his people's "wounds, bruises, and festering sores," to "mollify with oil" the injuries he inflicted? It is with good reason that Jonah could wonder whether it is not better to be among the torturers than among the tortured. His existential choice to take sides with the victims, *les vaincus*,[15] is radically questioned. What profit—to use a term of Qoheleth—is there in being among the friends of God rather than among God's enemies? As in the book of Job, with which Jonah has much in common (including a final divine discourse that conceals as much as it reveals), the issue is one of *justice*. For if God is not just, there is absolutely no justice in time or eternity. Justice is a myth, an opiate, a balloon as big as it is empty. And God, who presented himself as the champion of justice, the God who taught humanity the concept and the content of justice, is himself a balloon, for he stands or falls with justice.[16]

When Jonah wants to die (chap. 4), it is no childish whim. For where is the one who would choose to entertain relations so disastrous to oneself and to one's people? Who would opt for leaving one's city in shambles and mourning its dead in order to become, in the very city that committed the crime, the instrument of its forgiveness and salvation? Where is the Auschwitz survivor who would go to Berchtesgaden or Berlin carrying God's salvation? Qoheleth could not find any trace of justice in the world. Job and Jonah go still further, for they wonder whether there is justice in God himself, but then, "I'd rather die than live" (4:3, 8).

But we are anticipating, for the paradox consists in that while the prophet is interpreting God's commission as irrevocable, the Ninevites understand it differently. They introduce a "perhaps," which Jonah refused to entertain (see Jon. 4:9; see also chap. 4, above). Now those who change the meaning of the apodictic pronouncement are no casuists but the very inhabitants of Nineveh, "where are more than six score thousand persons that cannot discern between their right hand and their left hand"! Despite the absence of any conditional clause in the oracle, these simple-minded "goys" are able to transform determinism into indeterminacy; the future is unfathomable. They bring a conclusion of their own to the prophetic sentence and make it say more than Jonah intended. "Who knows? The divinity might turn and repent. He might turn away from his burning anger, and we shall not perish" (vs. 9). They thus raise a doubt as to the irrevocability of the oracle. They open, by the power of their creative imagination, an issue in what looked like a "no exit" situation. In other words, the message becomes entirely different from that carried in the messenger's interpretation. Hence they are said to have believed *God*, not Jonah (vs. 5).

The text becomes at this point ironic, even comic. Although Jonah speaks in a vengeful spirit (unless it is with indifference?), thus sealing the deadly fate of Nineveh, and utters his oracle without nuance, without pity, without love or affect, its very brutality unexpectedly brings the message home to the Ninevites and they repent! The whole thing looks really too easy. The reader of the tale is left unsatisfied. The dramatic confrontation seems to have been sidestepped by the author. It does not take much imagination to picture the intense dialogue that might have transpired between the prophet and the Ninevites on a public square of the city, perhaps "spiced" with a scornful rejoinder to the prophet's presumptuous and arrogant attitude of judgment. Such a dramatic debate among the inhabitants of the city on the issue raised by the prophet would not be out of place here. But it does not occur in the actual book of Jonah.[17] The theme of Nineveh's repentance is given short shrift. The point of the story clearly does not lie in the romantic description of the psychological debate of the soul with itself. Perhaps the reason for this shortcut has been rightly intimated by Wolf Mankowitz, who argues that Jonah reveals to the Ninevites something they already know without admitting it to themselves:

> *Jonah (to the King of Nineveh)*: Oh, so *your* little bird tells *me* a hundred times nightly to come to Nineveh and inform *you* that in forty days from now *you* are completely in liquidation. And that's what *I'm* telling *you*? It's a madhouse here![18]

Be that as it may, the irony of the matter is that the Ninevites' interpretation of God's intent is more appropriate than that of the prophet. We really are dealing with a *satura menippea* (see chap. 2, above). The Ninevites "choose life in order to live," a staggering phenomenon about which we must say more. For the moment, however, a warning note must be struck: the conversion of Nineveh is *not* the goal of the book. If it were, there would be no reason for the tale to continue with chapter 4. In fact, the Ninevites' mourning rites only pave the way for something that is of greater importance to the storyteller and his original audience.

But the conversion of Nineveh is no small thing in the book. As before in the case of the sailors, the Ninevites' attitude is integral to the progression of the story. It makes an ironic contrast with Israel's expected attitude toward heathens. Instead of passively waiting for forty days before undergoing their own death, instead of escaping the problem (as Jonah had done in chap. 1), instead of indulging in self-pity, the Ninevites confront the issue head-on; they telescope the forty days into the "today" of their repentance, and make present an event that is not due to come until later, namely, their own death. They mourn and grieve. In a remarkable and highly unusual move, they choose not to spend the rest of their short existence in pleasure. Even though they are in the situation of one who is "condemned" by physicians as terminally ill, they choose not to heed Horace's exhortation "Carpe diem" as long as it is still possible. They use wisely the time before death and they say: "Who knows?" And, since there are infinitely more chances to meet the catastrophe announced by the prophet or the physician than there are to be granted a reprieve, they have at least enough imagination to see themselves already dead, and they proceed to their own interment. Instead of feeling helpless and ultimately unconcerned about an event over which they have no control, they reflect upon their past; they review their foul deeds; they unravel the image of their wicked soul, and they mourn. It might well be a gratuitous move that is essentially incapable, in their own eyes, of altering the course of their destiny, but at least the Ninevites choose to respond humanly to a situation that involves humans and not things. In other words, what is important to realize at this point is that however we name the reaction of the Ninevites, they do *respond* to a "dictate," which they transform into a *challenge*—to themselves and, beyond, to destiny.

It is a tremendous step, a formidable wager, to hope that perhaps all is not said in the prophet's oracle.[19] Perhaps death is not the final divine word. André Neher writes:

> Yes, all *may* be, all is possible; nothing is either too atrocious to be impossible in the world and in history, nor too sublime to be impossible in human conscience and action. . . . At Nineveh's gates, saved by its repentance, this is the lesson taught by God to Jonah whose soul strived after automatic certainties. These are pulverized by the fiery fugue of *Perhaps.*[20]

The miracle is that the "perhaps" of the Ninevites corresponds to the secret desire of God in sending his prophet to Nineveh. From the start, the oracle destined for the Ninevites was no unconditional prediction. True, the message could be interpreted as of the same nature as "a law of the Medes and Persians which altereth not" (Dan. 6:10, 13, 16). Then indeed the Ninevites would have effectively granted to the prophet's oracle the character of a brazen law and left to themselves no other alternative but fatalism. But it is also up to them to tip God's word the other way. Such a choice is so real that indeed the repentance forfeits the ineluctability of the impending doom. It is true that it might be for a

time only. Tobit 14:4, for example, intimates that God's pardon
of Nineveh is to be understood as a temporary remission. "I believe," says Tobit, "in the word of God upon Nineveh which Jonah
spoke."[21] The present episode thus falls in parallel with other re-
missions of penalty, as for instance that in behalf of David (2 Sam.
12), of King Hezekiah (Isa. 38), or of King Ahab (1 Kings 20).

The narrator of course does not exclude the eventual "overthrow" of Nineveh. It actually occurred in history in 612 B.C.E.,
and all of his audience of the third century knew it. Similarly, all
readers of the tale know that it is the question here of gracious
delay given to the Assyrian city. What is thus emphasized by the
text is not the newly discovered virtues of the Ninevites, but the
divine grace. The spotlight is upon God, not upon the Assyrians.
God was not wrong regarding the gravity of the city's crimes. The
fact that the Ninevites mourn shows that there is no ambiguity in
that respect. They know that they will undergo the fate described
by Jonah, because it is the just effect of a cause they acknowledge
as such. But they also intuit that they are not locked in the impasse of divine determinism. Behind the apparent firmness of the
inflexible oracle, they sense something like a crack, a slight hesi-
tation perhaps, the shade of an unexpressed prophetic doubt (see
4:2). They draw a conclusion with the shrewdness and the clear-
sightedness that are obtained only in the "minute of truth." They
have felt that the crack in the blind wall was nothing else but the
prophet's fear that they, the Ninevites, discover the truth about a
God who is so different from their own unchangeable, immuta-
ble, but also "futile" (2:9) divinities. The almost undiscernible
shaking in the prophet's voice is the reflection of the weakness of
Israel's God who wants not the sinners' death but that they live.[22]

The repentance of the Ninevites is prophetic because it echoes the profound accents of the prophetic "provocation" of humanity by God. They have heard a word of God and now they
speak his very language! For what they say could be said by an
Israelite; it is worthy of Daniel's companions (Dan. 3:17–18), of
the prophet Joel (2:14), or of the prophet Amos (5:15): "who
knows whether God will not turn and repent and turn away from
his burning anger that we perish not?" Here, it is the nonspecu-
lative "who knows?" that people of hope oppose to hopelessness.
As Sartre would have it: the Ninevites bring into the realm of the

"thinkable" an unthinkable situation so as to transcend it at least in spirit. The French philosopher writes in *The Flies*, "human life starts across the river of despair."[23]

But, if every aspect of the Ninevites' future is thereby changed, it also changes Jonah's whole universe. As far as he is concerned, the "contract" has not been respected by God. The prophet had come to Nineveh with a program, and the program is changed in the course of its realization. Originally, God had so stubbornly clung to his intent for Nineveh that he had mobilized wind, sea, and shark to swallow Jonah in their monstrous spirals. God was so sure that Nineveh had to be overthrown that nothing could prevent him from confronting the Ninevites with a proclamation of their doom. Even the cosmic "unalterable" laws were changed to ensure that Jonah would go and, on behalf of his Lord, spit in the face of the cursed city. But now that the time of realization has come, God sides with the Ninevites and "repents from the evil that he said he would do unto them" (vs. 10).

We should pause at this point to recall that the book of Jonah is a satire written in the community of the restoration against the party in power in Jerusalem (see above, chap. 2). The author appears to be saying that if only the community would open itself up to the world instead of recoiling within itself, a miracle could happen that would, in fact, usher in the long-awaited restoration. This is so true that even hesitant or utterly hostile Jonah is highly successful in his mission, even though his conception of success did not prepare him for that type of accomplishment!

The totally unexpected repentance of Nineveh occurs even though the prophet has done nothing to provoke it. He even considers the reprieve as a terrible personal failure. Jonah in no way plays the role of a missionary, zealous or reluctant. He, rather, represents the ideologists in Jerusalem who refuse even to consider that the good news might be spread outside Zion. Jonah is thus a foil for the author's opinion that he only suggests by indirection. For the book is a plea for radical change of policy. The ground of the exhortation is that the restoration has not been realized, despite the proclamation of theocracy in the Temple by the priests. The restoration, intimates the author of Jonah, will occur only *with* the nations, not without them. And if one asks by what unfathomable means such an event might be possible, one should first take the pains to "go to Nineveh"! But Jonah is repulsed by the sparing of Nineveh, in the name of sacred principles; he refuses to be the instrument of what he considers God's betrayal of his covenant with Israel. God, however, "has his reasons that reason does not comprehend" (Pascal).

One thing entails another. There occurs a chain-reaction as soon as one "impossibility" has become not only possible but actual. The repentance of the Ninevites is extraordinary, but not so much as its sequel. God is "found by those who did not seek" him in the past (see Isa. 65:1). The repentance of the wicked city stirs the repentance of God, and who knows how far this concatenation of cause and effects will go? Perhaps to the celebration by all the nations of the feast of Succoth on Mount Zion as dreamed by Zechariah (chap. 14)? The dream is "impossible," but by the power of God not unrealizable! In the I-Thou relationship that Jonah indirectly restores between God and the Ninevites, there is a striking reciprocity of feelings and reactions. We said above that the Ninevites' move corresponded to God's secret desire in the first place. We must now go one step further and reflect upon the verb used in Jonah 3 to describe God's repentance (vss. 9, 10; 4:2). As André Neher writes:

> God's repentance is, assuredly, one of those biblical notions introducing the theme of failure in its sharpest form. . . . The Hebrew term which expresses this repentance is *neḥama* which at the same time means repentance but also *consolation* . . . resilience in the face of failure; it is the will, the energy, the taking over again of the task, it is hope. Thus failure and hope are not two separate moments of the divine work, they inherently belong to each other as two facing poles. One single term expresses their concomitance so that, in the biblical text, failure and hope are read in the same word; they are seized in the same hinge of the biblical adventure.[24]

God is consoled by Nineveh's repentance. It is now clear that, before the Ninevites bet on the possibility of escape from the impasse ("Who knows whether God will not turn and repent?" vs. 9), God had placed a wager upon the Ninevites, just as he had placed a wager upon Jonah when he called him to "cry against Nineveh," and upon Job, according to the prologue of that book. The very fact that Jonah is sent to Nineveh is paradoxically the demonstration that the future is not forgone. For if it were, from the Jewish point of view, it would be nonsensical to go to Nineveh and to "cry against her." For Greek tragedy, it makes sense to oppose someone's *hybris* with *moira* ("fate"). Tragedy can intellectually conceive of a world from which humanity is absent. Its vision is cosmocentric, not anthropocentric as is the Hebrew conception. Greek "Truth" can exist without humanity and thus can be proclaimed for its own sake. Not so for Israel, for the "Truth" here is the truth of God *and* humanity in the making, not an Idea. In other words, "Yet forty days, and Nineveh shall be overthrown" must not become a Procrustean bed for the Jewish conception. From the outset, Jonah's commission is *prophetic*, not just predictive. The prophet is not a soothsayer in Israel, and if his word is understood as operative, it is not because it is magical but because it participates in the history it describes.[25]

We have already contrasted God's will with "the law of the Medes and Persians which altereth not," according to the testimony of the books of Esther and Daniel. The rabbis broadened this perspective and opposed the human judges, who cannot revoke their sentence, to God, who can. Philo sees here the divine attribute of omnipotence at work,[26] which is correct enough but still needs qualification. For the "omnipotence" of God appears here, embarrassingly enough, as weakness. Jonah makes this point clear in his plea to God (4:2). From all we know of omnipotence, through our experience with human tyrants and despots, discretionary power is but another term for obduracy and capriciousness. But the unalterable aspect of omnipotence receives a fatal blow here, as the God of Israel paradoxically expresses his sovereign liberty by changing his mind. As for the other aspect of omnipotence, namely, capriciousness, it too is out of the question here. God's decision to relent from "the evil which he said he would do unto them" (vs. 10) is no moody gesture but in fact corresponds to his original desire and expresses not his unreliability but his "graciousness, compassion, long-suffering, and abundance in mercy" (4:2).

No people are more aware than those living after Auschwitz of the impossibility of speaking without qualification of the "omnipotence" of God. As can be seen here, the book of Jonah already sounds a *caveat* in this respect. God is compassionate (Jer. 15:6; Ps. 19:13; Judg. 2:18); he comforts himself in repentance (both his own and that of the Ninevites). For this indeed is his "omnipotence," that he can so totally change the hearts of human beings that their collusion in wickedness shifts into unanimous penance.

Verse 5 insists on that point, showing that the mourning rites extend to include the leaders themselves (vs. 6). This sequential order is important, for it shows that repentance is a spontaneous popular decision. They begin to mourn without first checking with the authorities for their approval.

The move initiated by the populace is nonetheless condoned and made official by the "king of Nineveh" who in the process sheds his attributes of kingship along with all autocracy, totalitarianism, and dictatorship. The "king of Nineveh"[27] was the "king of kings," but he appears here to be extremely accessible, in contrast to the inhuman and cruel image given historically by the Assyrians. One result of repentance, the author seems to say, is the retrieval of one's humanity and the dropping of all pretentious roles.[28]

At the other extreme of the social ladder, the reader is struck by the mention of the beasts' participation in the ritual (vss. 7–8; cf. 4:11). This motif appears during the Persian era in Jewish literature (see Joel 1:20; cf., later, the book of Judith whose fictional context is Persian, see 4:10). It was apparently a Persian custom to include animals in funerals (Herodotus, *Hist.* IX, 24; Plutarch, *Alexander* 72; see also Vergil, *Fifth Eclogue* 24ff.; some modern scholars call attention to the attire of horses during present-day funerals). The point is not only that the animals form a "topocosm," as Theodor H. Gaster notes,[29] but also that, along with the Ninevites' passage from a, so to speak, "nonkosher" state to a "kosher" one, all that belongs to them also passes into the realm of redemption. It is, one could say, the reverse of the *ḥerem* ("the ban") in the Bible, whereby people and their possessions, including animals and plantations, were smitten. In other words, in the process of human repentance, the whole of nature is also transfigured. In the image of Isaiah 11:6ff., it could be said that we have here a taste of paradise!

No wonder, then, that human repentance has the extraordinary effect of changing God's mind. Such, in particular, had been the striking discovery of the Hebrew prophets during the exile. This parallel introduces us to a crucial issue in the understanding of Jonah.

Although there are several texts of the sixth-century prophets that stress God's versatility, the *locus classicus* among them is Jeremiah 18:7–10, which Bickerman believes Jonah opposes because of the unconditional character of its prophetic declarations ("... if the nation which I have threatened turns back from its wicked ways, then I repent of the evil I had in mind to bring on it"). According to the critic of Columbia, Jonah "refused to accept the perspective of Jeremiah and Ezekiel, in which the prophet is no longer God's herald but a watchman who blows a horn to warn his people of coming danger (Ezek. 3:16; 33:1–9)."[30] But Bickerman's point is self-defeating. He fails to realize that the radical change of milieus from Jeremiah to Jonah makes their respective problematics entirely different from, and even opposed to, one another. Our thesis in contradistinction to that author's viewpoint can be summarized thus: despite the generality of terms used by the prophets Jeremiah and Ezekiel, what they actually have in mind is strictly and exclusively the fate of *Judah* and not the fate of all nations. The author of Jonah, therefore, cannot take advantage of "universalistic" statements of the prophets of exile and simply apply them to Nineveh. For he is dealing with a *new* problem, and the very least one can say about it is that it is far from evident that it has been "solved" by Jonah's predecessors. Indeed, they probably never envisaged it.

Thus, when we realize that the invitation addressed to the Ninevites in Jonah 3:8, "Let them turn everyone from his evil way," is found verbatim in Jeremiah 25:5, we must be careful to stress the point that in Jeremiah it is addressed to Judah (see vs. 1). The parallel, therefore, far from being consistent, is paradoxical and shocking. The "universalism" of Jeremiah had a very limited scope: God's graciousness toward his captive people. The same applies to Jeremiah 26:3 (see vs. 2) and to 36:3, 7 (which text is all the more interesting as vs. 3 comes as a restrictive provision to vs. 2). Jeremiah 18:11 is still clearer; the message is for "the men of Judah and the inhabitants of Jerusalem," and the prophet says: "for you . . . against you," as if to indicate a very particular move of God in behalf of his people. We find the same phenomenon in 23:22 ("my people") and in 35:15 (see vs. 13).

We have already mentioned Jeremiah 36. This chapter has been taken as a model by the author of Jonah. "It is here and there the same course of events: divine threat (Jon. 3:4; Jer. 36:7b); publication of an extraordinary and general fasting with, here and there, the use of an expression unparalleled elsewhere *qarah rom* (Jon. 3:5; Jer. 36:9); the king and his court happen to hear the news (Jon. 3:6; Jer. 36:12–20)."[31] But in Jeremiah's scene, nobody is impressed, including above all King Jehoiakim of Jerusalem (vss. 29–31). "Exposed to the same word of the Lord as Nineveh, Jerusalem, the king of Judah and his ministers do not relent from their evil ways so that the Lord may forgive them."[32] Consequently there will follow destruction of "man and beast"; whereas in Jonah there is general repentance, which entails the salvation of humans and beasts (3:6–8, 10; 4:11)—but the trees must not conceal the forest. In Jeremiah the oracle is entirely conditioned by the particular convenantal relationship that exists between God and "the house of Judah" (vs. 3). In Jonah, on the contrary, we stand outside that unique framework. There is nothing in Jeremiah or Ezekiel to make us extend that which is valid for God's people to God's foes.

St. Jerome is certainly right when, in his explanation of Ezekiel, he says that the prophets foretell punishment in order to make it unnecessary. This statement is correct as long as one remembers that such oracles are directed to Jerusalem, not to Nineveh. To the contrary, the contemporaries of the author, who share with him in the fiction of a Jewish prophet sent to the pagan city par excellence, are third-century people, a butt for sarcasms and taunts from arrogant strangers who settled in their cities and countryside. It is certainly far from evident to them that Jeremiah's and Ezekiel's statements concerning *exceptional* divine actions in favor of the Jewish exiles in Babylon are to be extended to include Nineveh. If indeed they are, it cannot be automatic but must follow a decision taken *de novo* by God. Furthermore, the same divine action that was once the motive for Israel to rejoice and praise becomes here at the very least a cause of puzzlement. Are the Ninevites on the same plane with the Israelites? Does God's grace and compassion for his people in the dungeon create a precedent by which to extend the grace to the jailers?

The paradox of the book of Jonah is compounded by a feature to which André Feuillet has called attention. Not only did the Ninevites repent, moved as they were by an extraordinary theological insight ("who knows . . . ?"), but as we stressed earlier, they did so "from the greatest of them unto the least of them" (vs. 5). This expression, it is well-known, is Jeremian (cf. 5:4–5; 6:13; 8:10; 44:12). "In Jeremiah's book, it is only with the coming of the messianic era that all shall know YHWH from the least of them even to the greatest of them (31:34); in Nineveh, with Jonah's message that marvelous fulfillment is already at work!"[33] The point is important here. It recalls a Jewish tradition according to which, when a non-Jew turns to God and repents, he becomes right away greater even than Israel's high priest, and the day when this happens greater than Yom Kippur, and the place that witnesses it holier than the Holy of Holies![34] In this Gentile, Judaism sees the purest fruit of its preaching (cf. Matt. 8:10; 15:28). In the words of Jesus "there will be greater joy in heaven over one sinner who repents than over ninety-nine righteous people who do not need to repent" (Luke 15:7).

It is true that the Ninevites, even before they are given the benefit of the *covenantal* attributes of Israel's God, as they are described in 4:2,[35] display a disposition that is strikingly close to a Jewish attitude in similar situations. Our preceding review of the parallels that exist between Jonah 3 and the book of Jeremiah has shown this clearly. The Ninevites' fasting and repentance closely follow the model of Jewish repentance and mourning rites. What is said in Jonah 3 concerning the Ninevites could be said without the slightest alteration—except perhaps for the use of YHWH instead of Elohim—about Israelites. This is not a lack of imagination on the part of the author of the tale, for what he intends to prove is that non-Jews can indeed become "greater than the high priest." The sailors of chapter 1 "offered a sacrifice to YHWH and made vows" (vs. 16; cf. Mal. 1:11); the Ninevites turn to God and repent, thereby inaugurating what Jeremiah hails as the messianic era, not in Jerusalem, however, but in Assyria!

Critics are generally at a loss to explain the presence of such so-called universalistic themes in Second Zechariah, Malachi, or Jonah. Feuillet, for example, writes, "Universalism comes suddenly to the fore, in contrast with the rather particularistic tone [that prevailed earlier]."[36] But this remarkable shift should not be overstressed. It is too easy to oppose "universalism" and "particularism." In fact, "universalism" does not stand in contrast to "particularism." The sailors sacrifice to YHWH[37] and the Ninevites convert to Jonah's God because, in their contact with the Jew Jonah, they are "Israelitized." Not that it is a question of conformism with or adoption of "Judaism"—although, of course, this can be a sign of that too. *Israel* is the name given to the human relation-with-God. Israel's tie with the divine, Israel's election by God and election of God, are precisely what makes Israel universal, for these are what bind Israel to the human.[38] Nothing, in point of fact, is truly human without a divine dimension. Neither is anything divine without its human incorporation. As Bonhoeffer put it: "Einen Gott den es gibt, gibt es nicht" ("A God which there is, is not at all"). God is the one in relation-with-Israel. The contrast, therefore, is not between particularism and universalism but between election and paganism. The nations are barbarian, "goy" in every respect, for they prevent the fulfillment of their humanity. E. M. Cioran wrote, "The common man is the unfulfilled Jew."[39]

The sailors and the Ninevites both realize this much, and they adhere to the community of Israel, throwing themselves (for a while or forever) into the stream of its history.

NOTES

1. Already in 1799, J. C. Nachtigal made a distinction between Jon. 2:3 to 4:11, on the one hand, and 1:1 to 2:2, on the other. The former passage was written during the exile against Jewish particularism, the latter in the time of Ezra-Nehemiah. More recently this thesis has been adopted by A. Thoma, "Die

Entstehung des Büchleins Jona," *Theol. St. u. Krit.* (1911): 47ff. Cf. Nachtigal in *Eichhorns allegemeine Bibliothek der biblischen Literatur* (Lips: Weidmannschen Buchhandlung, 1799), vol. 9, pp. 221ff.

2. Cf. Bettelheim, ". . . the dominant feeling a myth conveys is: this is absolutely unique; it could not have happened to any other person, or in any other setting; such events are grandiose, all-inspiring and could not possibly happen to an ordinary mortal like you or me" (*The Uses of Enchantment* [New York: Knopf, 1976], p. 37).

3. "A second time" is, however, also understood in Jewish tradition as being restrictive, namely, there is no third time, which sanctions Jonah's looking "for the glory of the son (Israel), but not of the father (God)" (*Mekilta on Exodus* 2a on 12:1).

4. R. D. Laing writes: "To be eaten does not necessarily mean to lose one's identity. Jonah was very much himself even within the belly of the whale" (*The Divided Self* [Baltimore: Penguin Books, 1965], p. 49).

5. Wilhelm Rudolph, *Joel-Amos-Obadja-Jona* (Gütersloh: Mohn, 1971), pp. 357–58.

6. "The Ninevites might be the source of dramatic suspense in easily imaginable variations of the plot. But the biblical book is about Jonah" (Bickerman, *Four Strange Books* [New York: Schocken Books, 1967], p. 9).

7. See "extravagance" in *The Oxford Universal Dictionary* (1955), s.v. "extravagant."

8. Melville, *Moby Dick* (New York: Holt, Rinehart & Winston, 1957), p. 47.

9. Ps. 11:5 uses the word *ḥāmās* in connection with Sodom and Gomorrah. Redaq in the Middle Ages had already called attention to the necessary connection with the fate of Sodom and Gomorrah. Long before him, Cyril of Alexandria had made the same point (see Bickerman, *Four Strange Books*, p. 13).

10. YHWH is the proper name of the God in covenant with Israel, whereas Elohim is a common noun and can be translated "God," "the divine," "the divinity," etc. On the decisive importance of the use of YHWH and Elohim for the understanding of biblical texts, see LaCocque, "Job or the Impotence of Religion," *Semeia* 19 (1981): 33–52.

11. *ʾAbot de Rabbi Nathan* 1:8.

12. Again here, behaviorism seems to miss the real existential issue. With the book of Jonah we are far from a statement like the one that follows, by H. J. Eysenck, that "there is no neurosis underlying the symptom but merely the symptom itself. Get rid of the symptom, and you have eliminated the neurosis" (*Behavior Therapy and the Neuroses* [Oxford: Pergamon Press, 1960], p. 9). It is to be noted that Wolpe's systematic desensitization therapy is based on this credo.

13. Or, as the book of Jonah entertains the fiction of an eighth-century B.C.E. prophet speaking to Nineveh, that wicked city is destined some day to assault Jerusalem and its Temple.

14. See J. Blenkinsopp, *A History of Prophecy in Israel* (Philadelphia: Westminster Press, 1983), p. 271: ". . . the book [of Jonah] is theologically crucial since it breaks once and for all the bond of what might be called prophetic causality by its emphasis on the divine freedom."

15. This choice is illustrated by the novel of A. Camus, *The Plague*.

16. As mentioned earlier (chap. 2 n46), above, the problem of Jonah's is echoed in second-century C.E. apocalypses. ". . . for I have seen how you endure those

who sin, and have spared those who act wickedly, and have destroyed your people, and have preserved your enemies, and have not shown to anyone how your ways may be comprehended. Are the deeds of Babylon better than those of Zion?" (4 Esdras 3:30f., 34–36; 4:28ff.; 5:29f.).

17. As W. Booth says, "A *Candide* twice as long would be half as good!" About irony, he says that it "is a swift communication of meanings that make the reader himself feel clever for seeing so much in so little, the less the better" (*A Rhetoric of Irony* [Chicago: University of Chicago Press, 1974], p. 206).

18. W. Mankowitz, "It Should Happen to a Dog," *Religious Drama*, vol. 3, selected and introduced by M. Halverson (Meridian, N.Y.: Living Age Books, 1959), p. 131.

19. Cf. Servius ad Vergil, *Aeneid* 4.696: "Sunt fata quae dicuntur denuntiativa, sunt alia fata quae condicionalia vocantur. Denuntiativa sunt quae omnimodo eventura decernunt . . . non potest aliter evenire." ("The relevation of destiny can be unconditional—*denuntiativa;* it then occurs in any case, nothing else can happen.") Quoted by E. Bickerman, "Les deux erreurs du Prophète Jonas," *RHPR* 45 (1965): 252 n75.

20. "R. Ami wept when he came upon the [following] verse: 'let him put his mouth in the dust, perhaps there may be hope' (Lam. 3:29). He said: 'All this for a Perhaps!?' (*Hagiga* 4b; cf. Zeph. 2:3; Joel 2:14)." See A. Neher, *The Exile of the Word*, Philadephia: Jewish Publication Society of America, 1981, p. 238.

21. According to the so-called "short text"; cf. Josephus, *Ant.* 9.10.1 §214.

22. See Ricoeur, *The Symbolism of Evil* (Boston: Beacon Press, 1967), p. 68: "If, then, history is revealed as chastisement only through the ministration of prophecy that interprets in this way, the bare occurrence can be prophesied as irrevocable and its meaning as revocable." According to the rabbis (*Sanhedrin* 89b), "Jonah did not know whether Nineveh would be 'overthrown' towards good (convert), or if it would be overthrown by evil." In a somewhat similar vein, St. Augustine says that from a material point of view, it is true Jonah appears to be a liar, but from a spiritual viewpoint it is true that sinful Nineveh was "overthrown" (quoted by Bickerman, "Les deux erreurs," p. 225). *Yalqut* to Jon. 3:3 (§550) says that because Ninevites did penance, God restrained his wrath for forty years in accord with the forty days of the oracle.

23. Sartre, *The Flies*, act 3, scene 2, *in fine.*

24. Neher, *L'exil de la parole* (Paris: Seuil, 1970), p.254–55 (our English trans.).

25. We must, however, credit Bickerman for pointing out the difference between Jewish "repentance" and Greek *metanoia*. Whereas the former is contrition of heart, the latter implies a mere intellectual value judgment (see A. D. Nock, *Conversion* [Oxford: Clarendon Press, 1933], p. 181) and is oriented toward future behavior rather than the moral condemnation of the past. Similarly note the contrast between the Hebrew concept of revolt against God and the Greek *hamartia;* cf. Bickerman, "It's not sin, it's a mistake" ("Les deux erreurs," p. 257 n90 [our English trans.]). See also A. LaCocque, "Sin and Guilt," *Encyclopedia of Religion* (New York: Macmillan, 1987), vol.13, pp. 325–31.

26. Philo, *De Jona* (quoted by Bickerman, *Four Strange Books*, p. 47).

27. The title is startling and may be a token of the age in which Jonah was written. But Landes warns that this should not be pressed, for the formula "X king of Y" is a Hebrew form of identification (1 Kings 21:1; 2 Kings 1:3). The same phenomenon is present in Neo-Assyrian inscriptions (Landes, "Jonah," *IDB Sup.*, p. 490).

28. "Thus the heathen ruler, in consequence of his faith, becomes the model of a king as he actually should have been in Israel according to Deuteronomy 17:20, someone who does not lift his heart over his brethren . . . but is an example in the fear of God" (H. W. Wolff, *Studien zum Jonabuch* [Neukirchen-Vluyn: Neukirchener Vlg., 1947], p. 126; our English trans.).

29. T. H. Gaster, *Myth, Legend, and Custom in the Old Testament* (New York: Harper & Row, 1975), vol. 2, p. 655. That figure is overstylized but has the merit to make us go to the possible origins of wearing a sac. The sac was generally of goatskin. Hence R. Hiyya b. Abba's commentary (about 300 C.E.), "Thereby we mean that we are demeaned to the rank of cattle" (*Taanit* 16a).

30. Bickerman, *Four Strange Books*, p. 40.

31. André Feuillet, *Études d'Exégèse et de Théologie Biblique, Ancient Testament* (Paris: Gabalda, 1975), p. 422 (our English trans.).

32. Wilhelm Vischer, "Jonas," *EThR* 24 (1949): 119.

33. Feuillet, *Études d'Exégèse*, p. 422 (our English trans.).

34. See *Sanhedrin* 59a; *BQ* 38a; *'Aboda Zara* 3a; *Sifra Shemoth* 13 (ed. Weiss, 86b).

35. Bickerman remarks that God is all that Jon. 4:2 says he is, within the framework of his covenant with Israel. That he appears to act with other nations as he does with Israel is as shocking to Israel as it is to a wife who witnesses her husband's infidelity!

36. Feuillet, *Études d'Exégèse*, p. 427 (our English trans.).

37. The Tetragammaton is judiciously used here as the tale makes sure that we understand the sailors' move to be one of conversion, and not a religiously vague act. We shall therefore take exception here to Ibn Ezra's remark (on 1:1) that the text does not say anything about the destruction by the heathens of their altars and idols. For Bickerman as well, there is no mention of the conversion of pagans in Jewish literature before 2 Maccabees. "The Ninevites (and the sailors on the ship) simply acknowledge the power of the Lord" ("Les deux erreurs," p. 250 n67 [our English trans.).

38. See LaCocque, *But as for Me* (Atlanta: John Knox Press, 1979).

39. E. M. Cioran, *La tentation d'exister* (Paris: Gallimard, 1956), p. 82 (our English trans.).

SEVEN

A MATTER OF JUSTICE
(Jonah 4)

... beyond justice and anger lies the mystery of compassion.
Abraham J. Heschel, *The Prophets*
(New York: Harper Torchbooks, 1971), vol. 2, p. 67.

In the preceding examination of Jonah 3 we remarked that, under certain conditions, the narrative could have started there. The book could also have ended with the conclusion of chapter 3. All seems to be said there, for the repentance of the Ninevites brings about the repentance of God. But after reaching this edifying peak, the author draws us again into the depths of despair. For, as far as Jonah is concerned, to accept the resolution of the tension of the narrative through the direct reconciliation of God and Nineveh would mean that he, the Israelite prophet, shares in another *Heilsgeschichte*. It would mean that he can commit himself to a history other than that of his own community, that he can identify with Nineveh rather than with Jerusalem, and lose his very personality, which has been until now so closely associated with his people's.

But Jonah does not fall into this trap; the narrative at this point rebounds with the theme of his anger. The noun "anger" appears no fewer than three times, and there is one occurrence of the verb in the chapter. Jonah, we are told, reacts with anger to God's forgiveness of Nineveh (vs. 1). Thus, God, who is "slow to anger" (vs. 2, but the Hebrew term here is different) raises an unexpected question about Jonah's anger (vss. 4, 9): "Does your anger become you?" That is: Does anger open up your understanding to what is happening?[1] It is clearly a didactic kind of question in the expectation of a "sensible" answer. We have seen, however, that Jonah's logic cannot be so easily dismissed. In the words of L. C. Allen:"[Jonah] considers it intolerable that Israel's experience of Ex. 32 should be mirrored in Nineveh; he cannot stomach Yahweh's cheapening his mercy by offering it to all and sundry."[2]

The rabbis of old had a sharp exegetical insight when they interpreted Jonah's reasoning in the following way: "since the heathens are nearer to repentance, I might be causing Israel to be condemned. Rather I would die" (4.3, 8; cf. 1:12).[3]

The Lord is present here, as he was in chapter 2 where Jonah was transformed in the process. Here, however, the text stresses the prophet's attitude as radically different. He does not like this new experience of the divine Presence. The rationale for such displeasure is also clearly stated. The whole issue, as Cohn has shown, pivots around the term *raᶜ* ("evil") used in the narrative.[4] God does not seem to take the evil with all the necessary seriousness. Jonah began by addressing himself to *raᶜatam* of the Ninevites (1:2) and he brings them back *middarkam haraᶜah,* from their evil way (3:10), thus averting their punishment. God repents of the *raᶜah* which he had intended to do to them (3:10). But this precisely is *raᶜah gedolah,* a great evil (4:1) in Jonah's eyes. And Cohn adds: "It is his very zeal *for* God that turns Jonah against God."[5] St. Jerome follows the rabbis and states: "[Jonah's] despair is about Israel's salvation. . . . He is not saddened, as some think, by the salvation of pagan multitudes, but fears that Israel would perish."[6]

In other words, Jonah clearly expected the literal fulfillment of his oracle of doom against Nineveh. He preached to the Ninevites, not in order to bring them to repentance but in a spirit of vengeance that is without parallel in Israelite prophecy except for Nahum precisely at the occasion of Nineveh's ruin in 612 (see 1:3, 7; 2:1; 3:4–7, 19). Such an ethos of avenging rage, common to Nahum and Jonah, is already enough of a reason why not to belittle the importance of the city's name in Jonah, as if one could swap it with any other pagan city's name (cf. P. Trible; R. E. Clements) or even with Jerusalem (see above, chap. 2, where we discuss that point).

For ancient Israel, being is inseparable from performing. Abraham *is* the one who leaves Ur and becomes the father of the faith; Jacob *is* the one who fights with the angel and deserves to be called Israel; Amalek *is* the wicked one who tries to thwart the fulfillment of Israel's destiny. Similarly, Nineveh is the destroyer of Jerusalem, the concentration camp for God's people. God's decision to spare it perpetuates a fatal threat to Israel. One must always bear in mind the *historical* character of the reality about which the Bible speaks.

It is furthermore in the name of the historical integrity of the "actors" and their acts that Jonah is also as much message as messenger. He feels totally implicated in the Ninevite affair, vis-à-vis which he keeps no objectivity. When the oracle's outcome is the antipode of the prophet's expectation, it is clear that Jonah is left with an unbearable split of his personality. He was wholly committed to his message "yet forty days and Nineveh shall be overthrown." A reprieve of the sentence or, worse, a verdict of cancellation is violation of his person.

On the other hand, however, determinism is passionately rejected by Israel in the category of the penultimate. The Nineveh of tomorrow is not necessarily the same as the Nineveh of yesterday. This, in part, is the lesson of the book of Jonah. But for this metamorphosis to happen, no less than a miracle must occur. Only a miracle can alter the unswerving course of heavenly bodies, but Jonah's "logic of faith" militates against such a hypothesis, not only because history is not made up of miracles, but when they do occur it is precisely in Bethlehem, in Judah, in Palestine. That they can actually happen in Nineveh is in Jonah's eyes such a remote possibility that it is not to be envisaged. For all practical purposes Nineveh is what it represents; it represents evil.

Jonah's anger does not, therefore, emerge from solipsism and parochialism. It is a righteous wrath for which Jonah feels no shame. J. T. Hower writes: "Every man's anger is righteous indignation in his own eyes. Every man feels his anger is legitimate because it is due to a violation of his personal code of 'how things ought to be.' "[7]

God says to Jonah, "Does your anger become you?" and by the same token the anger of Jonah is exposed to another kind of light. Jonah has perhaps the best motives to be indignant, but they do not prevent his attitude from being too harsh for those who had become his "parishioners." Later in the narrative, this anger of his will be replaced by its ironical contrary, pity—but it is addressed to a tree! Meanwhile, Jonah is convinced that he is right to be angered. If he does not answer the question raised by God, it is not because he chooses to be arrogant, but because in fact he thinks that he is right in his indignation whatever God thinks of it.[8] He wishes he were dead.

At this point we recall J. D. Crossan: ". . . the hearer expects prophets to obey God, and pagans such as the Ninevites, especially, to disobey God. But the speaker tells a story in which a prophet disobeys and the Ninevites obey beyond all belief."[9] We are thus in the midst of extravagance. "God's folly" (1 Cor. 1:25) spares the very city that is to destroy Israel (see Hos. 9:3; 11:5, 11; Amos 5:27; cf. Ps. 137:7–9). Jonah had said, yet forty days and Nineveh will become like Sodom. But there was a crack in the iron-clad declaration: "Sodom" escapes through that crack; it is spared!

If Jonah is disappointed, he is not really surprised. From the beginning, as he himself confesses (4:2), he has suspected that his oracle would not come true. There was a conflict in his mind between the traditional affirmation that the Lord changes not (Isa. 45:23; Mal. 3:6; Num. 3:19; 2 Sam. 12), and a strong intuition that God wants to be defeated by his children in Nineveh. One day, St. Paul will forcefully say that the power of God "comes to its full strength in weakness" (2 Cor. 12:9), but Jonah does not deal with paradoxes. God's weakness irritates him; it is a feeling that he cannot tolerate in the super-ego, as he does not tolerate it in himself.[10] And not only weakness, but non credibility vis-à-vis others and more gravely vis-à-vis self. From this perspective there also arises the problem of unfulfilled prophecy, which indeed makes of Jonah a liar (see Deut. 18) and stirs within him a profound suspicion of himself. Might it be that he misunderstood his mission from the beginning? Was he wrong about the meaning of the message? Has he been really called? Or is all this only illusion, phantasm, absurdity? Is there really still a meaning to life

when all the balloons of our secret causes blow up? In such conditions, there remains only one solution, suicide, the wish to die.
So it was for Elijah and Jeremiah, so it was for Job. It is true that
those men had other reasons than bad temper to wish that the
end of their torments come soon. The author of Jonah is a full-
fledged satirist, and he counts on the fact that we shall draw the
parallel. The rationale of Jonah, in comparison with his famous
predecessors, is much less honorable. He rejects divine pity, of
which he himself was the beneficiary, because now it is addressed
to others than his people. One expected more generosity; especially in the light of chapter 2 where Jonah showed faith in the
unchangeable love of God and celebrated God's graciousness,
which endures forever. In chapter 2 he transformed a dirge into a
cry of victory, but now that the Ninevites come out of the abyss of
their nothingness, his voice becomes again a lamentation. Jonah
is the man of inopportune reactions.

As we mentioned in chapter 6, above, the problem of God's
forgiveness of the wicked city was not settled in the minds of Jonah's readers. Especially bothering is the chronological sequence of
God's anger followed by his repentance and his forgiveness. This
psychologizing diachrony of God's feelings leads head-on to apo-
rias. If one agrees with Scripture that there is no other religious
language but the one of divine anthropomorphisms, at least these
must be qualified by the imperatives of transcendence. This
encounter of the contingent and the absolute is much better expressed synchronically. The God of the book of Jonah is *simultaneously* angry and compassionate. Simultaneously, he condemns
and forgives; he lets die and makes alive, he wounds and he heals
(see Deut. 32:39; 1 Sam. 2:6). The mistake of Jonah is when he
sees as mutually exclusive the concomitant aspects of God's attitude. He sees God as a "simple body": God is curse for Nineveh;
he is benediction for Zion. Although he has the intuition, expressed in verse 2, that the contradiction belongs to the essence of
God, the relationship with God is rendered highly uncomfortable.

Many before and after Jonah had the same experience. The
late text (second century B.C.E.?), Tobit 14:4, as we saw, says "I
believe the word of God upon Nineveh which Jonah spoke" (see

above, chap. 6). For Tobit, the repentance of God about Nineveh's fate can only be temporary. Philo also tries to assuage Jonah's sharp feelings in the following imagined dialogue between Jonah and God: "Thou mayest say, O prophet, . . . from My humiliation didst thou receive honor. . . . If thou art perturbed about the falseness of thy proclamation, thy accusation is against Me and not thee, O prophet. For thou preached not what thou wished but what thou received" (*De Jona* 6:41, 48).[11] Philo's reasoning is a bit too neat. In the words of Harry Stack Sullivan, ". . . anger, in either its mild or severe grades, is one of the most common masking operations for anxiety."[12] Indeed, Jonah's anger appears to him to be more pleasant (or "becoming") than anxiety before God's display of weakness. Jonah dares say to God: "It is unfair; all this for naught?" All the humiliation and danger, the descent into the netherworld, the guilt feelings, the victory over oneself, the confrontation with the Ninevite crowd—was it for such an empty result? Nothing will really change Nineveh; it will continue to be evil as before; repentance is shallow and short-lived. It is as if you trusted a sleeping dragon. In time, it will change into "a beast dreadful and terrible . . . it will devour and break in pieces and stamp the residue with its feet" (Dan. 7:7).

Jonah's indignation is precisely what prevents him from choking to death. Rather than explode with outrage and die, it is better that Jonah vent his anger, even if he risks being blasted by God's thunder. His strength lies in the fact that life is no longer his most precious good. He has nothing to lose, he is ready to die (vss. 3, 8). Not that he be tempted by self-destruction, but he is anxious not to be vulnerable to the accusation of complicity with the one who hurts him. God has become his adversary and Jonah says it loud and clear. He also knows that he is up against an insurmountable obstacle; his foe is absolutely invincible. Nothing escapes him, of the acts or intentions of Jonah. Even under the most horrible circumstances, in the death camps of Nazi Germany, rare exceptional people still believed that "thoughts are free" (*Die Gedanken sind frei*). But in the case of Jonah, even his intimate reflections are known by the Other. And Jonah refuses to resort to mimicking his jailer—like some camp inmates who behaved and even dressed like the SS. His refusal falls in line with

Job's attitude vis-à-vis deceitful "friends," and vis-à-vis God. Jonah will not be subdued or manipulated; rather, he will be either a free man or a martyr for the right cause.

Jonah, a martyr? The statement seems foolish if we remain within the boundaries of psychological explanations of the prophet's feelings. From that standpoint, the hero indeed is so close to us that we recognize ourselves in him. Psychology sheds light on the common human denominator between him and us. Jonah's anger is a feeling that we immediately understand. We can appreciate its intensity, so that the wish to die, expressed by the prophet, does not utterly surprise us. But psychology gives only a partial grasp of the rationale for Jonah's anger. It is within the concreteness of his Jewish involvement that we must understand it. His anger is not just bad temper when replaced in its theological context. On the contrary it has its full depth within the context of his dialogue with God.

Jonah's theology is not one-sided; he cannot be accused of believing in an authoritarian God who would lack the attributes of mercy and compassion. He proved this in one of the most terse and pointed summaries of the whole Bible (vs. 2). Such a creed derives from a longer list of God's attributes in Exodus 34. One can also refer to Psalm 103:8, Nahum 1:3, and, especially, Joel 2:13, where we find the exact wording of Jonah 4:3. Joel besides may have served as a model, for Jonah, we now know, dates from the third century B.C.E.[13] Jonah, therefore, simply *chooses* to call into question the exercise of divine mercy toward Nineveh. This, he thinks, is tantamount to warming a snake on one's breast.

The dramatic tension in the tale is enhanced by the necessity, on the part of the reader, of acknowledging that God has been right all along: first of all, by sending Jonah to Nineveh with an oracle of doom against the city and, second, by forgiving Nineveh after it repented (see 4:11). But Jonah's reluctance to obey may be still more correct! Clearly, the prophet does not seek to protect himself; he, rather, puts himself in jeopardy, as he did on the boat, showing to all that he is not a coward. Rebel with a cause, selfish survival is the last thing he has in mind. He rejects any idea of an absurd existence where justice is flouted by the very one who is its initiator, its founder, and its guardian.[14]

The question that Jonah raises could be expressed thus: What is to prevail when there is a conflict between God's partiality and one's fidelity to and love for one's suffering people? Or between the demand of loving one's enemy and the imperative not to betray one's own flesh and blood? Jonah, for one, chooses not to relinquish his humanity in blind obedience to a debasing commandment. He does the *only* thing that is left to a *free* person: he refuses and so puts his life on the line. This is, properly speaking, the virtue of disobedience. It is indeed a virtue and it is clearly so when put in contrast with its contrary. If Jonah had made no objection to God's command, he would have become a puppet, a straw man, not a prophet. Paradoxically, it is only the disobedient Jonah who deserves our attention; perhaps only the disobedient Jonah is truly obedient. And perhaps God, from the outset, does not wish to be obeyed. It might be that Jonah fulfills the expectation of God in not belittling the crime of Nineveh against his people. What is at stake in the book of Jonah is not the clash between an omniscient and all-wise God, on the one hand, and a narrow-minded, petty, chauvinistic Jew, on the other. This would indeed offer little interest. Rather, two different conceptions of justice and grace confront one another. As said in Jonah 4:2, the prophet "knew [from the beginning] that God is a gracious God and compassionate, long suffering, and abundant in mercy. . . . *therefore* [he fled beforehand] unto Tarshish." These divine attributes are generally admirable; but are they applicable particularly to a Julius Eichmann? Cyril of Alexandria (PG LXXI) was well inspired when he stated that Jonah was sent to Nineveh and not, for example, to Tyre in order to show that God is merciful even toward the *worst* of all sinners.[15]

Jonah's flight to Tarshish is no blot on his reputation. On the contrary, we love him because he fled; we admire him because he put his life on the line rather than make God an accomplice of murderers. The Christian scholar Rupert of Deutz (twelfth century) was right when he stated that Jonah refused to obey God out of pity to his people. That is why, he said, God was not very angry at Jonah. Long before Rupert, the difference of interpretation between Origen (185–254 C.E.) and Jerome (347–420 C.E.) on this issue brings us directly to the point. Origen insisted upon the full pardon of the repentant sinner; at the end, even the devil will be converted. Jerome reacted to this opinion with indignation, rhetorically asking whether ultimately there will be no difference between the Virgin Mary and a prostitute, between the angel Gabriel and the devil, between the martyrs and their torturers.

The question is a perennial one. The rabbis dared say that even the *yeṣer haraᶜ* ("the evil inclination") could be redeemed. That also was said by the Creator to be "very good" (see *Genesis Rabbah* 14:4). One recognizes here an attempt similar to the one of the subversive postexilic literature to shatter the stronghold of the "ideologists" in Jerusalem, which is precisely the aim of the book of Jonah. But let us stress once again the point that their position is far from being ridiculed. It is the one of Jerome in his discussion with Origen. It takes evil seriously and, above all, it takes the victim of crime seriously. However, it is not retained by the rabbis, nor by Christianity, nor by Jewish mysticism, for evil can and must be redeemed. Augustine, to recall, could not conceive of a definition of evil from which the term "good" would be absent. Evil, he said, is "amissio boni, privatio boni"—but, after Auschwitz, these mystical and theological oratory flights appear perhaps too optimistic. Some even say with St. Jerome that they are offensive. Can we today seriously and responsibly affirm that evil is but the reverse of good? Where are the "sparks" of the Spirit among the SS of Dachau?

It remains, for the author of Jonah and for the community of the disciples of a Second Zechariah, for example, that Nineveh must be warned about its wickedness, and perhaps in this way be brought to repentance and salvation. This belongs to the vocation of Jonah-Israel toward the nations, and the prophet's feelings and convictions cannot become the ultimate criteria for what is right and wrong. But then, following Jeremiah (20:7), Jonah is entitled to complain: "Oh my Lord, Thou hast enticed me, and I was enticed, Thou hast overcome me, and hast prevailed. I am become a laughing stock all the day, everyone mocketh me." Jonah is not compelled to debase himself; until the end, he maintains his liberty as a human being and rebukes God for a justice that is nothing but injustice. In so doing, Jonah is not so much envious of the Ninevites' salvation as he is jealous for the honor of his people and, through his people, the vindication of the *innocent.*

Despite their divergences, the "visionaries" and the "ideologists" of Jerusalem agree on one point. Whether the "missionary" is zealous or reluctant, it is only from him that the nations can hear the word of God. The indispensable mouthpiece of God is Jonah. Nineveh owes its salvation to no one else, "for salvation comes from the Jews." Without Jonah, Nineveh is like Sodom or Gomorrah, which nothing can save.[16]

From this standpoint at least, Jonah is not to be confused with a professional psychologist. From a psychological point of view, no one better than a Ninevite knows the psyche of his fellow citizens and how to speak effectively to them. Genuine counseling must include many guarantees, such as commonality of language between advisers and advisees, empathy, and interpersonal qualities that will facilitate communication. According to Carl Rogers, at least six basic conditions are necessary if positive personality change is to occur in the therapeutic process: warmth, permissiveness, acceptance, genuineness, internal frame of reference, and unconditional positive regard (respect).[17] Strikingly enough, *all* of these features are absent in Jonah's relations with the Ninevites![18]

In short, there are human phenomena that do not belong entirely in the realm of psychology, as for instance, love, God's calling, the prophet's discourse. They can be approached but not exhausted by psychological analysis. It is certainly for this very reason that the Ninevites' conversion in Jonah 3–4 is so tersely presented. The singer of tales wants us to understand this occurrence as a "beyondness" that is irreducible to any human explanation.

Parallel to the irrationality of the Ninevites' unexpected repentance, Jonah's anger is also to some extent illogical. God asks him: "Does anger become you?" Does it open your eyes to the meaning of what is happening? (vss. 4, 9). The first time this question is raised by God (vs. 4) it remains unanswered. This is all the more surprising as here God is conversing directly with Jonah for the first time in the tale, apart from his calling in chapter 1. Jonah should be happy, especially since God appears moved, patient, and comforting; in short, God seems to understand the prophet. So, in effect, Jonah's anger is problematic. But the situation is not unheard of. A parallel imposes itself. There is indeed a famous predecessor to Jonah, to whom also God twice addressed a question in a form of reproach: Elijah on Mount Horeb (1 Kings 19). This kinship between the two personages must, besides, be broadened, for the correspondence between Elijah and Jonah is the very key to the understanding of Jonah 4 and more generally to many a detail within the narrative.

For we are now at the point of the narrative's development that allows us, without any shred of doubt, to specify the model that the author of Jonah followed in constructing his satire (see above, chap. 2). The story of Jonah and the cycle of Elijah (1 Kings 17–19; 2 Kings 1–2) stand in parallel and contrast.

The attitude of Jonah closely recalls the one of the prophet of the ninth century, but Jonah seems to do everything Elijah would not do in similar circumstances. While the Tishbite finds himself most often, and physically, in elevated situations, Jonah as far as he is concerned chooses often to "go down" ever lower.[19] In 1 Kings 17, Elijah is in an upper room; in chapter 18, he is on the top of Mount Carmel; in chapter 19 on Mount Horeb. Those he is dealing with also occupy increasingly elevated positions (social and spiritual): a widow in Sarepta, the whole of Israel. This pattern is repeated in two episodes of 2 Kings 1–2: Elijah is on the top of an unnamed mountain and he confronts the troops of the king. The prophet goes up to heaven in a fiery chariot. As to Jonah, one remembers that he "goes down" to Joppa (1:3), into a ship (1:3), then to the vessel's hold (1:5). Finally he is hurled into the waters of the sea (1:15). He says: "To the base of the mountains I descended; of the earth the bars were forever locked on me" (2:7). Those he is dealing with are increasingly less important, from God to a chaotic monster via the captain of the vessel and his crew. "While Elijah is taken up in a fiery chariot in the midst of a whirlwind, Jonah is taken down by a water monster to the netherworld and the storm above his head comes down."[20] There is too much water in the time of Jonah for three days, but no rain in the time of Elijah for three years. In the ninth century, only fire remains: a fire that consumes everything in 1 Kings 18;

in 2 Kings 1 it devours two squadrons; in 2 Kings 2 it takes Elijah to the heavens. For Jonah, Nineveh is another Sodom, hence in forty days it shall be destroyed by the fire of heaven as also was Gomorrah. But instead of this it is, rather, "the heavenly dew" that comes down upon Nineveh (see Deut. 32:2; Isa. 45:7). The burning sun and the scorching wind from the east are reserved to Jonah! There is opposition between the unwittingness of Jonah to execute the command of God and the eagerness of Elijah to obey. The one and the other receive vocation, however, in the same terms: "Get up, go." But the one goes to fulfill the call, while the other goes "to flee" (see 1 Kings 17:9–10 and Jon. 1:2–3). The destination of each is a foreign land (1 Kings 17:9). Jesus recalls Elijah's positive attitude toward the Sidonian widow; he would have been at a loss to say the same about Jonah toward the Ninevites (see Luke 4:24–26).

The parallels between the two traditions go further. Without pretending to be exhaustive, it is useful, we believe, to pursue our inquiry. Among the points of comparison, one will notice in both cases that the king is identified simply by mentioning his capital. In 1 Kings 21:1, Ahab is "the king of Samaria"; in Jonah 3:6, the Assyrian king is "the king of Nineveh."[21] In both texts, there is a royal edict (see 1 Kings 21:8), and the courtiers proclaim a fast (see 1 Kings 21:9). Above all, Ahab and the king of Nineveh both repent and their mourning rites are detailed in both texts (see 1 Kings 21:27). In both cases also there is a reprieve to the catastrophe (1 Kings 21:28 and Jon. 4:1–2). So, in one sense, the earlier prophecy of woe is made pointless.

The stories of Elijah and Jonah insist upon the kingship of God over nature. God appoints a shark, the sea, the wind, the sun, a plant, a worm—Nineveh's salvation is a corollary of that doctrine of the creator God. In the cycle of Elijah, God controls dryness and rains, dew and heavenly fire, winds and earthquakes, ravens and angels/messengers. Paul Ferguson says pointedly that such a parallel between the two prophets has sense only for an audience that revered Elijah as a national hero. Later, Jewish tradition made Jonah the son of the widow of Sarepta whom Elijah revived.

Chapter 4 of Jonah particularly is interspersed with reminiscences of Elijah. Above, in chapter 1 of this book, we mentioned a certain number of parallels between the two prophets. Elijah goes into a cave and waits; Jonah sits at the east of the city. God addresses the one and the other twice with a question-reproach (1 Kings 19:9, 13 and Jon. 4:4, 9). The one and the other sit under a desert plant (1 Kings 19:4 and Jon. 4:6). They are both convinced of being right (1 Kings 19:14 and Jon. 4:9). Let us also notice the similarity of the storm wind in 1 Kings 19:11 (cf. 2 Kings 2:11) and the "eastern scorching wind" of Jonah 4. About this, it is interesting to note that both Elijah and Jonah have first the experience of the whirlwind, then of the earthquake, finally of the fire; another trilogy in Jonah shows the worm that "strikes" the plant that provided its shade, then the eastern wind, and finally the sun that strikes upon his head. In verse 2, Jonah must confess the compassion of God when, in fact, he wishes that God's anger be unleashed upon Nineveh. Elijah also, and especially he, is known for his insensitivity and his hardness; but in 1 Kings 19:12, God is found neither in the whirlwind, nor in the earthquake, nor in the fire. God is in "the sound of a tenuous silence"!

The parallel set by the author of Jonah in chapter 4 with the prophet Elijah in 1 Kings 19 conveys to his theme the dimension of what Robert Culley[22] calls "a visitation in the wilderness," as in Genesis 16:6–14 and 21:14–19. In both of these texts, it is the question of salvation in extremis of Hagar threatened by death in the desert. There is hunger and thirst in the case of Hagar and Elijah, there is unbearable heat in the case of Jonah. Help comes through the intermediary of a messenger to Hagar and to Elijah, an element that allows the story in both cases to reach its apex. To Hagar is promised a glorious posterity. To Elijah is revealed the presence of God, and a prophetic commission is given. Is there such a "following up" as regards Jonah? At any rate, like Elijah, Jonah thinks that he alone remained faithful to YHWH. The irony of the matter is that, on the contrary, there are at least 120,000 "faithful"!

According to the rabbis, "Elijah honored the Father but not the Son" (i.e., Israel), while Jonah honored the Son but not the Father (see above, chap. 6). Indeed, the distinction is clear between Elijah who condemned the unfaithfulness in Israel, a charge that isolated him from his own people, and Jonah condemning Nineveh, the enemy of Zion. In a way, however, the result is the same for the two men. They are isolated, "I remained alone," says Elijah. A similar "jealousy for the Lord" (1 Kings 19:10) moves both. What appears at first glance to be egotism on their part is in fact an act of defense of God's honor. Is a God who changes his mind and "repents" still credible? Is a justice that allows itself to be influenced by personal interpretation still justice?²³ Elijah became exhausted in the relationship with such a God. Jonah, in his turn, grows exhausted in the dialogue with Someone who is so unpredictable. When God seems to be at some place, he is elsewhere. The revelation on Mount Sinai had taught us that God is in the whirlwind, the earthquake, the fire. But for Elijah, God is not any longer in those unleashed natural elements. Is God then in the sea storm, in the fish's belly, in a wicked city? In any case, God is not where one looks for him. "What do you do here, Elijah?" "Does anger become you, Jonah?" First there is no answer from the prophet because he only now begins to "be-seen-by-God." Ricoeur writes:

> The primordial significance of this seeing is to constitute the *truth* of my situation, the justness and the justice of the ethical judgment that can be passed on my existence. That is why this seeing, far from preventing the birth of the Self, gives rise to self awareness. . . . I desire to know myself as I am known (Ps. 139:23–24). The preferred form of this act of awareness is interrogation, the putting in question of the meaning of acts and motives.²⁴

This development has shown how much the author ironically wanted to present Jonah as an anti-Elijah. The end of the story of the Tishbite will show it once more. In 2 Kings 2:1, "YHWH took up Elijah to heaven in a whirlwind (sa‘arah)"; Jonah also finds himself from the beginning in a great "sa‘ar" (1:4, [11], 12, [13]). For Elijah, the tempest or the storm is the framework of theophany (cf. Job 38:1; 40:6; Ezek. 1:4; etc.); for Jonah, however, it is radical distance. Moreover, Jonah will also experience rapture— but by a sea monster and toward the depths of the abyss (2:1). However, the two prophets join on the main point: both are scandalous. Jonah contributes against his will to the preservation of Nineveh, which sometime in the future is to overwhelm the Holy Land and to invade Jerusalem. Elijah left a poisoned bequest to his people. He anointed Hazael the Aramean who proved so effective in massacring Israelites (1 Kings 19:15, 17; 2 Kings 8:12).

The personal ground for anger in these two prophets plays, therefore, a minor role here. The matter transcends their persons. "What are you doing here, Elijah?" "Does your anger become you, Jonah?" Elijah's and Jonah's momentary slackening in the accomplishment of their mission is not, however, a time out to the extent that God seizes this opportunity for dialoguing with his messengers. With Elijah, the stage is the most formidable and most fascinating place of biblical geography, Mount Horeb. What about Jonah? With Jonah it is something else. What a fall from the top of Sinai! The irony of the whole development is that one would expect the dialogue to take place in the Temple of Jerusalem, but Jonah fled the divine presence precisely to prevent God from speaking with him. However, the "Temple" is not far, nor is the face-to-face with God, as we already saw in Jonah 2. Once more, here, he breaks the contact with God. He abstracts himself from the dialogue started between God and the wicked city; he distances himself from the city and leaves God behind, if he wants to stay there. With stubbornness he sits "at the east of the city," an expression that is a pun on the Hebrew *qedem,* meaning "the east" or "the past." Jonah as a matter of fact sees Nineveh only from the standpoint of its past, a past that proclaims its guilt. "At the east of the city" unmistakably recalls Genesis narratives of origins. Adam and Eve settle at the east of Eden; Cain is exiled there. It seems as if the author of Jonah drew a parallel between the prophet's anger and Cain's anger: both reach a murderous level. As W. I. Thompson says pointedly:

All through history, from Abraham to Mao, prophets have left the city behind them to insist upon a vision of things greater than they are; but in the double nature of all phenomena, the abandoning of the city for the wilderness is also the pattern of madness: the psychotic leaves the social structure of sanity. From the psychotic's point of view, one could paraphrase Voltaire who says that sanity is the lie commonly agreed upon. Those left behind in the city define themselves as responsible and sane and see the wanderer as a madman. The wanderer defines himself as the only sane person in a city of the insane and walks out in search of other possibilities. All history seems to pulse in this rhythm of urban views and pastoral visions.[25]

Let us note here the process of "distanciation" of which Erik Erikson has so aptly spoken:

> The counterpart of intimacy is *distanciation:* the readiness to repudiate, isolate, and, if necessary, destroy those forces and people whose essence seems dangerous to one's own. . . . *Isolation* . . . [is] the incapacity to take chances with one's identity by sharing [in] true intimacy.[26]

Despite the opinion of some that verse 5 is out of place here and should follow Jonah 3:4,[27] it is, to the contrary, understandable that at this point Jonah would set himself to watch the course of events. Perhaps after all God will again change his mind and destroy Nineveh (cf. Redaq in the Middle Ages). Jonah's attitude may even be construed as defiance of God's decision to spare the city. Nineveh's wickedness may prove stronger than God's leniency. The prophet therefore builds a *sukkāh*, which is reminiscent of the exodus from Egypt when the Hebrews dwelled in booths in the desert (Lev. 23:43). Thus Jonah insists upon two points: he considers Nineveh to be another Egypt, which he leaves behind to its own fate, and by the same token he reminds God of his covenant with Israel, which he chose from among all nations (Exod. 19:4–5; Deut. 10:14–15). At any rate, there is a contrasting effect between Jonah sitting comfortably in the shade of his *sukkāh* and the king of Nineveh who sits, with a sackcloth around his loins, on ashes.[28] J. S. Ackerman[29] sees a key to the understanding of this motif in the continual quest of Jonah for shelter (see 1:5; 2:1). God responds here with a "super-shelter" which will provide more surely a false feeling of security, namely, the *qîqāyôn* (sometimes translated as "gourd"). Thus, if it were still necessary, the text shows once more in what follows that the *sukkāh* is not functional here but purely symbolical.[30] Were it not so, its replacement by a plant that God lets grow in one night would make no sense. Similarly, "the shade" that the one and the other are supposed to provide to the prophet is to be metaphorically understood, as is often the case in the Bible, as meaning protection (see Ps. 121:5).

The parallel established earlier with the story of Elijah suggests that the motif of the *sukkāh* corresponds to the one of the cave on Mount Horeb where the Tishbite took refuge. If so, the temporary habitat, here and there, represents a place of expectation for theophany. Besides, Psalm 76:3 shows that the *sukkāh* can be synonymous with the Temple in Jerusalem (see as well, Ps. 27:4–5, ". . . He will *protect* me in his *sukkāh*. He will *hide* me under the *cover* of his tent"). The *sukkāh* has thus at least two functions deserving attention, the function of cover and the one of expectation. As to the former one, it echoes a theme already met earlier, the *regressio ad uterum* of Jonah. Mircea Eliade writes: "In many regions, there is a hut for initiations in the bush. It is there that young candidates undergo a part of their ordeals and are instructed in the secret traditions of the tribe. And the initiation-cabin symbolizes the maternal womb."[31]

As to the function of expectation, Elijah's anticipation was frustrated, then transcended by an unexpected revelation. Similarly, Jonah does not receive the expected answer: he cannot contemplate, as Abraham did, the smoldering ruins of the annihilated city (see Gen. 19:27–28), but he must surrender to the evidence of the divine point of view (Jon. 4:10–11).

Shelter and expectation, instinct and faith, regression and progression, withdrawal and anticipation, the *sukkāh* is above all a plea to God to remember, "remember your covenant with us!" (Jer. 14:21). Jonah is waiting: will his call, his recall to God of the covenant, which binds him with his people, be heard? Will the prophet's silent rebuke have a bearing upon YHWH? It will, but not as Jonah expected. God's pedagogy manifests itself in an intervention that contrasts with earlier models like the sea storm with its waves and its streams and its monsters: he lets a plant grow above Jonah to provide shade. And Jonah feels a great joy because of the *qîqāyôn*. God reaches out better and more efficiently to the prophet in this way than through words (see vs. 4). But this conclusion in a serious mode is not without a certain aftertaste of embarrassment. There has been a change in the focus of the text, as when the camera makes a grotesque scene succeed a violent one. From the impending destruction of a whole city, one has shifted to the egoistic pleasure of an individual who, until then, was incommoded by the heat of the day. From a whole population, shrouded in bereavement and tears because of absence, one is now oriented toward a man deeply satisfied to be taken in charge, to be inundated by Presence.[32]

All the more so, as the *qîqāyôn* seems to indicate that God agrees with Jonah and confirms him in his expectation. The *qîqāyôn*, with its abundant shade (vs. 6) is superior to the *sukkāh* as the permanent to the temporary, and the divine protection to a man-made booth (vs. 5). Assuredly God remembers his covenant with Israel. The respite here is the correspondence to the big fish of chapter 2, or to the bush in the story of Elijah (1 Kings 19:5). It indicates the care of God for his prophet (1 Kings 19:7). God expresses his compassion for Jonah so that the declaration of verse 2—the pivotal text of the whole book—acquires a different meaning by now. It is no more a reproach but a thanksgiving hymn. Jonah is freed from his anger to the very extent that his attention is diverted from a hated city to a tree of delights or, in more noble terms, from the wickedness of the earth to the divine grace toward Israel.[33]

The *qîqāyôn* ("gourd") appears only here in the entire Bible. One has thought, on the basis of cognate Semitic languages, of the *ricinus communis*, "which grows rapidly, has wide spreading branches and large leaves, and can reach a height of forty feet, though only an annual."[34] But, just as the *sukkāh* was symbolic, the mention of the *qîqāyôn* or the *ricinus* suggests that we are dealing with a metaphor. We can even think now that part of its symbolism refers to a feeling of sturdiness of a tree, a feeling that is, besides, belied by its short life. So that the sign of "permanence," in replacement of the temporary in the case of the *sukkāh*, is itself deceiving. The shelter that the booth could not provide has not become better.[35] We are with the one and the other motifs within the symbolism of the Temple. The *sukkāh* does represent it without doubt, as we see attested by Psalm 76:3, where it designates specifically the Temple, or by Psalm 27:45, both quoted above.

As to the gourd, J. Ackerman is right to refer to the well-known motif in the ancient Near East of the tree of life blooming on the divine mountain (the Temple), but that a snake or a worm attacks. In the poem Enuma Elish, the snake grasps the plant of life and disappears with it. In Genesis 3, the tree is put in relation with the snake generator of death. In the northern traditions of the Edda, the axial tree sees itself attacked by a "worm" or snake at its root.[36]

The *qîqāyôn* therefore is not replacing the symbol of the booth but strengthening it. That is why it is unnecessary to wonder what happened, meanwhile, to the booth that would justify the growing of the gourd. The booth and the plant are both one object, the Temple. Or, in a broader sense, the plant represents life. It is a symbol of perenniality. The tree pictures the cycle of life-death-regeneration.[37] As such, it is the *axis mundi* connecting heaven and earth, and channeling a vital sap downward to the cosmos.[38] To Jonah, it is also a channel of communication with a message that the context of Jonah 4 renders clearly: God has decisive reasons for deciding to save Nineveh.

Hence, God speaks first through a symbol, before resorting to direct discourse in the rest of the chapter. Through participation with the transcendent reality, the *qîqāyôn* communicates also, along with the message, life to Jonah and, it is hoped, a renewed sense of the sacred, for the tree is a symbol charged with sacred forces. In the words of Eliade: ". . . it is vertical, it grows, it loses its leaves and regains them and is thus regenerated times without number . . . because of the *power* it expresses; and if it becomes a *cosmic tree*, it is because what it expresses is a perfect reproduction of what the cosmos expresses."[39]

At this point, we must deal with the totally unexpected word *qîqāyôn* in this passage. A clear parallel to the motif of a desert plant is provided by Elijah's rest under a "juniper tree" in 1 Kings 19:4–5. But as much as the latter term is well known, so the word *qîqāyôn* is unknown. It is a *hapax* that challenges the understanding of the rationale behind its selection by the author. Etymologists and botanists have turned their attention in the wrong direction, toward Mesopotamia; the results have been disappointing.[40] The mistaken dating of Jonah has here again misled the scholars. By establishing that Jonah's composition occurred in Hellenistic times, however, the perfect similarity of the Hebrew *qîqāyôn* with the Greek *kukeyon* is evident. *Kukeyon* designates in the Eleusinian Mysteries an initiatory beverage made of a barley concoction (in Greek, *kakeon* means "medley"). True, from a tree to an initiatory potion, the distance is great. But, from a symbolic perspective, there is between the two a common denominator. The *kukeyon* celebrates the passage of the grain from death to life, and from the worthlessness of wild grass to evolved edible staple, from "wild rye" (in French *ivraie*, i.e., tares) to wheat, corn, and so forth. In other words, what is celebrated here is the advent of cultivation and civilized life. To the initiate is shown an ear of wheat whose miraculous growth and maturation is emphasized. As W. F. Otto writes, ". . . there can be no doubt of the miraculous nature of the event. The ear of wheat growing and maturing with a supernatural suddenness is just as much a part of the mysteries of Demeter as the vine growing in a few hours is part of the revels of Dionysus."[41] The seed represents immortality, for the seed "never dies."[42]

In Hesiod's "Hymns to Demeter," Homer allegedly said that, instead of wine, Demeter rather chose to drink the *kukeyon*, the refreshing potion of the harvesters, as well as the sacred cup offered to the faithful at Eleusis.[43] One will think here of the important theme of the shade in Jonah 4. Furthermore, after Nineveh's conversion, Jonah is figuratively a harvester.

But Jonah passes from the shade again to the sun's scorching heat. In Eleusinian terms, it is a sign of continuing initiation. Strikingly, Demeter is described as "baking" Demophoön, son of Queen Metaneira, to make him immortal. Thus the issue is again one of survival. Besides, during the Mysteries, the final vision, called *epopteia*, occurred in a flooding light although the rites were taking place at night. At that supreme moment, the initiate became an *epoptes*, a "seer." The motif recalls the role played by the sun in Jonah 4. In both cases, the light opposes the darkness of Hades. Hades is called "the sunless west" in the so-called "Homeric" Hymn to Demeter.

It is important to notice that all along the initiate remained passive. Aristotle says that the *mystoi* were not suppposed to learn "whatsoever but to endure and be moved."[44] Revelation occurs in silence, something emphasized by Hippolytus in his *Philosophymena* (5.38–41).

There is no implausibility in the third century B.C.E. author of Jonah being aware of Greek religious terms like *kukeyon*. If anything, the Mysteries were a great subject of conversation among the Hellenes and Hellenizers in Palestine and elsewhere.[45] One is referred to the classic work of Martin Hengel.[46] Cicero (106–43 B.C.E.) said that no contribution of Athens is more important than "those mysteries that made us emerge from our rustic and wild mode of existence to a cultivated and refined state of civilization" (*De legibus* II.36). Let us note in passing the Eleusinian ring of this statement. This quotation from Cicero is far-reaching. It shows that, for many people, even the most sophisticated, the Mysteries appeared as the privileged means of Hellenization. In the course of the present essay and especially, above, in chapter 2, we have discussed the impact of Greek ideas upon Palestinian Judaism. At the turn of the first century B.C.E., 3 Maccabees—a material generally legendary but with historical elements—shows that Jews let themselves be initiated into the Dionysos Mysteries (2:30ff.; see 3:21). Strikingly, Jewish tradition claims that Jonah witnessed great mysteries while in the monster's belly (a tradition picked up by Paracelsus[47]). In *Pirqe de Rabbi Eliezer* 10, it is said, "Jonah entered its mouth just as a man enters the great synagogue, and he stood there. The two eyes of the fish were like windows of a glass giving light to Jonah. Rabbi Meir said: One pearl was suspended inside the belly of the fish and it gave illumination to Jonah, like this sun which shines all its might at noon, and it showed to Jonah all that was in the sea and in the depths."[48]

Jonah 4 draws a contrasting parallel to Jonah 2. Jonah 2's hymn was an upward surge, an ascension. Jonah 4 and its *qîqāyôn* motif is a regression. The tree that was supposed to be, for the prophet, a breakthrough toward the sacred dies in one night. The only "mystery" discovered by Jonah is the trivialilty of choking under the sun.

Kukeyon, in Jonah's usage, is ironic. The sign, like the Eleusis ear of wheat, should initiate the prophet into the mysteries of the integration of the self into the cosmic cycle of life, including in a very special way the revival after death, and consequently, the possibility for Nineveh to be alive again after its ritual burial (Jonah 3). But instead, the sign is removed by God overnight and it is revealed that Jonah did not see the signified beyond the signifier. The sign filled the horizon. At no point was the prophet oblivious of himself. Like the *sukkāh,* the *qîqāyôn* was at his service and for his comfort. He felt relieved from the heat and that was enough for him to conclude that he was in the right. He drew a wrong conclusion because he did not allow the sign to be completed *by its very removal.* To the extent that the *qîqāyôn* gave a feeling of security, of comfort, of rectitude, to the extent that the tree was a symbol of the Temple in the ideologists' eyes, it had to go. The message, therefore, moved from the presence of the tree to its removal. The lesson is that there is no inherent sacrality to a plant, a system, or a shrine that would operate by magic, *ex opere operato.* Jonah and the Jerusalem ideologists are content (Jon. 4:6) to sit in the shade of an *axis mundi,* and they believe that they are protected forever from all unpredictability.

"Nineveh," or more exactly Nineveh's conversion, is the unpredictable that withers the *qîqāyôn* in no time. Understandably, Jonah is angry. But is it really the moment for anger? Does it become Jonah at this point? The removal of the *qîqāyôn* is no capricious move of God. It is the disposal of a sham security, as deceptive as the cyclical recurrence of sameness. Nineveh's repentance is the extravagance that cancels the routine, the worm that eats the heart of the gourd.

It is doubtful whether one should see in the worm a snake in reduction, thus drawing a parallel with the serpent that eats the plant of life in the Gilgamesh Epic, or that tempts the primeval human couple in Genesis 3. The worm is no adversary of God but is appointed by God, like the storm or the scorching wind, to fulfill God's designs. In focus is not the worm, but the action of the worm that kills the *qîqāyôn.* There is here no room for allegory. Rather, we are dealing with a parable. It says what the turn of events regarding Nineveh looks like, and consequently how Jonah's interpretation is wrong. The worm is, in the parable, the little, insignificant element that changes the whole. It is like the small stone in Daniel 2, or the mustard seed of Jesus' parable (that also becomes a big tree, like the apocalyptic stone that became a high mountain).

Once again, the *setting in life* of the book of Jonah is clear: in the context of the mystique of the Temple and of the proclamation of theocracy of the postexilic community, the author of Jonah recalls a fundamental dimension of exile, which must not be lost in the course of the restoration process. The exile in the midst of foreign nations has been also a means for Israel to reach out to the ends of the earth, thus providing to the "Ninevites" of the world the opportunity to repent and to live (see Ezek. 18:23, 32). While some in the Temple milieu speculated upon the impending destruction of the nations and the vindication of the sole Judean people, others had a vision of the eschatological conversion of the non-Jews and of their coming to Jerusalem to adore Israel's God (see Isa. 55:3–5; Zech. 14; Joel 3). In their views, the conservative party in Jerusalem was wrong, since it led the people astray in the name of a cultic reality that was only "penultimate" in regard to that which is authentically ultimate. For, in fact, there is no fulfillment of history in isolation from the world. If there is a lesson to be drawn from the exile in Babylon it is that the "world out there" must somehow be brought "in here," first into the consciousness of Israel but ultimately also into the geographical and historical, the spatial and temporal center of the universe.[49] It is precisely in order to avoid acknowledging this that Jonah builds a *sukkāh*. Our interpretation above fits the symbolism of the house, as Mircea Eliade and others have shown. The house is a private and impregnable world. But, as in reality it is destructible and its inhabitants know it within themselves, the house implies also the expectation of its ruin, *thanatos*.[50] As James Ackerman says:

> It can be seen as a subtle critique of the reestablishment of the Zion/temple emphasis in postexilic Judaism. . . . the combined anti-temple and universalistic thrust may be

aimed at the "Temple Presence" theology of the postexilic Zadokite priesthood, yet the Book of Jonah cannot be easily set within the categories of "proto apocalyptic" thought. This must be left for others to resolve.[51]

At any rate, the *qîqāyôn* finally is the only thing in this narrative that knows death, although at each chapter a certain number of people were threatened with destruction. For if the Temple underwent the fate that we know in 587, it can again experience the same catastrophe in the future. And if the city of life can die in one night, the city of death, to the contrary, can come back to life someday. To miss this pendulumlike movement in the book of Jonah is to miss the whole of its message. It is possible that the author is dependent, for this dialectical thinking, upon a famous predecessor, the prophet son of Amotz. In Isaiah 1:8, as a matter of fact, one reads this: "The daughter of Zion is left like a *sukkāh* in a vineyard . . . ," but in verse 9 it is a question of Sodom and Gomorrah, those old cities that were "overthrown," as Nineveh must be overthrown: ". . . we would soon be like Sodom, no better than Gomorrah" (had God not kept for us a little remnant). The *sukkāh* therefore is here a symbol of Israel and of its vulnerability. Isaiah 4:6 combines the theme of the *sukkāh* with the one of the shade: "there will be a shelter providing a shade from the heat by day . . ." Then the text passes right away to a metaphor of the vineyard that yields bitter fruits, so that it is neither pruned nor hoed but put in ruin (vs. 6). Verse 7 cancels all ambiguity when it says that the vineyard "is the house of Israel."[52]

In Jonah's dogmatics, the notion of retributive justice is at the center. Not only must Nineveh be destroyed within forty days, but from the outset of the narrative, retribution has underpinned the narrative. For example, when Jonah advised the sailors to throw him overboard, it was with the conviction that, once the guilty is chastised (the culprit he acknowledges to be), God will spare the innocent. And in his view, if the sailors are unblamable, that is what the Ninevites are *not*. But Jonah's judgment, although it is not wrong, is, however, narrow-minded. Indeed, it is not in the name of their innocence that God will spare the Ninevites but through exercising his *ḥus*, his disposition of grace. "It is here," says Thayer S. Warshaw, "the great lesson that Jonah must learn: compassion is not simply a capricious and negative suspension of 'faith and order,' but a positive act of love."[53]

But before we turn to the use of *hus* in Jonah 4, we must set the discussion within the appropriate perspective. The concept of distributive justice unavoidably leads to determinism. Evidently, Jonah favors the unswerving realization of God's judgment over the Assyrian city. Now, the object of mystery religions is to celebrate victory over the goddess Tyche ("chance," *fortuna*) as she manifests herself as *anangkè* ("necessity") or *heimarmenè* ("destiny"). As recalled by Eliade, in the Mysteries of Isis, the goddess reassures the initiate that she can prolong life beyond its end fixed by destiny. In *Praises to Isis and Osiris,* the goddess proclaims: "I conquered Fate, Fate obeys me."[54]

The application of this conception to Jonah 4 is self-evident.[55] By their repentance, the Ninevites have broken the circle of determinism. Fate is overcome by the possibility of the "perhaps" of 3:9. The wager is won, for God, using a logic that is as Stoic as it is biblical, takes into account the attitude of the Ninevites; this changes the course of events. As a matter of fact, the Stoics had amended the astrological amorality and reinterpreted Fate as Providence, thus valuing ethics. It is such a conception, which nothing in the Bible invalidates, that explains God's arguments to Jonah in verses 10–11. One of the major contributions of the book of Jonah is the demonstration that the astral determinism of the Gentiles finds no prophetic substitute in Israel. The prophet (Jonah) is no diviner, no soothsayer. The authority of God's word does not lie in being unalterable; it lies in its power of transformation, i.e., of creation. Nineveh's people gone through repentance is not any longer the people whose "wickedness came up" to God (Jon. 1:2). They are a people deserving *pity* (4:11).

In the Near East, the verb *hus*, "to pity," designates an arbitrary act of clemency of the king. It is thus a fitting term for the divine attitude vis-à-vis Nineveh (vs. 11). In Israel, as a matter of fact, *hus* finds its place in the framework of faithfulness to the covenant (*hesed*; see Neh. 13:22, "spare me according to your steadfast love").[56] That Jonah would exercise it vis-a-vis a plant behooves a bitter irony. All the more so as no one is blinded by Jonah's move. He does not pity the *qîqāyôn* but regrets its shade; likewise, his care is not for Nineveh but for his own religious convictions.[57]

Would God really be the only one who does not see that for Jonah the *qîqāyôn* has been only a utility? Does Jonah really pity the tree? Does he not, rather, pity himself? God's argument would indeed remain cryptic or naïve were it not for the fact of the Cynic influence detectable here. The issue is that Jonah, facing external circumstances, does not remain indifferent (*apathès*) as a Cynic philosopher should. To the contrary, the prophet is deeply moved by what Stoic philosophers call *eunoia* or *eupatheia*.[58] It is for Stoics a virtue, not a flaw as it is for Cynics. Stoics are even going further: they put on a par divine and human virtue.[59] Therefore, if Jonah is justified in his own eyes to react with *ḥus* to circumstances, how much more so is God when he feels *ḥus* for the Ninevites!

Furthermore, if *ḥus* is in itself a virtue, is Jonah's *ḥus* for the *qîqāyôn* (or rather, before the *qîqāyôn*) a grounded reaction? A negative response is demanded by the context. Thus the "how much more so" in the divine argument has bearing upon the premise of the analogy: if Jonah feels justified to be sorry (a groundless feeling) for the loss of a tree that he did not plant or care for, how much more justified is God when he prospectively sheds tears on the loss of Nineveh that he created and kept alive in the past!

But Jonah represents more than himself; and the *qîqāyôn*, more than an ephemeral plant. The Jerusalem ideologists must learn that it is intolerable that they cry over a destroyed temple, and remain deaf to the fate of the surrounding world. "You have pity on the gourd . . . which came up in a night, and perished in a night; and should I not have pity on Nineveh that great city wherein are more than one hundred and twenty thousand people who do not know their right hand from their left, and also much cattle?" (vss. 10–11).

Abraham J. Heschel wrote:

God's answer to Jonah, stressing the supremacy of compassion, upsets the possibility of looking for a rational coherence of God's ways with the world. History would be more intelligible if God's word were the last word, final and unambiguous like a dogma or an unconditional decree. . . . Yet, beyond justice and anger lies the mystery of compassion.[60]

From the prophet's own person, or from solipsistic, isolated concerns and pride, the author wants to shift the attention of his contemporaries to the world and its sufferings. When all arguments are exhausted in the theological debate, what ultimately remains is love. The mistake of Job's friends, or of the theocratists, contemporaries of Jonah's author, consists not of a weakness in their theological dialectics but of a lack of love. God is the first one who causes love to triumph over anything else, even his own justice. This truth, which is so often and so forcefully stressed in rabbinic Judaism, stands at the heart of the message of Jonah. "Nowhere in the Hebrew Bible," writes S. H. Blank, "do the 'person-hood' of God and his entanglement in the human situation stand more clearly revealed."[61] At the basis of love lies an immense compassion for the inadequacy of humanity. Nineveh is a city of "a dozen myriads" of people (as Wilhelm Rudolph renders the text of vs. 11) "that cannot discern between their right hand and their left hand."

This latter motif has stirred much discussion. Are we to understand this literally, "little children and simple people whom you, Jonah, certainly will not be able to prove to be sinners," as St. Jerome says?[62] Or should we see in "right" and "left" symbols of good and evil, as do André Parrot, Wilhem Vischer, Jacques Ellul, and the *Traduction Oecuménique de la Bible*? This latter reading is not necessarily confirmed by texts such as Deuteronomy 5:29 (32) and Joshua 1:7, but it is undeniable that pagans are sometimes described as boors in comparison with Israel. It is, we think, something of that conception that is expressed in Amos 3:2, "you only have I known of all the families of the earth, therefore, I will visit upon you all your iniquities." The nations are not guilty in the same sense as Israel can be called guilty, for, in comparison with the latter, the former are only children or ignoramuses.

In the same vein, the connection in the text with "much cattle" prompts Rudolph to comment that "the people of Nineveh are as guiltless as the animals that would be drawn into the catastrophe."[63] But A. D. Martin, it seems to us, has expressed the idea of this verse perfectly: "They might be adult in years, but in character they were children—willful, passionate, perishing without vision yet not without value . . . disciplined and overgrown children yet also the work of God's hands."[64] Inadequacy of the Ninevites. But is it very different from the inadequacy of Jonah, so egotistic and so indifferent to those myriads suffering and "perishing without vision."?[65]

Such is the end of the book or, rather, its unendedness. In the words of Elias Bickerman, ". . . we are left to believe that the Lord's rebuke convinced Jonah of his second error just as the episode of the sea monster had shown him the uselessness of his flight."[66] But one may wonder whether Bickerman's opinion is correct. Is Jonah really convinced? Perhaps the story returns to its beginning. Perhaps the hero is still to live other exhausting experiences before he understands God's will. Is this not the case of most of those who encountered God? There will perhaps be for Jonah still another ship and another "shark." Or perhaps this time there will be no ship, no fish, and the prophet will plummet piteously to the bottom of the sea and into oblivion. No past victory can guarantee a future triumph.

We have repeatedly expressed admiration for the author of the narrative because he left it open and unfinished. Those for whom he has told his tale in the first place were themselves left with the uncomfortable necessity of creating a proper end for Jonah's story. No two ends will be alike, depending upon the taste of the interpreters. As Dostoevsky wrote in the conclusion of his novel *Crime and Punishment,* "this is another story." It is a story that he does not even presume to tell because it is beyond all expression and so personal to each respondent that it would be of no avail to generalize it.

Besides, Jonah is not more or less noble if he is convinced or remains skeptical. God is right and Jonah is right. But their respective stances are mutually exclusive. Who will tip the balance one way or the other?[67] Voicing doubt as to God's justice and equanimity may appear more "Jewish," and pleading for it more "Christian." Perhaps the book of Jonah takes us to the very heart of the Jewish-Christian problem.[68] If so, we must, like the author of the biblical book, leave the narrative without conclusion. Jonah-Israel does not surrender to the theological rationality of an argument that will satisfy the mind in general while it is nothing other than a slap in the face of the victim in particular. Is this to say that the particular smothers the general? Does the tree hide the forest? Does the admonition to "turn and offer your other cheek" (Matt. 5:39) mean that it is not true that "after Auschwitz the Jew has received the commandment to survive" (Fackenheim)? Both commandments are true. They must accompany one another until the end of this world. And even then, one will not prevail over the other, but they will be reconciled like Hillel and Shammai, the rival rabbis of the first century c.e., who, when they died—according to the Talmud—looked like twins.

NOTES

1. There is an interesting parallel here with the ending of the book of Job when God asks Job, "Where were you?" and especially with the questions posed by God to Elijah on Mount Horeb (see below).

2. Allen, *The Books of Joel, Obadiah, Jonah, and Micah* (Grand Rapids: Eerdmans, 1976), p. 227. Allen makes the constant mistake, however, of depicting the audience of the tale as antipathetic to Jonah. On the contrary, those for whom the narrative was conceived in the first place, namely, the ideologists of Jerusalem, must have been perfectly attuned to Jonah's reaction. The *grandeur* of Jonah lies in the fact that such a stance, although rejected by the author, is not subjected to wholesale ridicule. To be sure, irony and satire are present here, but only in light strokes and with discretion.

3. *Mekilta*, tractate *Pisha* I, 80–92 (ed. Lauterbach).

4. Gabriel Cohn, *Das Buch Jona* (Assen: Van Gorcum, 1969), ad loc. 4:1.

5. Cohn, *Das Buch Jona*, p. 100 ("Es ist der Eifer für Gott, welcher Jona sich *gegen* Gott wenden lässt").

6. Quoted by Wilhelm Rudolph (*Joel-Amos-Obadja-Jona* (Gütersloh: Mohn, 1971), ad loc. 4:1; "desperat de salute Israelis. . . . Non contristatur, ut quidam putant, guod gentium multitudo salvetur, sed quod pereat Israel"). Rudolph also quotes Andrea di S. Vittore (d. 1175): "penitencia gencium ruina Judaeorum."

Let us add that the gospel shares the same perspective. Matt. 12:41 says: "at Judgment when this generation is on trial, the men of Nineveh will appear against it and ensure its condemnation for they repented at the preaching of Jonah; and what is here is greater than Jonah." There is an interesting parallel to this in the Midrash on Lamentations (*Midrash Ekah Rabbati* on Zeph. 3:1, the repentance of the Ninevites in contrast to the hardening of Israel's heart led to the latter's exile).

7. J. T. Hower, "The Misunderstanding and Mishandling of Anger," *J. of Psy. and Theol.* 2 (1974): 270.

8. See R. B. Y. Scott, "The Sign of Jonah," *Interp.* 19 (1965): 25: "In the name of divine justice [those who had suffered so much at the hands of enemies] were all too sure of their *right* to be angry."

9. John Crossan, *The Dark Interval* (Niles, Ill.: Argus, 1975), p. 76.

10. Cohn, following Wolff (*Studien zum Jonabuch* [Neukirchen-Vluyn: Neubirchener Vlg., 1947], p. 118), calls attention to the prophet's use (nine times) of the first-person singular in vss. 2–3. Wisd. of Sol. 11:23–24 is the counterpart of Jonah. Where the latter saw God's weakness, Wis. of Sol. sees omnipotence. "You are compassionate with all because you can do everything."

11. In an Armenian text translated by Bickerman, *Four Strange Books* (New York: Schocken Books, 1967), p. 34.

12. Harry S. Sullivan, *The Psychiatric Interview* (New York: W. W. Norton, 1954), p. 135.

13. In 4 Esdras 7:132ff. there are also seven terms describing God's qualities (including the three terms of Jon. 4:2).

14. According to *Yalquṭ* on Jon. 4, God said to the prophet, "You 'saved my face' in fleeing me on the sea, I also 'saved your face' in rescuing you from the Sheol's belly."

15. Bickerman, *Four Strange Books,* p. 44.

16. Hence the strange insistence of God that Jonah, no one else, has to go to Nineveh (Jon. 1–2).

17. Carl Rogers, "The Necessary and Sufficient Conditions of Therapeutic Personality Change," *Journal of Consulting Psychology* 21 (1957): 95–103; or *Client-Centered Therapy* (Boston: Houghton Mifflin, 1951).

18. Hebrew documents offer many examples of imperative orders followed by their execution. Above, we mentioned the call narratives of Abraham, Moses, Jeremiah, and Ezekiel. The same situation prevails in the New Testament where the call to discipleship is equally abrupt and extravagant, but efficient. See, e.g., Matt. 9:9 with its echo in Acts 9:4. No psychological explanation is sufficient for justifying Paul's or Matthew's moves. Their inner change (conversion) transcends all explanation.

19. This point was made in a seminar on Jonah by my assistant, Paul Ferguson.

20. Quoted from Paul Ferguson.

21. In the Elisha cycle, one also finds "the king of Israel" and "the king of Aram," without the mention of their names.

22. Robert Culley, *Studies in the Structure of Hebrew Narrative* (Missoula, Mont.: Scholars Press, 1976), p. 43.

23. "One of the things people need most is a feeling of living in a world they understand" (M. Neuman and B. Berkowitz, *How to Be Your Own Best Friend* [New York: Ballantine Books, 1971], p. 46). When such an understanding collapses, as in the case of Elijah or Jonah, despair or depression results. L. Bellak writes, ". . . depression is the equivalent of intra-aggression" (in *Specialized Techniques in Psychotherapy,* ed. E. Bychowski and L. J. Despert [New York: Grove Press, 1952], p. 328).

24. Paul Ricoeur, *Finitude et culpabilité.* Vol. 2: *La Symbolique du mal* (Paris: Aubier Montaigne, 1960), pp. 85–86 (our English trans.).

A MATTER OF JUSTICE

25. W. I. Thompson, *At the Edge of History* (New York: Harper & Row, 1972), quoted by H. Schneidau, *Sacred Discontent, the Bible and Western Tradition* (Berkeley: University of California Press, 1976), p. 119.

26. Erik Erikson, *Identity, Youth and Crisis* (New York: W. W. Norton, 1968), pp. 136–37.

27. Cf. H. Winckler, "Zum Buche Jona," *Altoriental. Forsch.* 2 (1900): 260–65; A. Rofé, "Classes in the Prophetical Stories: Didactic, Legends, and Parables," *Studies in Prophecy, VTSup.* 26 (Leiden: Brill, 1974), p. 157 n71; Sellin, in KAT series; Weiser, in ATD series; Robinson, in HAT series; von Rad, *Theologie*, Vol. 2, p. 299 n16; Trible, "Studies in the Book of Jonah" (unpublished); Rudolph, *Joel-Amos-Obadja-Jona*, p. 362; Lohfink, "Und Jona ging . . . ," *BZ* 5, no. 2 (1961): 185–203; Allen, *Joel, Obadiah, Jonah, and Micah*, p. 231; Wolff, *Studien*, pp. 44–48; Cohn, *Das Buch Jona*, p. 57.

28. Cf. J. Magonet, *Form and Meaning: Studies in Literary Techniques in the Book of Jonah* (Bern and Frankfurt: H. et P. Lang, 1976), pp. 19–20.

29. J. S. Ackerman, "Satire and Symbolism in the Song of Jonah," in *Traditions in Transformation: Turning Points in Biblical Faith*, F. M. Cross 60th Birthday Festschrift, ed. B. Halpern and J. D. Levenson (Winona Lake, IN, Eisenbrauns, 1981), pp. 213–46.

30. Even Rudolph, who denies all allegorical interpretations of the book of Jonah, acknowledges that the *sukkāh* refers to the *Laubhütten* festival. On this very basis, he adds, it may be said that its roof was not sufficient for an effective protection against the sun (*Joel-Amos-Obadja-Jona*, p. 365).

31. Eliade, *Myths, Dreams and Mysteries* (New York: Harper & Row, 1960), p. 198.

32. On the meaning of remembrance in the book of Jonah, see above, chap. 5. The motif of rejoicing is common in liturgical contexts. See Deut. 12:12, 18; 27:7.

33. "God is good, compassionate, and kind, and hesitant to punish. In origin this formula belongs firmly to an Israelite setting of application" (Allen, *The Books of Joel, Obadiah, Jonah, and Micah*, p. 193).

34. Emil Kraeling, *Commentary on the Prophets* (Camden, N.J.: Nelson, 1966), vol. 2, pp. 202–3.

35. In Jon. 4 the motif of the *sukkāh* is set in balance with Jon. 1:3, e.g., "the Lord's Presence."
At this point, let us mention the interesting reading of C. H. H. Wright ("The Book of Jonah Considered from an Allegorical Point of View," *Biblical Essays: or Exegetical Studies on the Books of Job and Jonah* [Edinburgh: T. & T. Clark, 1886], pp. 55ff.), who sees in this chapter of Jonah a symbol of the activity of Israel during the restoration. So the oracle of Nineveh's doom corresponds to the often predicted downfall of the nations (especially the Persian empire); the booth represents the "poor shelter in their desolated country"; Jonah's displeasure reflects the frustration at the nonfulfillment of exilic prophecies; the plant is Zerubbabel (cf. Ezra 1:8; 1 Chron. 3:19)—like the *qîqāyôn*, Zerubbabel disappeared "overnight" from the scene. With regard to the identification of Zerubbabel with the *qîqāyôn* of Jonah, one will remember the use of the term *ṣemaḥ* in Zechariah with its messianic overtones.

36. See J. Campbell, *The Mythic Image* (Princeton: Princeton University Press, 1974), vol. 2, p. 192; and O. Keel, *The Symbolism of the Biblical World* (New York: Seabury, 1978), pp. 51–52, and plates 45, 46, 47.

37. See Eliade, *Patterns in Comparative Religion* (New York: Sheed & Ward, 1958), p. 306: ". . . trees are simply another expression of the inexhaustible life and reality which the earth represents too."

38. In Jewish mysticism (in the Zohar, e.g.), the cosmic tree is described as upside-down with its roots in heaven.

39. Eliade, *Patterns*, pp. 268–69.

40. The Akkadian word *kukkanitu* would designate an unknown plant. The problem is as obscure as it ever was!

41. W. F. Otto, "The Meaning of the Eleusinian Mysteries," in Joseph Campbell, ed., *The Mysteries* (Eranos Yearbook II), trans. Ralph Mannheim (New York: Pantheon Books, 1955), p. 25.

42. C. Kerenyi ("Kore," in C. Jung and C. Kerenyi, *Essays on a Science of Mythology*, trans. R. F. C. Hull [Princeton: Princeton University Press, 1963], pp. 101–55) writes that "the primary Eleusinian theme [is] the vision of birth as the source from which life, growth, and replenishment spring in inexhaustible plenty" (p. 146).

43. See H. G. Evelyn-White, *Hesiod, the Homeric Hymns and Homerica* (New York: Macmillan, 1914), p. 303.

44. Quoted by W. F. Otto, "Eleusinian Mysteries," p. 24.

45. See Ptolemy Philopator (221–203 B.C.E.). He was deeply attached to the orgiastic cults of the Great Mother (Demeter) and of Dionysos. In Palestine itself, the *polis* promoted the mysticism of the Mystery cults as well as Dionysian orgies. The pig used as sacrifice animal on the Jerusalem altar and elsewhere was consecrated to Demeter and was used as an important element in the purification rites of Eleusinian Mysteries.

46. Martin Hengel, *Judaism and Hellenism* (Philadelphia: Fortress Press, 1974), passim.

47. Paracelsus, *Liber Azoth*.

48. Quoted by C. Jung, *Symbols of Transformation* (1956), p. 330.

49. On Zech. 14, see, e.g., A. LaCocque, "II Zacharie," CAT XIb (Neuchatel: Delachaux et Niestlé, 1981).

50. On the motif of destruction in this chapter, see Phyllis Trible, "Studies in the Book of Jonah," pp. 195–96. The theme, she says, "is central in the legend." See Eliade, *Myths, Dreams and Mysteries*, p. 198.

51. Ackerman, "Satire and Symbolism," p. 246. We take up the challenge in the appendix, below.

52. In the same chap. 1 of Isaiah, one finds the same vegetal symbolism. Here it is a question of oak: "You shall be as an oak whose leaf withers" (1:30). Joel also uses vegetal metaphors to designate Israel: "my vine . . . my fig tree" (1:7). In 1:12 are added the pomegranate tree, the palm tree, the apple tree, all the trees of the field. In Jonah, it is a *qîqāyôn* tree.

53. T. S. Warshaw, "The Book of Jonah," in K. R. R. GrosLouis, ed., *Literary Interpretations of Biblical Narratives* (Nashville: Abingdon, 1974), p. 194.

54. Eliade, *A History of Religious Ideas*, Chicago: University Press, 1982, vol. 2, par. 205.

55. That speculations around Isis were known in Palestine of the time is proved by a text such as Prov. 8, built on an Isis aretalogy.

56. Cf. Joel 2:17; Jer. 21:7; Ps. 72:13.

57. G. M. Landes ("Jonah: A Mašal?" in *Israelite Wisdom: Theological and Literary Essays in Honor of Samuel Terrien*, ed J. G. Gamie [Missoula, Mont.: Scholars Press, 1978], pp. 137–58) stresses the contrast: the Ninevites respond to God with

faith and repentance and they live; Jonah responds with anger and complaint, and he desires to die. The ensuing episodes, says Landes, are to move the prophet to do what both the Ninevites and God have done: change one's mind (p. 147).

58. Cf. H. von Arnim, *Stoicorum Veterum Fragmenta*, vol. 3, pp. 105ff. (frgmts. 431–32, 438–39).

59. Ibid., pp. 58–59 (frgmts. 245–52).

60. A. J. Heschel, *The Prophets* (New York: Harper Torchbooks, 1971), vol. 2, p. 67.

61. S. H. Blank, "Doest Thou Well to Be Angry? A Study in Self-Pity," *HUCA* 26 (1955): 41. The rabbis said, "As Jonah did not pity the Ninevites nor call them to repentance, he found himself in need. He had to beg God to rule His world with the measure of compassion, cf. Daniel 9:9 (so as to be himself at the benefit of that disposition)" (*Yalquṭ* on Jon. 4:8).

In turn, Fromm writes, "God's answer to Jonah is to be understood symbolically. God explains to Jonah that the essence of love is to 'labor' for something and 'to make something grow,' that love and labor are inseparable. One loves that for which one labors, and one labors for that which one loves" (*The Art of Loving* [New York: Harper & Row, 1956], p. 23).

62. So in the Bible of the French Rabbinate, the Jerusalem Bible, the *Interpreter's Bible* (W. Neil), the ATD (A. Weiser), the ICC (J. Bewer), etc.

63. Rudolph, *Joel-Amos-Obadja-Jona*, p. 368.

64. A. D. Martin, *The Prophet Jonah: The Book and the Sign* (London/New York: Longmans, Green and Co., 1926), p. 87.

65. The motif of "120,000" is found again in Judith 2:5, 15 (cf. Rev. 7:4 where 144,000 = 12,000 × 12).

66. Bickerman, *Four Strange Books*, p. 14.

67. As Rudolph, in a very Kantian vein, so aptly writes regarding the lack of an ending here: "Das gift zu denken" (*Joel-Amos-Obadja-Jona*, p. 368).

68. If it seems to some that the problem of the relationship between Judaism and Christianity is artificial here, suffice it to recall that from the time of the fathers of the church until our own day, the book of Jonah has been used argumentatively to prove the "superiority" of Christianity. Bickerman recalls the pamphlet of a Protestant minister, published in a time ominously close to the irruption of German Nazism in 1920: *Biblisher Antisemitismus, Der Juden Weltgeschichtlicher Charakter, Schuld und Ende in des Propheten Jona Judenspiegel* ("Biblical Anti-Semitism: The Universal Character, Sin, and End of the Jews in the Mirror of Jewish Soul Provided by the Prophet Jonah").

PART III

EXISTENTIAL MESSAGE

EIGHT

THE CALL TO AUTHENTICITY:
Listening to the Outer Voice

[Love and conscience are the two] most striking manifestations of . . . the capacity of self-transcendence. Man transcends himself either toward another human being or toward meaning. Love, I would say, is that capacity which enables him to grasp the other human being in his very uniqueness. Conscience is that capacity which empowers him to seize the meaning of a situation in its very uniqueness.

Viktor Frankl, *The Will to Meaning*
(New York: New American Library, 1969), pp. 18–19.

Jonah's vocation, like that of anyone else, is strictly personal. The masses of Israel were not under the commandment to move to Nineveh and to proclaim the message of God to the wicked city. But, paradoxically, the particularism of the vocation does not exclude its universalism; to the contrary, it grounds it.[1] Particular in its recipient, the vocation is universal in its structure and implications. Jonah at Nineveh is paradigmatic for Israel in its relation with the nations. So that, if the contents of the message is always different in each case, according to the circumstances that constitute its setting in life, and to the personality of the herald, the unity is guaranteed by the oneness of the Caller and the congruity of the Caller's will. The vocation participates in the absoluteness of the one who commands and is thus definitely "ethical" because, for the Bible, the knowledge of good and evil is founded on the authority of the one who issues the order to choose the former and reject the latter.

The book of Jonah is no exception. If, ultimately, Jonah goes to Nineveh despite his inner resistance to the idea of delivering a message to the arch-enemies of his people, it is because of the authority of the command-giver. His personal ethics leaves room to a divine will that transcends his norms and standards. In other words, the obedience of Jonah is not the fruit of an ethical maturation or the outcome of a deepening of his personal reflection and sensitivity, but the passage to another dimension, which frees Jonah from Jonah, in the same way that a butterfly is freed from its cocoon. Jonah, without the commandment of the "outer voice,"[2] is indeed deprived of his singularity, promise of a chrysalis without its fulfillment. For we believe no one can be said truly to exist without the commandment that is addressed to that person. What this means is that the human is a "gerundive,"[3] in the words of Van der Leeuw. The human becomes. The human is his or her own project. Jonah testifies to this. He is torn between his desire not to leave the static existence in the motherly womb (of the land where he was born, for instance), and the necessity created by the call of the Outer Voice to surpass himself, which is also to fulfill himself. He must give birth to the grown-up man in him (see 1 Cor. 13:11).

Using a psychological language, one could characterize the "first" birth as being-for-oneself, and the "second" as being-for-the-world. "To be-for-the-world" defies our most natural instincts. It requires that we have the courage to discover and to adopt a reality that transcends the limits of our subjective world. It requires that we change the order of our priorities and feel responsible for others. The problem with this last existential option is that it is unpopular as it questions other attitudes more preoccupied with solipsistic security. It thus runs the risk of being overtly or, more probably, covertly ostracized. Rejection, hence loneliness, is what we dread most. Instinctively we sense that solitude, especially if prolonged, is at bottom a confrontation with death. It is also an experience susceptible to break into pieces our dreams of being incomparable, invulnerable, and immortal.

But not to be "reborn" is to be like stars lost in the immensity of a universe without beginning and without end. As long as Jonah does not respond to his vocation to have a world—even though it be Nineveh—he is like the ship he boarded, tossed aimlessly here and there, moving in all directions and in no direction. Only death, as the negation of all movement, can put an end to such a groundless and meaningless pitching. Death-in-life, then, is the clearest manifestation of what has been Jonah's condition from the beginning. Even before he started to live, at his first "birth," such a Jonah was dead, that is, "soulless," a "not-Jonah," just as the prophet Hosea says that Israel, in forfeiting its vocation, becomes "Not-My-People."

Individual identity is constituted by the person's project. It is the latter in its quality of *ex*pression of the self that makes one unique and irreplaceable. It is not a "soul" added to human nature, for Israel affirms persons' integrity—spiritual and carnal, sensible and sensitive—in the integrity of their project, that is, in the personal response to *vocation*. If, for instance, we say with the French Constitution that all people are by nature equal, or with the American Constitution that they are so by creation, we must interpret this biblically as an equality of people under a call. For, apart from the vocation to become fully human, nothing else equalizes us that would not be accidental. The enormous differences between the privileged and the disfranchised, to take only one example, are self-evident. To proclaim their equality is a pious or a deceitful lie. But all people, irrespective of their political and economic situation or philosophical stance, are facing their human responsibility. This, really, takes them out of their undifferentiated common animality—their equality by a lower common denominator—and promotes them to the freeing Difference. However one calls that particular character of the person, it is, we believe, the very foundation of our authenticity.

In brief, one has received the commandment to be. Samson R. Hirsch said, "Gabe ist Aufgabe"—"Bequest is behest," one is one's task. The whole of my being is the wager I risk on the existential decision to accept or to refuse the vocation addressed to me and which, in fact, *is me*. So is explained that often-quoted word in Deuteronomy 30, "I have set before you life and death . . . choose life in order to live."

As Eliade continuously points out, our era is one of desacralization. "Vocation" is one of those words that today smacks of an obsolete religious parlance that stirs little echo in our contemporaries. They, rather, have recourse to trivializing explanations about human drives and external conditions, and the most surprising is that they seem satisfied with them. Yet these intellectual constructions are often shallow as they confuse effects for causes, and the explanations explain nothing. Even the genes for that matter are as many invitations to the human to be. They represent less a deterministic orientation in the existence than a broad spectrum, so that human liberty is exercised, not in the indifference of equalized options, but in the contrasted universe of choices that are existentially (thus, not necessarily essentially) good or evil. Even the motherly womb is a given milieu where communication is initiated with the embryo in a *dia*logue, a back-and-forth movement, a give-and-take commerce; in short, an apprenticeship for the fetus to become itself. From that moment of our proto-history, and on for the rest of our existence, we shall spell out our response to that fundamental calling; "Before I formed you in the womb I knew you" (Jer. 1:5). When Noam Chomsky, reflecting on the child's acquisition of language, suspects that "from the start, . . . we are dealing with a species-specific capacity with a largely innate component,"[4] we wonder about the nature of such a component. Innate in us is no Platonic Idea, but the *energy*, the *potential*. Universal is the will, the capability of fulfilling one's vocation, of responding to the message as it is perceived.

These last words are important. Existence as a whole is interpretation. Understand this term not only with the sense of *decipherment*, but also of *performance*. The human presence to the world, and the world's presence to the human, happen in the *logos*, a logos that is both voiceless and articulate. "What do you see, Jeremiah? . . . I see a branch of almond tree. . . . You have seen well, for I watch over my word to perform it" (Jer. 1:12). There is here a pun in Hebrew that we do not need to go into.[5] What is important is that without Jeremiah's interpretation, the almond tree as inarticulate message remains unheeded and vain. But in Jeremiah's *encounter* with the soliciting world, something happens that is an exchange, a relationship, indeed, a mutual creation.

However, the other alternative for Jeremiah would have been perfectly possible. In contrast to Jonah's refusal to "see" Nineveh and its six-score thousand persons, an evidence that is staring him in the face, Jeremiah's indifference to a tree would have been a lot more understandable. For an almond tree is such for anyone. No one needs to be Jeremiah in order to see it. Only Jeremiah, however, sees it in the *way* that he sees it, so that the almond branch *becomes* different from what it is for anyone else. In fact, it becomes for the first time what it strove to be from the beginning! For Jeremiah "is a particular individual with his unique personal characteristics who experiences a unique historical context in a world which has special opportunities and obligations reserved for him alone," Frankl writes.[6] He says further:

> Thus, the ultimate meaning is no longer a matter of intellectual cognition [an almond tree] but of existential commitment ["You have seen well, for . . ."]. One might as well say that a meaning can be understood, but that the ultimate meaning must be interpreted. An interpretation, however, involves a decision.[7]

So, to say that one *is* one's choice or that there is in each of us a vocation that we have chosen from the time of our conception does not make us solipsistic beings. To the contrary, in Israel's conception of vocation, we are taken away from our solipsism and made participants in the dialogue with the world. We have been conceived through communication. We are born from and for communication. From the outset we are in relation (and even for a while in symbiosis) with another being.[8] This positive fact does not imply, it must again be said, determinism, for we are free to negate and sterilize what the Creator wanted "good." This is true on the physical plane as well as on the spiritual or ethical.

It is only seemingly paradoxical to say that everyone is called to prophecy, to priesthood, or to kingship.[9] Priesthood is universal, and so are prophecy and kingship. Each individual has a word to utter, each is gifted with a logos that is indispensable for the integrity of human discourse. Each can express a prophetic message in a unique and irreplaceable way. Jonah's prophecy is prophecy *according* to Jonah. It is marked with his personality. It is so entirely his responsibility that it remains until the end to be wondered whether he rightly interpreted his call. Was he really to say,"Yet forty days and Nineveh shall be overthrown"? Be that as it may, Jonah's word, in the form he transmitted it, is immediately understood by the Ninevites, for the prophet speaks to potential prophets. Were it not for this, Jonah would have spoken for himself only, in a soliloquy. But the prophet is heard. As Andras Angyal has said:

> A poem written in a language that no one can read does not exist as a poem. Neither do we exist in a human sense until someone decodes us. A man in the most crucial way is a symbol, a message that comes to life only by being understood, acknowledged by someone. . . .[10]

Vocation consists of *one call* among a thousand and one other possible ones, which is destined for that person and that person alone.[11] Israel has taken the strong stand that our calling, that which actually makes us *persons* ("but a little lower than God," and "crowned with glory and honor," as Ps. 8:6 says), comes from God, from the Ground of Being (Tillich). Theology seeks to disclose the ultimate meaning and import of what modern human sciences rediscover today about human beings on the psychological level. For the encounter with God of which Israel speaks is nothing other than the authentic encounter with "the other," which in psychological terms makes one fully human. In the words of Alfred Adler, ". . . the individual as a complete being cannot be dragged out of his connection with life—perhaps it would be better to say, with the community."[12]

That is why the question here is not so much what the person expects from the community but what the community expects from the person—provided that the person is not envisaged as a mere cogwheel in the state's machine—not so much what the individual expects from life as what life expects from the person,[13] notwithstanding the modern tendency to place the individual at the center of attention. This is not to say that the individual should be lost sight of in the anonymity of the crowd, as we see happening in some political regimes where the citizens are leveled to the rank of uniformed mediocrity. But, as beings-for-the-world we must, by the necessity of our creaturely nature, choose from among many possible alternatives the one(s) which is (are) creative in the richest meaning of the word. Life itself is such a constant selection because the resistance against the regression to animalhood is a constant and ceaseless struggle. Paradoxically, the human is truly a being-for-the-world only in choosing transcendence. Roberto Assagioli writes:

> . . . to "decide" very often means to *choose;* that is, a selection must be made from among various possibilities. But to choose implies to *prefer;* and to prefer some one thing, one action, one way, necessarily demands the discarding or eliminating of others. . . . an important criterion in choosing is to foresee in the clearest possible manner what *effects* the choice will have: not only the immediate but also the long-term ones, since the latter can turn out to be different from, and indeed opposite to, the former. . . . The act of will and intention then involves a decision to accept or not accept an impulse. Authenticity does not consist in giving in to a bad motive simply because it exists.[14]

This contrasts with what Maslow wrote in 1968 in a Hobbesian vein of sorts: "the only way we can ever know what is right for us is that it feels better subjectively than any alternative"; and again: "what tastes good is also, in the growth sense, 'better' for us."[15] The terms "feel" and "subjectively" as criteria for "growth" appear especially deceiving. They have a ring of the pre-Freudian era, even of the Enlightenment, when individual autocratism triumphed.[16] It is simply contrary to truth that one "grows" by choosing "what tastes good." In many cases the opposite is true. If Abraham Maslow were right in this, there would have been no Israel in human history. For "Israel" is precisely the name given to those who, like Abraham, prefer to leave "their own country, kindred, their own father's house" in the pursuit of an "impossible dream." Psychologically speaking, the least one can say about an Abraham who chooses to stay in Ur in Chaldea for the reason that it "feels better" is that he has missed the train of history and, hence, his own destiny. Abram, then, would never become Abraham, just as Jonah, by staying in his country because the "milk and honey" taste so good there, would never become Jonah!

During the last fifty years humanistic psychologists seem to have promoted conflicting trends. Although they agree on basic tenets such as the human being self-determined, free to choose, unique, and so forth, they still diverge in their understanding of human purpose and vocation. Some, like Kurt Goldstein, emphasize the organismic need to maintain a tensionless equilibrium (called here "homeostasis" or "principle of equalization").[17] Others, like Maslow, go one step further. They assert that when those fundamental biological needs are fulfilled, "meta-needs" can come to the fore, but these are "less urgent or demanding, weaker."[18] "Self-actualization means working to do well the thing that one *wants* to do."[19]

The language is revealing. "Self-actualization" is totally different from "self-transcendence." It does not raise the issue of the meaning of life, unless as a luxury, a thing "less urgent or demanding, weaker." Thinkers like Jung, Allport, May, and Frankl utterly disagree with the reduction of the human to biological components and dictates, although they do not negate or in any way deny human "basic needs." For example, they emphasize the constructive and necessary aspect of anxiety. Says Frankl:

> What man actually needs is not a tensionless state but rather the striving and struggling for some goal worthy of him. . . . What man needs is not homeostasis but what I call "noo-dynamics," . . . the spiritual dynamics in a polar field of tension where one pole is represented by a meaning to be fulfilled and the other pole by the man who must fulfill it.[20]

Human self-actualization here is not "an end-state" as Maslow or Rogers suggests, but only a by-product in the realization of values, and in "the fulfillment of meaning potentialities which are to be found in the world rather than within himself. . . ."[21] This last group of thinkers also asserts that one must select among various immanent potentialities and aim at what is most ethically meaningful. Frankl concludes: "Man must make his choice concerning the mass of present potentials: which will be condemned to non-being and which will be actualized."[22]

As proposed, the program does not lack interest, although it is not necessarily very clear what is meant by terms such as "the world" and especially "authenticity." The latter seems even to cover divergent and directly conflicting anthropological notions.[23] There is a cause-and-effect relationship between one's belief system and specific actions as they are inspired or dictated by that system. We may pose the problem in the following way: Is authenticity the conformity of actions to any set of beliefs or convictions? Such a general understanding of being "true" or "genuine" lends itself to vague relativism. *There would be as many authenticities as there are belief systems.* If one's beliefs are founded upon the ultimate value of happiness and "self-actualization," authenticity would consist precisely in realizing what "feels good" and rewarding. If, for instance, we take *Mein Kampf* as the expression of Adolf Hitler's belief system, the odious crimes of the German Führer could be said to make him authentic![24] Authenticity in this sense is a contextual notion; it does not convey in and of itself any ethical judgment. We therefore must rephrase our question. *When* there is "authenticity," that is, conformity of the action to a set of convictions, *toward what* goal is that authenticity oriented?

It appears that modern psychology too often uses the term "authenticity" with the same magical but empty content as Christian pietists use the word "faith," when faith per se has no salvific virtues.[25] Indeed, "having the faith" provides an insufficient ground for judgment, as long as it is not said in whom or in what; so also "authenticity" means little if anything. Value systems have sundry references. Even when there are between them resemblances from a phenomenological point of view, their respective meanings are nonetheless often divergent. Buddhic charity and Christian love may, for example, be seen from a certain angle as twins. But Henri de Lubac, for one, shows that it would be a mistake to be content with how they look on the surface.[26] On the other hand, if there is contradiction between Jonah-going-to-Tarshish and Jonah-under-the-commission-to-go-to-Nineveh, the son of Amittai is no less human, and probably no less religious, in one case than in the other. When he sails to Tarshish, it is with the conviction that "God" cannot conceivably demand that he betray his people. When he eventually fulfills the order to go to Nineveh, it is with the conviction that this indeed is his vocation. If all this brings him to the brink of a nervous breakdown, no wonder. As Erich Fromm said: "We can interpret neurosis as a private form of religion."[27]

Again, we must ask: Have faith *in whom*? Be authentic *to what*? It is the "reference" of authenticity that is decisive. In comparison with the imprecision of humanistic terms, deprived as they are of firm and substantial content, perhaps for fear of being accused of borrowing from the religious vocabulary, it must be said that biblical language at least has the advantage of being consistent. Here the criterion of "authenticity" is not to be found in the human soul. Abraham does not uncover in his mind a sudden impulse to travel abroad, or Jonah to visit a foreign city in Mesopotamia. Desire or impulse has little import here, for, before it orients someone in a given direction, vocation according to the Bible "dis-orients to re-orient," as Paul Ricoeur says. Maslow and many other psychologists, however, have no room in their systems for the disorientation. They envisage only an orientation imposed by nature, which they conceive as in no need of being re-aligned or restored. No one ignores, though, what it means to follow one's natural inclination—it is indeed an inclination, a descent.

We have, by now, reached an important curve toward a new development. We have learned that there are fundamentally two opposite concepts of authenticity: (*a*) authenticity to an *inner* voice, versus (*b*) authenticity to an *outer* voice. The "inner voice" can be called by numerous other names—inner potentials, inner drives, personal conscience, authentic self, and so forth. Individuals who listen to the inner voice fulfill their inmost potentialities according to their convictions, norms, values, or conscience. Such an option requires, one must say, a good deal of introspection. The results, in fact, are often highly respectable. One need only think of the evolved moral conscience that a sense of guilt implies in developed and mature societies. One has to acknowledge the enormous progress of conscientization in human history, through internalization, a far cry from the primitivist conception of taboo.

But the fact remains that human confrontation with conscience that leads to the realization of guilt, evaluates the fault with the skimpy yardstick of the *feeling* of fault. Paul Ricoeur says, that then "man is guilty as he feels guilty"! It demands a more refined conscience to recognize itself as captive, even misleading. It is a lesson that Freud has taught us: one must use suspicion toward conscience. From judging, it then becomes judged (Ricoeur). It is judged under two counts of indictment: on the one hand, the blame that conscience levies against itself is for selected sins that cover the very ones it should repent for. Furthermore, conscience hides in the background the self-deception of proper justice. In order precisely to cut short any such "stabilization of a conscience complacent with self-justice," the prophet proclaims a word of God that did not come up from the human heart and that "flesh and blood has not revealed" (see Matt. 16:17). This is what we call the "outer voice."[28]

To define such a voice is difficult because it is far from unequivocal. It is, by its nature, beyond our control. Its ambiguity resides in the fact that it is easy to confuse personally fabricated "voices" with the call that is "heard" as a message coming from without. Such ambiguity is always latent in even the best of situations. One can wonder, for example, what really prompted Jonah to advise the sailors to cast him overboard (1:12). Was it the voice of his conscience? Was it in response to a command from God? These are moot questions. Suffice it here to recall the case of the archcriminal David Berkowitz, self-named "son of Sam," who claimed to have been "ordered" from "without" to commit his horrendous murders! When asked by the psychiatrist Dr. Abrahamson, "Who told you to kill?" Berkowitz answered simply, "Sam."[29]

Again we are back to square one. In question is not so much the obedience to a call, either real or imagined, as is the intrinsic quality of the response (itself depending upon the quality of the command, as we shall see). So far in our analysis of Jonah, we have constantly probed the contents of his responses. These essentially derive from two elements, *who* spoke to him, *how* did he interpret (in the word's two meanings) the word? By contrast, the "son of Sam's" obedience comes out as a grotesque caricature. What kind of voice is that? Determinative in fact is the person communicating with the one who is called. Decisive is the *reference* of the discourse.

In the case of David Berkowitz, "Sam" is a sham reference. The alleged dialogue is a monologue with alternate voices. To the contrary, when one breaks the monologue with oneself and acknowledges a "Thou," one passes from what we might call a "prior-self stage" to an "authentic-self stage." The "prior-self stage"—or the stage of being-for-oneself—involves the innate concern for the self that is present in all human beings. Infants pull toward themselves everything they can reach. It belongs to an indispensable process of growth and maturation in all of us to discover the external world as an object that must be adapted to the self and the self to it. Yet, as we see it, ultimate maturity and personhood happens when the object is acknowledged as a subject, for only then is there dialogue and love. An individual in the process of encountering becomes someone engaged in the dialogical process. She or he becomes what Buber aptly calls *a person* (see below). In "surrendering" to the beloved One (Jon. 2), Jonah passes from anonymity to the stage of the authentic self. He has chosen life (see Deut. 30) and in fact, he lives! (Jon. 2:11). In the words of Martin Buber:

> An individual is just a certain uniqueness of a human being. . . . He may become more and more an individual without becoming more and more human. I know many examples of men having become very, very individual, very distinct from others, very developed in their such-and-suchness without being at all what I would like to call a man. The individual is just this uniqueness; being able to be developed thus and thus. But *a person . . . is an individual living really with the world. And with the world, I don't mean in the world*—just in real contact, in real reciprocity with the world in all the points in which the world can meet man. I don't say only with man, because sometimes we meet the world in other shapes than in that of man. . . . I'm against individuals and for persons.[30]

The "prior-self stage" is thus a preliminary stage, which prepares for an eventual existential breakthrough in becoming a person. This preliminary stage is also primordial; it must be transcended and not shed like an old skin. Jonah in chapter 2 or in chapter 3 is the same Jonah as in chapter 1. Similarly, the "authentic-self stage"—or the stage of being-for-the-world—is not built upon the ruins of the "prior-self stage." Instead of being a ready-made excuse to find refuge in a solipsistic abstentionism, the instinct of preservation shores up the will to transcend one's egotism and reach out to the other.

No one can win one's life unless one loses it, said the Nazarene. At the two poles is life, the life one loses and the life—the "same" one—one wins. Such is the paradox of the gospel declaration. Similarly, St. Paul exclaims, "It is no longer I who live, but Christ who lives in me" (Gal. 2:20). Paul's self is found present at both ends. The apostle does not pass, through absorption into another's personality, even Christ's, to a stage of "non-me." Rather than a metamorphosis, it is a question here of transfiguration.

Let us pursue further this dialectic notion, for it is, we believe, of fundamental import to the understanding of the Jonah story, presenting as it does a man going through *conversion* but not transmutation. The "authentic self-stage" is a complete reversal ("conversion") of the "prior-self stage" but not its abandonment, as in a dichotomy between "flesh" and "soul." Besides, the passage from the one to the other is ceaseless and never fulfilled. It is an ongoing self-decentralization, a "taking off." The springboard needs to be that with which we came to life in the first place, the self. This much must be acknowledged, lest we be left with a disincarnated spirit without flesh and, eventually, without reality.

But the "prior-self" is there as a means, not as a goal. It is endlessly sacrificed in a "living offering and a reasonable service" (Rom. 12:1) on the altar of the "I-Thou" relationship. One will remember at this point what the modern poet of that intimate relationship, Martin Buber, said about the necessity to begin with oneself "but not to end with oneself. . . . True, each [soul] is to know itself, purify itself, perfect itself, but not for its own sake . . . for the sake of the work it is destined to perform upon the world."[31] For the human is a person only in the process of dialoguing with a "Thou." To live means precisely to enter into the in-betweenness of the relation with the other. Ultimately, we believe, there is no other way to find life than by giving it up.[32] The phrase "to give up one's life" has a literal and metaphorical sense. It means running the supreme risk for the love of the other; leaving behind "having" for the sake of "being"; shunning power, because what good is it to gain the whole world, if one forfeits one's soul in the process? Or what will one give in return that would have the same value as life?—to paraphrase Jesus.

Clearly, however, the whole of me opposes that discovery. Nothing is more imperative in us than the instinct of survival.[33] But, applied to protect our solipsism, such an instinct becomes self-defeating. It is "as if a man fled from a lion and a bear met him; or went into the house and leaned his hand against the wall, and a serpent bit him" (Amos 5:19). What he confused with a lion was none else but his neighbor, his partner, his alter ego—himself. The Romans used a very closely related simile and described our fellow man as "a wolf for man." For, indeed, love that one would tend to consider as common in this world is in fact a very rare phenomenon. Often, what is called love is but the complicity between two people.

It is never easy to accede to a full mature existence by taking one's *responsibilities*. In doing so, one opens up the self to the outer world, when there are a thousand and one means to insulate oneself from the world. The deeply ingrained and universal wish to return to the golden age of the womb-stage has perennial importance. But the price to pay is enormous, no less than one's integrity, even identity.

Reaching authenticity is not reserved, however, to the "happy few." There are no two human races, one of which would be content with mediocrity, while the other would be made up of those touched by the fairy-wand striving toward an aristocratic "more being." The fact is that any human is infinitely complex—a complexity that comprises the need for others and the thirst for recognition. The negative side of this connatural striving is its caricature, conformism. As Buber explains:

Man's unacknowledged secret is his desire to be affirmed in his essence and in his existence by his fellow men. He wishes that they, in turn, would make it possible for him to affirm them, and for both affirmations to be conferred not merely within the family or perhaps at a party meeting or in a bar, but also in the course of neighborly encounters. . . . by so doing, each would let the other know that he endorses his presence. It is this endorsement that constitutes the indispensable minimum of man's humanity.[34]

Too often, individuals believe that they can use others and force upon them a role of mirror. It is a travesty of dialogue, sheer monologue with oneself. Here again, the story of Jonah is an illustration, for his encounter with the Ninevites is only a façade. Jonah is not engaged in a dialogue. He speaks without heeding. He rids himself of the burden of the message before an abstraction that he calls Nineveh. The abstraction, however, becomes undeniably concrete. The Ninevites repent and grieve over that caricature of themselves fabricated by the Gath-Hepher prophet.[35]

In its essence, narcissistic monologue is static and circular.[36] By contrast, dialogue is dynamic and linear. Encounter with another—so rare an occurrence as to be an extraordinary event each time[37]—is also encounter with the respective past and future of the two partners. That is why in his dialogue with Carl Rogers (April 18, 1957) Martin Buber insisted that any real relationship must begin with acceptance. He said that "confirming means first of all, accepting the whole potentiality of the other and making even a decisive difference in his potentiality. . . . I can recognize in him . . . the person he has been . . . created to become."[38]

Here the horizons are not clouded but, to the contrary, "the other fills the horizon" (Buber); the other constitutes the "referent" of otherwise meaningless strivings and impulses. The beloved other does not "blow your mind"—although this also may happen at times on the road to communion—but restores your mind, or perhaps gives you a sound mind for the first time. "Then," says our text, "Jonah prayed to the Lord his God out of the fish's belly. . . . I will sacrifice to Thee with the voice of thanksgiving!" (2:2, 10 [English 2:1, 9]).

The other fills the horizon, but does he not cloud it? It would be the case when the other is divinized, as is illustrated in courteous love ("l'amour courtois"), or in certain romantic understanding of love. It is not so when both partners are *called* to authenticity—personal and relational—by *someone else* whose presence and voice are enticing and commanding. We *are* not free, said Maimonides, but we have received the commandment *to be* free. Paraphrasing the Jewish philosopher, it can be said that we are not loving but, rather, we have received (*qua* humans and not just animals) the commandment to love. This is what is meant here by the "outer voice."

The phrase "the commandment to love" is problematic on two counts. First, *who* is the one who commands? Second, *why* must it be a command? With respect to the first question, the book of Jonah is written by an Israelite author who takes for granted that "the word *of the Lord* came unto Jonah" (1:1). Today, such statements are considered by many to be the products of groundless superstition. But perhaps this move is too precipitous. Maslow writes: ". . . the sacred is *in* the ordinary . . . it is to be found in one's daily life, in one's neighbors, friends, and family, in one's back yard."[39] We are not, therefore, speaking of a meta-reality that stands over and against our down-to-earth daily existence.[40] But there is a tendency within society to desacralize or devalue love, truth, respect for life and sex, in short, to shun any way of life based on the reverence for interpersonal relationship. True, it is only too easy to expose the hypocrisy of past mores when they had retained but the molds emptied of their ethical or religious content. It is out of the question to return to such deceptions, but it is to be wondered whether the alternative is any better, which offers to modern youth a chaotic and meaningless world. Both terms being unacceptable, it seems that the way to salvation is in giving back to life its sacred dimension and to acknowledge again the divine origin of values such as love and personal respect.[41]

However, to express the regret that a sense of the sacredness of life has been lost with the dechristianization of the West still says nothing about "the Lord" who, for Israel, is the author of the "outer voice" and the guarantor of its trustworthiness. Were we in a mythological environment—and it is indeed the environment of most of our contemporaries, despite their claims to be "liberated"—the personality of the god would be utterly definable, whether it be Zeus or Wotan, the Aryan "blood" or the American way of life, the will to power or the "quick buck," or again, at the level of the god-hero, Mao Tse Tung or the Olympic athlete. But there is an exorbitant price to pay for those comfortable religions: all those gods look benign, yet they actually are tyrants. They do cloud the horizon, ruthlessly grinding in their ideological or cultic machines those who could become a threat to their megalomania. Pol Pot eliminates close to one-third of his compatriots; Stalin had more material to which to apply his skill; it is estimated that his victims number 20 million.

To define the identity of the God of Israel will not be—thank God if one dares say—that easy. One cannot come nearer to God, but from a distance. It is only inductively that one can speak of God.

Our inquiry about who commands Jonah takes us first to considering the command itself. Here the commander and the command are essentially inseparable, the latter reflecting the personality of the former. There is no way to know who speaks other than to hear the word. Who is "the Lord" who speaks to Jonah but the one who tells him, "Arise, go to Nineveh"? Here we are entitled to take the commandment so seriously as to measure the quality of its author by that very norm. Speaker and speech build a gestalt. "God is the relation with God" (Buber). We are at the antipode of the mythological way of thinking. There a mute Zeus would still be Zeus. Who is he who could quote a memorable word of Zeus? It is an interesting exercise. Perhaps, if one cultivates the *belles lettres,* one will be able to think of such-or-such poetic sentence expressing, not so much the divinity of Zeus or Hera, but the genius of Homer or Sophocles. For these gods do not come with other laws but those of nature or of Anangke, Fate, to which they themselves must submit. Alone, the God of Israel reveals the divine will through apodictic (unconditional) laws that are not reducible to mere imperatives of natural reason.[42] Far from curtailing a congenitally natural human freedom, the commandment creates for the first time the indispensable conditions for its exercise, that is, the stipulations of reponsibility.[43] The commandment, as a matter of fact, is given to someone whose capability of free choice is acknowledged. The divine commandment is more inviting than coercing.[44]

In the Israelite tale of origin, the very first word addressed by the Creator to Adam is typically an order: "Be fruitful, multiply, fill the earth, and subdue it; have dominion," and so on (Gen. 1:28). It is properly an order-benediction, the fundamental blessing over all life. It already says all that we need to know about God, that God is Creator, that God is Love, Faith (Trust), Hope. In Israel's spiritual topology, what is decisive is the "in-between" space, which both separates and binds the speaker and the speaker's word, as well as the addresser and the addressee. Rather than zeroing in upon the message in its inalterability, Israel squarely focuses upon the process of the discourse, upon the event of the communication, upon the someone who is also a subject, that is, a *responsible* being capable of the best and the worst, of creating life with the Creator, and of destroying the world in an anti-God suicidal move.

From the same perspective, the Ten Commandments have shown their mettle. Some will perhaps be content to speak about them in terms of profound wisdom, of inspired knowledge, of human spirituality, and so on. Those compliments remain unsatisfactory, however, if only because they sound like lip-service paid to a cultural achievement that is as obsolete as it is admirable. We must, rather, ask *what* makes the Ten Words life-giving, *what* makes the commandment to Jonah a possibility for his rebirth? The book of Jonah demonstrates that the ground of the commandment, the support, as it were, of the "outer voice," is Love. Humans are under command because they are loved, and the order they receive makes them love in turn. The commandment pulls people up from animality to humanity. Buber writes, "Whoever goes forth to You (the other) with his whole being and carries to it all the being of the world, finds him whom one cannot seek."[45]

In summary, the human task is one of detection. One must detect not so much one's needs, desires, and aspirations, but the demands of life itself. That is why one must go beyond psychol-

ogy. One must also leave theology behind when it becomes so systematic as to leave no room for the *extravagance* of a divine will
that is not under the rules of reason. Such a theology is illustrated with profound genius by Job's friends. It is dramatically
echoed in Peter's exclamation, "God forbid, Lord, this shall never
happen to you" (Matt. 16:22). According to that system, God *cannot* demand that Jonah go to Nineveh. Similarly, when being ordered by God, Jonah *cannot* but readily obey. But it happens that
God demands the unimaginable, and that Jonah refuses to accept
it. The order of God is extravagant; it is also extravagant that
Jonah opt for "holy disobedience" in order to save God's honor
from the danger of being scoffed at in Nineveh.

Evidently, divine excess results in human excess. In the case
of Jonah versus God, it's a tie. God dared command the unthinkable; the prophet in turn dared ignore God's "folly."[46] Unless . . .
there is perhaps a still more surprising and constructive extravagance of which Jonah did not think or which he preferred not to
contemplate (see 4:2): the extravagance of divine repentance.

In any case, we are far beyond any ethical norm. What is
called here the "outer voice" is a commandment that transcends
the ethical realm. The latter is for penultimate realities only.
There we may heed the useful directions of respectable masters
such as Freud, Jung, Adler, Rank, and many others. They watch
our steps for a while, to a certain extent. They also serve as
judges of our progresses and regresses. But the movement of
Jonah that takes him to Nineveh in order to obey the exhorta-
tions of the "outer voice" belongs far less to anthropological ethics and depth psychology than to a divine Act.

NOTES

1. Susan Handelman strongly reacts against the Aristotelian categories of
the "general" versus the "particular." She writes: "Rabbinic thought will relativize
[those] concepts . . . and conceive their relationship in a more fluid way, as one of
extension and limitation rather than opposition, and will substitute a contextual
relationship for a proportional one." Furthermore, she reflects upon "the philosophical aspects of the Rabbinic system of interpretation," based precisely upon
the relation between the general and the particular, and she adds, "In contrast to
their use in Aristotelian logic, *general* and *particular* are above all semantic and

predicative categories. They are, therefore, relativized, as that which is *more general* or *more particular*, and not predicates preceded by the words *all* or *some*" (S. Handelman, *The Slayers of Moses: The Emergence of Rabbinic Interpretation in Modern Literary Theory* [Albany: State University of New York Press, 1982], pp. 13 and 65.

2. We are far from Socrates' definition of the voice of conscience as "Voice of God," according to Xenophon (*Apol.* 12).

3. Karl Jaspers said, "What man is, he ultimately becomes through the cause which he has made his own" (quoted by Frankl, *Psychotherapy and Existentialism* [New York: Washington Square Press, 1967], p. 9). G. van der Leeuw, *Religion in Essence and Manifestation, A Study in Phenomenology* (in German, 1933) [New York: Harper and Row, 1963, 2 vols.].

4. See Noam Chomsky, "Recent Contributions to the Theory of Innate Ideas," in *Boston Studies in the Philosophy of Science*, ed. R. Cohen and M. Wartofsky (Dordrecht: Reidel, 1968), vol. 3, p. 123.

5. Play of words on *shaked* (almond tree) and *shoked* (to watch), both of the same root in Hebrew because the almond tree is the first to blossom (to "wake up") in the spring. See Mircea Eliade, *The Sacred and the Profane* (New York: Harper & Row, 1961), p. 165: ". . . the world is neither mute nor opaque, . . . it is not an inert thing without purpose or significance. For religious man, the cosmos 'lives' and 'speaks.' "

6. Frankl, *Psychotherapy and Existentialism*, p. 44.

7. Ibid., p. 34.

8. "Community, of course, is implicit in the creature of flesh and blood by reason of his very origin in the mother's womb . . ." (Max Scheler, *On the Eternal in Man* [Garden City, New York: Doubleday, 1972], p. 374).

9. See Exod. 19:6; and A. LaCocque, *But as for Me* (Atlanta: John Knox Press, 1979).

10. Andras Angyal, *Neurosis and Treatment: A Holistic Theory* (New York: John Wiley & Sons, 1965), p. 18.

11. Frankl: "No man and no destiny can be compared with any other man or any other destiny. . . . no situation repeats itself, and each situation calls for a different response" (*Man's Search for Meaning* [Boston: Beacon Press, 1962], p. 77); "To compare yourself with anyone else is to do an injustice either to yourself or to the other person" (*The Doctor and the Soul* [New York: Knopf, 1955], p. 173).

12. Adler, *Social Interest* (New York: G. P. Putnam's Sons, 1964), p. 39.

13. See Frankl, *The Doctor and the Soul*, p. 80; *The Unconscious God* (New York: Simon & Schuster, 1975), pp. 23–24.

14. R. Assagioli, *The Act of Will* (Baltimore: Penguin Books, 1973), pp. 143, 166–68.

15. Maslow, *Toward a Psychology of Being* (Princeton: D. Van Nostrand, 1968), pp. 45, 48.

16. See Karl Barth, *Die Protestantische Theologie in 19. Jahrhundert* (Zurich: Evangelisher Vlg., 1952), chap. 1, "Man in the 18th Century."

17. Kurt Goldstein, *The Organism* (New York: American Book Co., 1939); also "Effect of Brain Damage on Personality," in *Theories of Psychopathology and Personality*, ed. T. Millon (Philadelphia: W. B. Saunders Co., 1973).

18. Maslow, *The Farther Reaches of Human Nature* (Baltimore: Penguin Books, 1971), p. 312. "Man's higher nature rests upon man's lower nature needing it as a foundation and collapsing without its foundation. . . . Man's higher nature is *inconceivable* without a satisfied lower nature as a base" (*Toward a Psychology of Being*,

p. 173, italics added). Maslow defines "self-actualization" as "the full use and exploitation of talents, capacities, potentialities . . ." (*Motivation and Personality* [New York: Harper & Row, 1970], p. 150).

19. Maslow, *The Farther Reaches of Human Nature*, p. 46.

20. Frankl, *Man's Search for Meaning*, p. 107.

21. Frankl, *Psychotherapy and Existentialism*, p. 68.

22. Ibid., p. 46. See also Assagioli, *The Act of Will*, pp. 143, 167–68.

23. A criticism already raised on the philosophical level by T. W. Adorno in *Der Jargon der Eigentlichkeit: Zur deutschen Ideologie* (Frankfurt a. R.: Suhrkamp Vlg., 1964).

24. As is well known, the Nazis used biblical passages as well as Luther's writings to support their propaganda.

25. For example, James Bugental (*The Search for Authenticity* [New York: Holt, Rinehart & Winston, 1965], pp. 45, 102ff.) says that man is authentic to the extent that he is conscious and responsible for his own decisions and actions. However, Bugental does not envisage the ethical ramifications of his views. No more than Maslow does he ask the question: Authentic to whom or to what, in view of whom or of what?

26. H. de Lubac, *Aspects du Bouddhisme* (Paris: Seuil, 1951), cf. chap. 1, "La charité bouddhique."

27. Fromm, *Psychoanalysis and Religion* (New Haven: Yale University Press, 1950), p. 27.

28. H. G. Gadamer writes: ". . . what points in the opposite direction. Whether he named this *nous* or God, either way it is ultimately what lies utterly outside us, just as the mystical submersion of the Christian ultimately attains inward reality" (*Reason in the Age of Science* [Cambridge, Mass.: M.I.T. Press, 1981], p. 18).

29. Although we are dealing with a man dangerously insane, the objectivation of the inner voice has its titles of nobility. So do, for instance, Homer's heroes when they speak with their *thumos* that one can define, with E. R. Dodds, as the organ of the senses. It is the warrior's *thumos* that tells him when he must kill his enemy. Dodds writes that "it commonly appears as an independent inner voice" (*The Greeks and the Irrational* [Berkeley: University of California Press, 1951], p. 16). M. P. Nilsson went further and concluded that Homer's heroes suffer from psychological instability (*psychische labilität*)! ("Götter und Psychologie bei Homer," *Archiv für Religionswissenschaft* 22 [1925]: 363ff); see also his *Geschichte der griechischen Religion* (Munich: Beck, 1941), pp. 120ff.

30. Buber, *Knowledge of Man* (New York: Harper & Row, 1965), p. 184 (italics added).

31. Buber, *The Way of Man* (New York: Citadel Press, 1967), pp. 31f., 34.

32. Similarly, Israel historicizes nature and spiritualizes matter. Nature and matter are the terrain of history and of spirit. As there is no tree without humus, there is nothing spiritual without the material. But the humus exists for the tree, not the tree for the humus. And what is true for a tree is a thousand times truer for a person. The ultimate scandal for Israel's tradition is that the human being, instead of becoming spirit, returns to humus!

33. In the first century B.C.E., Cicero was saying that the instinct of preservation is fundamental. "Love of the self was the first principle" (*De Finibus* III.5.16). Before him, Stoicism, to which Cicero owes so much, had recognized that truth. It taught that the fitting (*kathēkon*) consists in looking for the prefera-

ble (*proēgména*), i.e., the most usual goals of nature. But, added the Stoa, the sage goes beyond this up to the absolute virtue.

34. Buber, *The Way of Response*, ed. N. N. Glatzer (New York: Schocken Books, 1966), p. 207.

35. See 2 Kings 14:25.

36. The "Original guilt," Buber said, "consists in remaining with oneself" (*The Knowedge of Man*, p. 49).

37. "He only earns his freedom and existence who daily conquers them anew," said Goethe.

38. Buber, *The Knowledge of Man*, p. 182.

39. Maslow, *The Farther Reaches*, p. 333.

40. The dualistic conception shared by Christian institutions ever since the church fathers is the poison that has contaminated its "gospel" down to this day.

41. See, e.g., Maslow, *The Farther Reaches*, p. 48. The Brandeis scholar thus confirms what Jung said in 1933: ". . . we psychotherapists must occupy ourselves with problems which, strictly speaking, belong to the theologian" (p. 241, see the whole page).

42. See A. Alt, *Die Ursprünge des israelitischen Rechts* (Leipzig: S. Hirzel, 1934).

43. See Ricoeur, *The Conflict of Interpretations* (Evanston: Northwestern University Press, 1974), p. 433: "It is because I recognize my 'ought' that I recognize my 'could.' A being who is obligated is a being who presumes that he can do what he should do."

44. See J. Nabert, *Éléments pour une Éthique* (Paris: P.U.F., 1943), p. 141: "The order of duty contributes to the revelation to the self of a desire of being whose deepening is part and parcel with ethic itself."

45. Buber, *I and Thou* (New York: Charles Scribner's Sons, 1970), p. 127.

46. "God's folly is wiser than men" (1 Cor. 1:25).

NINE

THE JONAH COMPLEX
REVISITED

We have much data to indicate that the greatest threat and greatest cause for anxiety for contemporary western man, in the middle of the twentieth century, is not castration but ostracism: The terrible situation of being thrown out of the group. Many a contemporary man castrates himself or permits himself to be castrated, that is, gives up his power, originality, and independence, because of fearing exile if he does not. He renounces his power and conforms under the great threat and peril of ostracism.

Rollo May, *Existential Psychotherapy*
(Toronto: Bryant Press, 1967), p. 15.

In the crowd one feels no responsibility, but also no fear.

Carl G. Jung, "Concerning Rebirth" (1950),
The Archetypes and the Collective Unconscious
(Princeton: Princeton University Press, 1969), vol. 9i, p. 126.

This final chapter systematically studies the psychological complex of which we have followed different threads in the preceding chapters. We now must gather them together in a coherent whole. But, in order to do justice to the complexity, if we dare say, of the topic, we must preface our conclusion with a critical review of different psychological responses that have been given to a symptom called "the fear of success." It is, we believe, an indispensable introduction; it also broadens our study of the universal "Jonah complex" beyond the confines of the biblical tale. The reader, we hope, will forgive this relative and provisionary distancing from the scriptural text.

Conformism has always been considered a necessary element for group survival and inner harmony. But this primordial conformism is quickly outdone by another kind, because that which was originally meant as some kind of modesty soon enough becomes a uniformizing pattern. It is indeed for other, less natural reasons that men and women so generally opt for uniformity and for the trivial in life.

Research in social psychology has provided overwhelming evidence that peer pressure is such that most people resolve their existential difficulties by blindly complying with social norms and values abstracted from their original intentions. They use conformity as their main point of reference for judging the appropriateness of individual and social behaviors. As Harry Harlow points out, after reviewing the experimental research on conformity, "There appears to exist overwhelming pressure to conform to group norms, *even when such conformity is clearly at odds with the subject's own perceptions, attitudes or beliefs.*"[1] In fact, even the mere wish to be similar to other groups breeds attraction and conformity, as Darley and Berscheid so convincingly demonstrated.[2]

Social mimetism becomes a pathological phenomenon whenever it is used as the sole or the main point of reference for one's attitude toward life. Unhealthy conformity arises when it is compulsively idealized. In the words of Erich Fromm, we are then dealing with "automaton or compulsive conformity." He explains: "It means that one can be sure of oneself only if one lives up to the expectations of others."[3]

What is pathological conformity? It is "maintaining a protective coloring so that men won't be singled out from others," a kind of "death-in-life," says May.[4] He also writes: "It is a tendency of the individual to let himself be swallowed up in a sea of collective responses and attitudes. . . . it is a loss of awareness, the loss of your potentialities and sensitivities, the loss of whatever characterizes you or me as a unique and original being."[5]

Such automaton conformity is equivalent to "surrendering one's consciousness" and "destroying one's selfhood,"[6] thus leading a person to actualize a "pseudoself."[7] This mechanism, Fromm says, can be compared with the protective colorings of some animals; "they look so similar to their surroundings that they are hardly distinguishable from them."[8]

THE JONAH COMPLEX REVISITED

It is the purpose of this chapter to explore the psychological conditions giving rise to the temptation to run away from social responsibilities and growth; it is here called the "Jonah complex." Even though this pathological phenomenon is well known in literature, the interpretations of its causes differ. All agree that automaton conformity is a symptom of a more deeply rooted problem. In presenting an existential view on this complex, we shall take exception to the self-actualization group of psychological thinkers for whom listening to one's biological dictates and acting upon them represents the highest form of authenticity and constitutes the ultimate ethical criterion for ascribing "healthy" meanings in life. The Jonah syndrome, or complex, according to that group, is an avoidance of actualizing what "feels good" to the individual and a fear of the consequences it might bring to one's self-image. In contradistinction to this intrapsychic belief, it is here argued that what lies behind the pathological avoidance of social responsibility are two basic underlying psychological prods: the first is the fear of death, and the second is the desacralization of life and the trivialization of its meaning.[9]

But before we expand upon this definition of the Jonah complex, a look at the available psychological contributions on the psycho-dynamics underlying pathological conformity will be presented. Although we believe these not to do full justice to the complex under study here, they are nonetheless worth noting for their insights. One reason, for instance, that they often give to explain why so many people conform unhealthily is anticipated fear of unwanted consequences that success and knowledge of self may bring. To this problem we now turn.

As early as 1915, Freud noticed that during the treatment of psychoneuroses an unusual phenomenon arose in some of his patients: success in their work stirred in them acute anxieties.[10] He explained this by postulating that, for some, success meant the symbolic murder of the parent of the same sex. Such fantasy, in turn, would create intense anxiety and guilt feelings, precipitating a state of melancholy, which, in some cases, could last for years. Freud described these persons as "those wrecked by success."

As long as success remains a wish and not an actuality, Freud hypothesized, the "success neurosis" would not necessarily erupt. But when it becomes a reality, in the case of a person being promoted to a better position and salary, for example, it happens that the beneficiary cannot endure it, and may, indeed, become ill. Freud explained:

> People occasionally fall ill precisely because a deeply rooted and long-cherished wish has come to fulfillment. . . . It is not so very unusual for the ego to tolerate a wish as harmless as long as this exists in fantasy alone and seems remote from fulfillment, while it will defend itself hotly against such wish as soon as it approaches fulfillment and threatens to become an actuality.[11]

Freud was quite puzzled about the etiology of "success neuroses" and admitted not knowing where the censoring and punishing tendencies first originated. The "best" explanation he gave was an Oedipal one. One fears success and its repercussions, he thought, because one dreads surpassing the parent(s) in happiness, education, wealth, and status. To achieve such goals would imply the possible consequence of being a threat to the parents and of being rejected and ostracized by them.[12] Besides Freud's contribution, there have been numerous other endeavors to understand better the underlying causes of the fear of success. Some patients fear success, it is explained, because they do not feel worthy of it. Otto Fenichel says:

> Success may mean the achievement of something unmerited or "wrong" bringing inferiority or guilt into the open. . . . A success may not only mean something that must bring immediate punishment but also something that stimulates ambition and thus mobilizes fear concerning future failure and future punishment.[13]

The psychoanalyst Leon Tec also interprets such fear as the result of viewing the idealized success as not justified. To illustrate this point, he gives the example of a woman professor who was acknowledged as successful but internally she felt like a fraud. She said to Tec:

> At every point in my career, when I moved ahead I always felt that somehow "they" would find out I was not so good as I appeared to be, as others thought I was, and if I moved to a better, more successful position, "they" would eventually find out that I didn't belong there.[14]

Matina Horner went to great length to demonstrate that generally women have a much harder time integrating success than men.[15] To demonstrate her point she devised a simple experiment. She asked college women to rate a medical student named "Ann" after learning that at the end of the first term finals, she was at the top of her class. The ratings by these women were everything but flattering. Ann was described as unattractive, unhappy, lonely, man-starved, and a bookworm, among other pejorative adjectives.[16]

As much as we can see evidence for this specific syndrome or complex in clinical practice, we believe, however, that keeping the sexes apart in their experiences of responsibility avoidance does ultimately more harm than good. Our thesis is that the Jonah complex is universal and applicable to *both* men and women. True, it creeps up under different shapes and forms according to individual particularities. The apprehension here is of being ostracized, "killed," so to speak. Such is the fundamental fear because it portrays the universal dread of being alone and of confronting death (see below).

True, for most people change is frightening. For most, change is scary even if it means a better and happier life. To change one's view of oneself requires the leaving behind of old habits and images of ourselves. There is indeed *safety* in the predictable, even if it means predictable pain and suffering.[17] Knowledge and responsibility go hand in hand. Many people wish not to know their inner worlds because it would imply the possible discovery of unpleasant truths about themselves. To know means to own; and to own means to be responsible for such knowledge. In the words of Maslow:

> We tend to be afraid of any knowledge that could cause us to despise ourselves or to make us feel inferior, weak, worth-

less, evil, shameful. We protect ourselves and our ideal image of ourselves by repression and similar defenses, which are essentially techniques by which we avoid becoming conscious of unpleasant or dangerous truths.[18]

The more impersonal the knowledge, Maslow continues, the safer it is to learn it and contain it within the self. On the other hand, the more personal it becomes, that is, the more it pertains to our inner world, the more suspicious and ambivalent we tend to be.

As Bruno Bettelheim testifies, this ambivalence about change can already be detected in many children. It often appears as a fear of learning new things, that is, as a fear of knowledge.[19] He gives the example of a girl not learning biology because heredity is part of the subject matter. She refused to learn about the origin of life because it reminded her of how poorly her own had started. She had been abandoned by her mother and adopted by nonempathic substitute parents who never gave her a true sense of belonging or of being wanted. The wish to fail in school and also later in life, according to Bettelheim, is a protective device against facing more disturbing knowledge about the self. Indeed, the suppression of dangerous knowledge, of something *already known* to the self, serves the purpose of maintaining some sense of self-esteem and, literally, of keeping oneself unfragmented. As Maslow says:

Each step forward is a step into the unfamiliar and possibly dangerous. It also means giving up something familiar and good and satisfying. . . . It also often means giving up a simpler and easier and less effortful life, in exchange for a more demanding, more responsible, more difficult life.[20]

The temptation to run away from responsibility, pain, and loneliness has been widely acknowledged in psychotherapeutic literature.[21] Jung, in fact, calls this pathological wish to regress to a womblike state the "Jonah-and-the-Whale complex."[22] Social sciences, philosophy, psychology, and theology have shown that our fear of changes is the result of our attachment to old customs and attitudes.[23]

Frank Manual, a colleague and friend of Maslow, was the first to label this resistance to growth and authenticity the "Jonah syndrome." It is to Maslow himself, however, that we owe credit for elaborating upon this existential phenomenon in his attempt to integrate it within the framework of a theory of healthy growth and motivation. He first called this defense mechanism "fear of standing alone," "fear of one's greatness," "evasion of one's destiny," or "fear of knowledge" until he adopted Manual's term.

What precisely is the Jonah syndrome? Maslow writes:

> It is a falling short of what one could have been, and even one could say, of what one should have been. . . . We all have unused potentialities or not fully developed ones. . . . We enjoy and even thrill to the godlike possibilities we see in ourselves in such peak moments. And yet we simultaneously shiver with weakness, awe and fear before these very same possibilities. I have found it easy to demonstrate [the Jonah syndrome] to my students simply by asking . . . "Who aspires to be a saint, like Schweitzer, perhaps? Who among you will be a great leader?" Generally everybody starts giggling, blushing and squirming until I ask, "If not you, then who else?"[24]

It is interesting to note that both Maslow and Manual have wavered in their use of the expression "Jonah syndrome" or "Jonah complex" without ever defining either term. In fact, to our knowledge, neither scholar studied the biblical book of Jonah prior to introducing his concept. For example, Maslow's paper, "Neurosis as a Failure of Personal Growth," which first introduced the "Jonah syndrome," was published in 1967, but when it appeared in *The Farther Reaches of Human Nature* (1971), the "Jonah syndrome" had become the "Jonah complex" without an explanation of the switch in terms.[25] "Jonah complex" is to be preferred to "Jonah syndrome" because the latter would indicate sheer accidentalness and circumstantiality. The Jonah narrative, then, would be relevant only for some very specific, even unusual, occasions. A "Jonah syndrome," as the term is used in psychiatry and psychology, would represent a rare phenomenon (like Freud's success neurosis erupting in only a few nonrepresentative individuals). We must therefore go beyond Maslow's vision. The Jonah complex is universal. It affects us all, as we shall now argue.

One of the fundamental differences between Maslow's concept and ours lies in the context against which evasion from growth is interpreted. It can, of course, be viewed from a solipsistic point of reference, which interprets "happiness," "success," "meaning," and so forth solely in terms of the individual's private standards (or we could say in terms of a Voice from Within, thus formally imitating the "Inner Master" of St. Augustine). But another standpoint is possible for which the ambivalence toward one's greatness is the endeavor to reject the sublime (the Outer Voice, God).

The Jonah complex, as we see it, is a rejection of our Godlike potentialities (e.g., our unique capacity for concern—as Heidegger says[26]—charity, and empathy). Like Moses (Exod. 4:13) and Jeremiah (Jer. 1), for example, we dread not having enough strength within ourselves to sustain the ethical demands of the Outer Voice. Indeed, to be concerned and feel responsible for others' welfare requires such an enormous amount of energy and compassion that seldom do we find anyone willing to make this existential leap. To do so, individuals must overcome the narcissistic preoccupations that bind them to solipsism. If we call the Jonah complex that human resistance to the Call, then the notion is applicable to everyone; it is universal. The Jonah complex means that, for all and always, there is a congenital fear of one's humanness and of one's vocation to universality.[27]

Now, one must admit that, thus far, the fear of success has been interpreted in the psychological literature basically as a neurosis present in a few nonrepresentative individuals. It is thus hard to feel implicated in such a clinical curiosity. But this conception is too narrow. The fear of knowledge—as Socrates well understood—or the fear of responsibility, or of change, is a universal phenomenon. If therefore we decide to call "patients" those suffering from such fears, we must add that the doctor is no less "contaminated." In other words, if we want to go further in our research, we must be sensitive to the question of value. The fear of what success are we speaking about? Is there, for instance, a true success that we should not fear? We must proceed to define success.

Obviously, for a four-year-old girl practicing riding a bicycle, success means to keep her balance. Hitler, as is well known, had a quite different definition in mind. While we can infer that in both cases there coexist simultaneously the desire to succeed and the fear to succeed, it would be, all the same, unjustified to disregard the intrinsic value of each object of desire and fear. If we take the fear of failure, shall we say that we are to treat Mother Teresa's anxieties, insomnia, depressions, on a par with Hitler's? At the center of the problem there is in both persons of our example a consciousness of our finitude and death, but its nature is wholly other, whether one speaks of the Sister or of the Führer. This remained apparently undetected by Maslow in his study of self-actualizing persons.[28] Emphasizing personal feeling as a criterion for values borders upon hedonism. We need to take into account the ethical grounds without which there is no mental health.

Conversely, psychotherapeutic treatments and self-analysis methods are no guarantee for having success in life. In any case, to put aside the question of ethical values amounts to using a "selective inattention," in the terms of Harry Stack Sullivan. One claims "to say everything," but the truth of the matter is that one says that which flatters the ego, even when the confession is painful. Hidden is the Judge. People beat their breast because they slept on the ship to Tarshish, but they leave unmentioned their vocation to go to Nineveh. They have decided—with what relief—that this does not belong to psychology, hence not to their deep self.

True success—if one insists on using that inappropriate term to designate the goal of life—is living an ethical life, a life filled with reverence and respect for all. "Having such a task makes the person irreplaceable and gives his life the value of uniqueness," says Frankl.[29] By contrast with those who fear success for *neurotic* reasons, there are persons shunning it for healthy, deserving motives. They are beings-for-the-world, like Mother Teresa, Martin Luther King, Jr., Gandhi, Albert Schweitzer. Here, fear or guilt feeling is produced by the consciousness of unworthiness before the universal call of God to love all that lives as related to our own life.

For many years Albert Schweitzer searched for a heuristic term expressing clearly the true meaning of success and life's purpose.[30] On a boat trip to N'Gomo where he was needed for medical services, 120 miles upstream from Lambaréné, Schweitzer decided that he would devote the entire trip to the problem "of how a culture could be brought into being that possessed a greater moral depth and energy than the one we lived in."[31] Page after page was filled with disconnected sentences seemingly getting nowhere. But on the third day he had an insight and the expression "reverence for life" came to his mind, a phrase that to his knowledge he had never heard before or read about. He gave the following definition:

> The great fault of all ethics hitherto has been that they believed themselves to have to deal with the relations of man to man. In reality, however, the question is what is his attitude to the world and all life that comes within his reach. A man is ethical only when life as such, is sacred to him, that of plants and animals as that of his fellow men, and when he devotes himself helpfully to all life that is in need of help. . . . Only by means of reverence for life can we establish a spiritual and humane relationship with both people and living creatures within our reach. . . . Through reverence for life, we become, in effect, *different persons* [i.e., beings-for-the world].[32]

"Success" now has acquired a different meaning. For Schweitzer, success has much less to do with one's paycheck or sense of well-being than it does with responding to the call to become beings-for-the-world. The outcome of such conscientization is what is here called the Jonah complex, namely a withdrawal before the divine that is, as we saw, another form of the fear of losing self-esteem and inner peace. Clearly, this ethical lifestyle does not protect anyone from pain and suffering. For the likes of Mother Teresa of Calcutta, Martin Luther King, Jr., Gandhi, and Albert Schweitzer, psychic pains and scars are present, indeed, are part of their daily experiences. They are not spared loneliness, emptiness, hopelessness. However, we suspect that what allows these modern saints to tolerate, perhaps even appreciate, their ordeals and sufferings is the conviction that there are no higher or richer spiritual meanings that can be detected in life than those found in the daily struggle to become beings-for-the-world. There is nothing more life-sustaining than having an ultimate purpose that transcends despair and emptiness into hope and meaning.

The problem therefore is not whether some have a vocation like Jonah, while some do not; the problem is for all men and women to fulfill their humanness.[33] Evasion of growth and pathological conformity, then, is counteracted by an ongoing *process* choosing to go *beyond* ourselves, beyond our potentialities precisely, and to be "attuned" to transcendence. Then do we discover the key to the meaning and purposefulness of life. It is an existential awareness that accentuates awe, wonder, and sacredness as primary foci for one's perceptions and beliefs, while not negating the wisdom of the biological. The latter, however, is not left to its dictates; it is put under the control of superior imperatives which at times may demand the subjugation of our natural desires and aspirations. This context of listening to the Outer Voice shifts one's fascination with oneself to a level of full humanness and respect for life. "The highest knowledge," Schweitzer once said, "is to know that we are surrounded by mystery."[34] And Albert Einstein echoes the Alsatian doctor: "The most beautiful emotion we can experience is the mystical. It is the sower of all true art and science. He to whom this emotion is a stranger, who can no longer wonder and stand rapt in awe, is as good as dead."[35]

Why do most people opt to listen to the Voice from Within and live in a state often referred to as one of a "spiritual lobotomy"?[36] Here Frank Haronian's thinking becomes particularly helpful. He defines the sublime as the realm in which men and women discover their feelings of brotherhood and sisterhood and their wish to get involved, with the direct intent of contributing to others' welfare.[37] Within that context, the Jonah complex is *repression of the sublime.* As that dedication "to the World" constitutes the highest human risk possible, it is understandable that Jonah's flight is also escape from death. To that point we now turn.

Above, we have equated the Jonah complex with the resistance to the pressing invitation or commandment of the Outer Voice. At least theoretically such reflection is puzzling. Those trained to carry "the yoke of the Torah" consider as evident that one must "choose life in order to live" (Deut. 30). The Outer Voice is to them closer than the Inner Voice. The reason for the suppression of the Outer Voice is well put by two modern thinkers:

> ... the more one is conscious of one's positive impulses, of one's urges toward the sublime, the more shame one feels for one's failure to give expression to these impulses. There ensues a painful burning of the conscience, a sense of guilt at not being what one could be, of not doing what one could do.[38]
>
> We fear the sublime because it is unknown and because if we admit the reality of higher values, we are committed to act in a more noble way.[39]

But, if it is not always true that "crime does not pay," certainly "to act in a noble way" shall remain without reward. Now, psychology insists upon the necessity of "reinforcement," that is, of a compensation system, if one expects a positive attitude from people. It is a golden rule in pedagogy. He who chooses to do good without expectation of being paid in return has therefore reached an unusually high degree of maturity. It is a supreme act of humanness, upon which Jewish Hasidism insists. "Lest a grain of wheat dies," says Jesus. But not everyone is Jesus Christ. At any rate, Jonah thinks twice before going to Nineveh. Who will be the first to throw a stone at him?

Death has nothing romantic about it. It is humanity's curse par excellence; it has a character of aggression that, common as it is, is however, the irruption of the unexpected. Death is not only the mark of our finitude; it is also the absolute negation of all meaning, the antilife, the antibeing. Sartre is right: it is always, and even in the best of cases, an accident—an accident that befalls kings as well as slaves. It is *derekh 'eretz*, the way of the earth (of all people), says Joshua 23:14, the terrible leveler that joins in the same embrace the righteous and the wicked, the murderer and the innocent. To fear such a gruesome monster is only natural. It does not mean that the fear of death is simple, however. In fact, it is extremely complex. Fear of death is also "life fear," fear

of loneliness and individuality.[40] It causes one to look for refuge
in pathological conformity and prompts Jonah to get lost in the
anonymity of the crowd en route to Tarshish. Thus, by "disap-
pearing" in the mass, the hope is to escape loneliness and the
awareness of death. People are often willing to sacrifice everything, including their own potentialities and humanness, to avoid
being singled out by the "eyes" of death. All this means that
death as much as life must be interpreted. It must be ferreted out
from its anonymity of blind fate.

Like life itself, death is no geometrical point at the end of a
line. It is a reality we carry with us all our lives. I live with my
death and my death is always present to me—so present that it is
even more intimate with me than a foreign body in my flesh, like
a stone in my kidney, a bullet in my leg; for I am pregnant with
my worst enemy, my death is me. In other words, I shape my
death as I shape my life. In consequence, death need not be negative; it can be made positive! The enemy can be made a friend.
Death is dialectical. It is not always where one expects it. *Tanhu-
mah b. Berakbot* 28b says: "the righteous even after their death may
be called living, whereas the wicked, both in life and in death may
be called dead." In the process of its transcendence, death has
changed its nature. As Reuven Bulka writes, "death makes life
meaningful," for "man would not be faced with an imperative to
act and accomplish if his life were endless. That his existence may be
terminated suddenly is a reality which forces, or should force, man
to utilize his allotted moments as meaningfully as possible."[41]

To live with the awareness that we are mortals transforms
our perception of the world. Everything is interpreted under a
new light, within a new context. Ultimately, in the very affirmation of the self lies the acceptance, even the appreciation, of one's
own death. Race, money, power, social status, education mean
very little. They do not redeem our lives.

Empathy—toward one another but also toward ourselves—is
asked of us because we all die. One aspect of the Jonah complex
is the refusal to accept that death binds us all into a human family. Death, our finitude, when brought to the level of consciousness, paradoxically provides a vantage point *sub specie aeternitatis.*
It puts things in perspective. It especially gives the philosopher or

the prophet a sense of compassion for those "humiliated and offended" by a life that is "a dying" from its start. Existence and its finitude cannot be stretched one inch beyond its "horizontal" span, but it can, indeed it must, be *fulfilled* "vertically." It has been stressed here all along that we live fully to the extent that we devote our lives to a vocation that is beyond our self-centered interests and accentuates the respect, protection, and enhancement of all that lives. One must start with oneself, but not end with oneself. "Sin," Paul Tillich once said, "is the turning towards ourselves, and making ourselves the center of our world."[42] Life is a loan that must be returned through death. Its ultimate meaning, therefore, lies in the response to this reality.[43]

Contrary to overoptimistic conceptions, it is to be emphasized that one, rather, listens to one's desires and libido, thus denying the uniqueness and dedication to a cause that would transcend one's animality and raise one to the level of humanness. By choosing a solipsistic context, one lives in a world where myth supersedes history, and where rites are substitutes for existential involvement. In this way it is again demonstrated that the human is H*omo religiosus*, as the person chooses magic and superstition. Thus Fromm may call neurosis a private form of religion. Religiosity indeed is in itself deprived of positive or negative sign. It is neutral as it applies to any kind of conviction, whether egotistic or altruistic, or even neurotic. Whatever meaning of life one opts for, one is always religious. The issue, therefore, is not whether one is or is not religious, but *how* one interprets one's religiosity. Even atheism is, according to Ricoeur, "a post-religious faith, a faith in a post-religious age."[44]

True, Eliade offers a more optimistic definition of the term "religious." Indeed, the historian of religions pinpoints its most respectable aspect. *Homo religiosus,* he says, is the one who believes in the sacred because such is the absolute reality of life; the sacred "transcends this world but manifests itself in this world, thereby sanctifying it and making it real. He *[Homo religiosus]* further believes that life has a sacred origin and that human existence realizes all of its potentialities in proportion as it is religious—that is, participates in reality."[45]

Clearly, such a definition is acceptable. It must, however, be complemented with the commitment unto God of which religiosity is only a premise. Ricoeur has this insightful statement:

> This is the first stage, the first level of thought that starts from symbols. But one cannot rest here; for the question of truth has not yet been posed. If a phenomenologist should give the name truth to internal coherence, to the systematization of the world of symbols, it is a truth without belief, truth at a distance, a reduced truth. From such truth this question has been eliminated: Do I myself believe that? What do I personally make of these symbolic meanings? Now this question cannot be raised as long as one remains at the level of comparativism, passing from one symbol to another without taking a stand. This stage can only be a stage, the stage of an understanding that is horizontal and panoramic, curious but not concerned. We now have to enter into a relationship with symbols that is emotionally intense and at the same time critical. To do so I must leave the comparativist point of view aside; I must follow the exegete and become implicated in the life of one symbol, one myth.[46]

The book of Jonah teaches that we are called to give unique responses to life's unique demands. There is only one answer per situation, the one that chooses "good and not evil, life and not death" (see Deut. 30). This response can be defined as a decision made in total honesty, integrity, and freedom. This positive option, we must add, is always against the background of the commitment to enhance the human condition. Such ethical choice is always through listening to the Voice from Without. For the principles of pleasure and of displeasure are not adequate arguments for or against the advisability of any decision or action. They are not within our grasp but exist only as side-effects of performing a meaningful task. To this also the book of Jonah testifies. At no point does the principle of happiness for the Ninevites come into consideration. Neither is Jonah to be content, nor are the inhabitants of Nineveh to "feel good" about themselves. Quite the contrary, Jonah must go whither he does not want to go, and he must accept the reality of Nineveh's pardon while he would rather see the city razed to the ground. Similarly, the Ninevites must not silence their guilt feelings and "autosuggest" to themselves that everything is for the best in the best possible world. They have to repent and to be forgiven.

All narcissism has subsided. The inner voice of a deceiving conscience (cf. Freud's exercise of suspicion) has been superseded by another Voice, which is not deceitful because it does not flatter, but does order and thus does respect our human responsibility; Jonah and the Ninevites hear the Voice from Without. The latter repent and are forgiven; the former—so we are left to believe—renounces his religious or theological constructions and allows God to be God.

NOTES

1. H. Harlow, *Learning to Love* (San Francisco: Albion Publishing Co., 1971), p. 98.

2. J. M. Darley, and E. Berscheid, "Increased Liking as a Result of the Anticipation of Personal Contact," *Human Relations* 20 (1967): 29–40. See also by the same authors, *Interpersonal Attraction* (New York: Addison-Wesley Publishing Co., 1978). See also T. W. Adorno, et al., *The Authoritarian Personality* (New York: Harper & Row, 1950); S. E. Asch, "Studies in Independence and Conformity: A Minority of One against Unanimous Majority," *Psychological Monograph* 70 (1956): whole #416; S. Milgram, *Obedience to Authority* (New York: Harper & Row, 1974); and S. Schachter, "Deviation, Rejection and Communication," *Journal of Abnormal and Social Psychology* 46 (1951): 190–207.

3. E. Fromm, *Escape from Freedom* (New York: Holt, Rinehart & Winston, 1941), p. 254.

4. R. May, "Modern Man's Image of Himself," *Chicago Theological Seminary Register* 52 (1962): 1–11; and "Existential Psychology and Human Freedom," *Chicago Theological Seminary Register* 52 (1962): 11–19.

5. R. May, *Man's Search for Himself* (New York: W. W. Norton, 1953), p. 55.

6. These expressions are May's, *Man's Search for Himself*, pp. 58, 88.

7. This term is coined by Fromm, *Escape from Freedom*, p. 205. See also D. W. Winnicott, "Ego Distortions in Terms of True and False Self" (1960), in Winnicott's *The Maturational Processes and the Facilitating Environment* (London: Hogarth Press, 1965), pp. 140–52.

8. Fromm, *Escape from Freedom*, p. 186.

9. The term "desacralization" was used by Mircea Eliade. He defines it as a refusal to detect awe, mystery, and the sublime in life. Maslow also has used the term to define neurotic behavior. Cf. Eliade, *The Sacred and the Profane* (New York: Harper & Row, 1961); see also Maslow's *The Psychology of Science* (Chicago: Henry

Regnery Co., 1966), esp. his chap. 14, "The Desacralization and the Resacralization of Science," pp. 138–53.

10. S. Freud, "Some Character-Types Met with in Psychoanalytic Work" (1915), in chap. 18 of his *Collected Papers* (New York: Basic Books, 1959), pp. 318–44.

11. Ibid., pp. 324, 325ff. For Melanie Klein, it is the fantasy *itself* that first promotes the anxiety. And this, regardless of whether it becomes reality or not. See esp. her paper, "Love, Guilt and Reparation," in M. Klein and J. Riviere, *Love, Hate, and Reparation* (1937; New York: W. W. Norton, 1964), pp. 57–119. Years later, Freud softened his stand on the relationship between fantasy and anxiety and held that indeed fantasies *alone* without their materialization in reality can themselves provoke disturbing emotional responses. See Freud's *Civilization and Its Discontents* (1930; W. W. Norton, 1961), p. 84.

12. Freud, "Some Character Types," p. 325, gives also the example of a university professor who for many years had longed one day to succeed his mentor and head of department. When the wish actually became a reality, as his mentor retired and his colleagues elected him in his stead, he fell into so deep a depression that it apparently took many years to overcome it.

13. O. Fenichel, *The Psychoanalytic Theory of Neurosis* (New York: W. W. Norton, 1945), p. 457. Fenichel has also a concept called "The Don Juan of Achievement" (pp. 502ff.) to explain why some people are not able to satiate their self-esteem through success. They go compulsively from success to success, never satisfied and always wanting more than previously achieved. Another opinion, shared by many, is the one given by Karen Horney. She explains that the "fear of success results from the fear of the begrudging envy of others and thus the loss of their affection. . . . The fear may appear also as a mere vague apprehension that one would lose friends if one were to have any success" (K. Horney, *The Neurotic Personality of Our Time* [New York: W. W. Norton, 1964], p. 214; see esp. chap. 12, "Recoiling from Competition," pp. 207–29).

In prescientific times, it is clear that the ambivalence toward success was also a known phenomenon. The Greeks expressed their view that the gods were always *jealous* of human success and happiness because these belong to the gods only. Too much success attracts supernatural dangers, think the primitives. Herodotus sees throughout history divine *phthonos* ("jealousy"). Only the nonsignificant, unpretentious person is safe (see Euripides, *Medeus*, 122–30). In a desacralized world, the eyes of "others" have replaced those of the gods.

14. Quoted by L. Tec, *The Fear of Success* (New York: Reader's Digest Press, 1976), p. 162.

15. M. S. Horner, "The Motive to Avoid Success and Changing Aspirations in College Women," in J. Bardwick, ed., *Readings on the Psychology of Women* (New York: Harper & Row, 1972), pp. 62–68; and "Toward an Understanding of Achievement-Related Conflicts in Women," *Journal of Social Issues* 28 (1972): 157–75.

16. Along these lines, Colette Dowling speaks of "the Cinderella complex" to describe the wish many women have to avoid taking charge of their lives by allowing men or "society" to dictate what they should think, do, or feel. Focusing exclusively on men, Dan Kiley speaks of the Peter Pan syndrome to describe those adult males displaying a refusal to "grow up" similar to J. M. Barrie's hero, Peter Pan. See C. Dowling, *The Cinderella Complex: Women's Hidden Fear of Independence* (New York: Pocket Books, 1981), esp. chap. 6, "Gender Panic," pp. 169–210. See also Helen Deutsch's contribution in *The Psychology of Women* (New York: Grune &

Stratton, 1944), and D. Kiley, *The Peter Pan Syndrome: Men Who Have Never Grown Up* (New York: Dodd, Mead & Co., 1983). Leon Tec also refers to the Peter Pan syndrome with similar connotations to Kiley's in his *Fear of Success* but does not elaborate much on his concept. For a psychological study of Peter Pan, see M. Karpe, "The Origin of Peter Pan," *Psychoanalytic Review* 43 (1956): 104–10; and F. Meisel, "The Myth of Peter Pan," *Psychoanalytic Study of the Child* 32 (1977): 545–63.

17. Such reluctance to change is even more pronounced among the psychotics. Ever since childhood many patients have had pressures exerted upon them not to change, not to try to individuate and separate from the parents lest they be abandoned and rejected. The psychotics, especially the schizophrenics, often equate individuation with a killing of sorts because the parents, directly or indirectly, have intimated that they would "die," that is, become insane. Because fathers are often, for one reason or another, out of the parenting picture (psychically and/or emotionally), it is the mothers who usually seem to exert such pressures not to wish change. These mothers often spare themselves a fullblown psychosis by setting up family relationships in which autonomous behaviors are neither allowed nor reinforced.

See M. Mahler, *On Human Symbiosis and the Vicissitudes of Individuation* (New York: International Universities Press, 1968); J. Masterson and D. Rinsley, "The Borderline Syndrome: The Role of the Mother in the Genesis and Psychic Structure of the Borderline Personality," *International Journal of Psychoanalysis* 56 (1975): 163–78; and Harold Searles, "Anxiety Concerning Change as Seen in Psychotherapy of Schizophrenic Patients—With Particular Reference to the Sense of Personal Identity" (1961), in Searles, *Collected Papers on Schizophrenia and Related Subjects* (New York: International Universities Press, 1965), pp. 443–64.

18. Maslow, *Toward a Psychology of Being* (Princeton: D. Van Nostrand, 1968), p. 60.

19. B. Bettelheim, *Love is Not Enough* (New York: Avon Books, 1950), esp. chap. 6, "The Challenge of Learning," pp. 146–83; and "The Decision to Fail," in Bettelheim, *Surviving* (New York: Vintage Books, 1960), pp. 142–68; and Bettelheim with K. Zelan, *Learning to Read* (New York: Alfred A. Knopf, 1982).

20. Maslow, *Toward a Psychology of Being*, p. 204.

21. See S. H. Cohen, "A Growth Theory of Neurotic Resistance to Therapy," *Journal of Humanistic Psychology* 1 (Spring 1961): 48–63; Frankl, *The Doctor and the Soul* (New York: Knopf, 1955), p. 67; and May, *Man's Search for Himself*, p. 250.

22. Jung, *Symbols of Transformation* (New York: Pantheon Books, 1967), p. 419. See also Roberto Assagioli, *The Act of Will* (Baltimore: Penguin Books, 1973), pp. 112–13. The courage to be alone has been widely acknowledged in psychotherapeutic literature as being an important aspect of mental health. May, for instance, in *Man's Search for Himself*, p. 121, speaks of the need for "cutting the psychological umbilical cord," while Jung, in *Symbols of Transformation*, p. 348, refers to the "battle of deliverance from the maternal grip." What both imply is that to reach maturity one must be able to get rid of morbid dependency ties that bind the person to significant others, e.g., parents.

23. On this, see n. 24, below.

24. Maslow, "Neurosis as a Failure of Personal Growth," *Humanitas* 3 (1967): 153–69, quotation from pp. 161, 163. Among Maslow's best contributions on the fear of knowledge is his paper "The Need to Know and the Fear of Knowing," *Toward a Psychology of Being*, pp. 60–71.

25. E.g., see Maslow, *The Farther Reaches of Human Nature* (New York: Penguin Books, 1971). See also *The Healthy Personality*, Maslow in collaboration with H. M. Chiang (New York: Van Nostrand Reinhold Co., 1969), esp. pp. 39, 46.

26. For Martin Heidegger, to be sure, the voice of conscience is not God's, nor is it an "outer voice." True, conscience, when authentic, speaks as a stranger, because we "fell" into a world of routine. But there is a more fundamental characteristic of the being-in-the-world that Heidegger calls *Sorge* ("care"). Through care human beings transcend themselves. Conscience makes me *responsible*. It is the "authentic I" that speaks to the "inauthentic I," as much to call it to responsibility as to declare it guilty. We are close to the Pauline *syneidesis* concerning the heathens (see Rom. 2:15). But Heidegger differs from St. Paul in that, for the former, a judging conscience and a judged conscience are one and the same. It is a doubling of the same, from me to myself. The "me" that acknowledges my own culpability is also the guilty "me"! Heidegger, however, defines guilt as a fact of nature, as a *"mal d'être."* Not being God's voice, conscience has no transcendent vocation. Heidegger regrets the options discarded by human choice, so that humans are never but a small aspect of what they could be.

The thesis we defend here is that Jonah, to become Jonah, has only one choice that authenticates him; it is the choice to go to Nineveh. True, opting not to go there is one of his privileges, but then he does not become fully Jonah. Franz Kafka understood that well. To recall, at the end of *The Trial* Joseph K. hears the chaplain's parable of the numerous doors giving access to "the law." But only *one* door is ascribed to each and every one. Moreover, that door is open before him or her, although it seems shut, as, for Jonah, is the road to Nineveh. In short, we feel closer to Martin Buber's interpretation according to which the voice of *my* conscience is nothing but the echo of the other's (and the Other's) voice. Guilt here is not human finitude, but self-centeredness. The "voice" says "Where are you?" (Gen. 3:9; Job 38:4; and Gen. 4:9), and human response includes dependence before the one who has been flouted and whose gifts have been squandered.

27. Though this point has not been emphasized yet, there are, of course, other Old Testament prophets whose names could be used to label the complex to which we refer here. Besides Jeremiah and Moses fearing God's commands, the reader will also remember similar reactions in Isaiah and Ezekiel, among others. Abraham Heschel speaks of the "Abraham complex" with similar connotations, but he does not elaborate. See *The Insecurity of Freedom* (New York: Farrar, Straus & Giroux, 1966).

28. See P.-E. Lacocque, "On the Search for Meaning," *Journal of Religion and Health* 21 (1982): 219–27.

29. Frankl, *The Doctor and the Soul* (New York: Alfred A. Knopf, 1955), p. 62.

30. See Schweitzer, *Out of My Life and Thought* (New York: Henry Holt & Co., 1933); and "The Ethics of Reverence of Life," *Christendom* 1 (1936): 225–39.

31. Schweitzer, *Reverence for Life* (New York: Philosophical Library, 1965), p. 56.

32. Schweitzer, *Albert Schweitzer: An Anthology*, ed. C. R. Joy (New York: Harper & Row, 1947), pp. 271–72.

33. See n. 28, above.

34. *The Wit and Wisdom of Albert Schweitzer*, ed. C. R. Joy (Boston: Beacon Press, 1949), p. 66.

35. Quoted in H. Meserve, "Nobody Here but Us Humanists," *Journal of Religion and Health* 21 (Fall 1982): 179–83, quotation from p. 182.

36. This expression is Assagioli's (see "The Synthetic Vision: A Conversation

with Roberto Assagioli," in *Voices and Visions,* ed. Sam Keen [New York: Harper & Row, 1974], p. 214).

37. Frank Haronian, "Repression of the Sublime," in *The Proper Study of Man* (New York: Macmillan, 1971), pp. 239–46.

38. Ibid., p. 245. Otto Fenichel explains that "repression is never performed once and for all but requires a constant expenditure of energy to maintain the repression, while the repressed constantly tries to find an outlet" (see *The Psychoanalytic Theory of Neurosis,* p. 150).

39. Assagioli, "The Synthetic Vision," p. 214.

40. See, e.g., Otto Rank, *Will Therapy and Truth and Reality* (1936; New York: Alfred A. Knopf, 1964), p. 124; and Yalom, *Existential Psychotherapy* (New York: Basic Books, 1980).

41. Reuven Bulka, "Death-in-Life—Talmudic and Logotherapeutic Affirmations," *Humanitas* 10 (February 1974): 33–43. In his interpretation of what characterizes a mentally healthy (i.e., a self-actualizing) individual, Maslow gave no great import to death awareness as incentive for living life more fully with added purpose and meaning. See Maslow, "Self-Actualizing People: A Study of Psychological Health," in *Motivation and Personality* (New York: Harper & Row, 1970), pp. 149, 180; Maslow, *Toward a Psychology of Being* and *The Farther Reaches of Human Nature;* and also Maslow with H.-M. Chiang, *The Healthy Personality.*

42. Paul Tillich, *The Eternal Now* (New York: Charles Scribner's Sons, 1963), p. 56. See also Buber on "Existential and Ontic Guilt," in his "Guilt and Guilt Feelings," *Psychiatry* 20 (May 1957): 114–29.

43. See P.-E. Lacocque, "On the Search for Meaning."

44. Paul Ricoeur, *The Symbolism of Evil* (New York: Harper & Row, 1967), pp. 247–48.

45. Eliade, *Le Sacré et le Profane* (Paris: NRF, 1965), p. 171; quotation from *The Sacred and the Profane* (New York: Harper & Row, 1961), p. 202.

46. Ricoeur, *The Conflict of Interpretations,* ed. D. Ihde (Evanston, Ill.: Northwestern University Press, 1974), p. 441.

CONCLUSION

At the end of this study of Jonah, the prophet and the "complex," it may be useful to look back to the ground covered and to embrace in one glance the whole countryside. The book of Jonah is a folktale and must be read as such. Oral versions of the narrative may have existed and may have been used by the biblical author for his own purpose. But in the third century B.C.E., the version given by the author of the book appears particularly fit as a polemical response to the isolationism of a powerful religious party among the returnees from Babylon in Jerusalem. Consequently, what had perhaps been an entertaining story seasoned all along with humor and irony became a satire in which irony is not absent, but whose bearing is all but for public amusement. It is a parable, a "world-subverting" tale meant to provide a merciless mirror for an awry and solipsistic attitude in life that deliberately ignored the fate of non-Jews.

To reach his goal, the author does not render his task facile. He has a profound understanding of the rationales behind his opponents' refusal to "go to Nineveh." It is the grandeur of his book that the "missionary" is no naïve ignoramus or a reluctantly acting petty bourgeois, nor are the "others" just "savages" ready for the proclamation of the gospel. The latter are symbolized by Ninevites, that is, by arch-enemies and torturers of Israel. In other words, the "prophet" Jonah has all the reasons not to bother with a nest of vipers from whose bites his people suffered so much. Until the end of the story, the reader is left with the most uneasy feeling that perhaps Jonah has been right from the first, and God's obstinacy in sending his Jew to Nineveh has been from the first wrong. There is a time when the greatest justice and the profoundest mercy in principle become outrageous injustice.

Such is the framework for a reflection that the author pursues without complacency. Is there any reason why God would call an unimportant man such as Jonah for such an unparalleled, important mission? What is exactly the message he is supposed to transmit? Does it accommodate nuances? Do we know the parameters within which God's call is uttered? Is there any law regulating the alternation of judgment and pardon in God? Is the divine promise to Jeremiah and Ezekiel to break the chain of determinism between generations also valid for others besides Israel? Are non-Jews also capable of repentance? Are foreigners susceptible to the word of the living God? Would such an opening of pagan hearts to Israel's God have an adverse bearing on the contrasting procrastination of the Jerusalemites? Under what conditions can a prophetic oracle remain unfulfilled and still be authentically commissioned by God?

This last question was especially relevant in the postexilic community of Jerusalem, agonizing about the nonfulfillment of solemn prophecies concerning the advent of eschatological conditions with the restoration. The author imagines a situation of nonaccomplishment of a prophecy of destruction to a pagan nation (instead of a promise of eschatological blossoming to the holy people). This seemingly only reverses the terms of the Jerusalem problem. The author even seems to elude the problem, when in fact he tackles it by indirection. Nineveh is the antipode of Jerusalem; its impending destruction is the very counterpart of the expected glory of Zion. Could it be, at the opposite, that its repentance, bringing about divine forgiveness, is a foil for the arrogance of some in Jerusalem bringing about divine punishment in the form of nonfulfillment of prophecies? As for Nineveh, the lack of accomplishment spells out salvation, and it is initiated by its repentance; but as far as Jerusalem is concerned, the sparing of Nineveh spells doom, and it is wrought by the callous solipsism of a complacent establishment. Perhaps one would wish for the reversal of the situation, that is, for the glorification of Zion and the "overthrow" of Nineveh, but the book of Jonah indicates that this cannot be accomplished by a simple algebraic operation (cf. Jon. 4:10–11). For if the revocation of God's decision regarding Nineveh resulted from the repentance of the whole population, it is implied that the realization of prophetic promises regarding Zion will require a profound transformation of the situation in Jerusalem.

CONCLUSION

Clearly, this theological kerygma could have been presented in another form by the author of Jonah. But he chose to be a "singer of tales," using the genre of the Menippean satire, and this should be taken with the utmost seriousness. If the "content" is decisive for the "form," as a river opens up its own bed, the "form" reflects upon the content and is instrumental in restricting or enlarging its sway. No literary genre is more encompassing than the narrative. Even when it conveys a very focused message—as is the case of Jonah—narrative makes the message immediately universal because it is presented as a human experience mirroring innumerable similar experiences. In other words, the story renders paradigmatic a situation or an event that otherwise could appear as isolated in time and limited in scope. Furthermore, when the narrative happens to be a satire, its universality is compounded by a corrosive action of its own. It is so for the ridiculed institution and, by extension, for all institutions. It attacks a specific form of conformism, but by the same token, all conformism is scorned. It is ambivalent also for the readers. The latter instinctively place themselves in the camp of the critics, but soon they discover that they also might be *alazons* under the sting of the *eiron*. It is especially true when the weakness mocked is no idiosyncrasy of an isolated individual or group, but a human universal complex.

The story of Jonah is not only a religious manifesto; it is also a psychological tableau of the human condition. Jonah is not just a Jew of Palestine called out of his anonymity by a commissioning Voice from Without. He is human, he is everyone. The theological beam focuses on a specific and known prophet (2 Kings 14:25) with a specific and unique task: to preach the destruction of Nineveh. But the psychological pencil of rays reveals very human characteristics, and stirs up within us what Ricoeur calls the process of suspicion vis-à-vis ourselves. Jonah, *qua* human, exemplifies our call to task. He is also a paradigm of our resistance to God's election, for nothing is more repulsive to us than to be designated (elected, chosen) by the Outer Voice for a self-transcending task, when we would rather follow our inner voice and our biological dictates ("what feels good") for our self-satisfaction and our self-aggrandizement.

CONCLUSION

This universal resistance to a vocation that breaks our solipsism and thus provides with a sense of responsibility the authentic liberty, we call "the Jonah complex." This is an anthropological pronouncement. What it implies is that always and everywhere the human is "distinguished" by the Outer Voice for a task of communication. The very meaning of life is the love of others for their own sake, in their own right, even if they are "Ninevites." That is why such a love transcends *eros* and is antiheroic (which is narcissistic); it is antideterministic (and therefore "bears all things, believes all things, hopes all things, endures all things"), and antifunctional (it does not expect recompense). Ethically speaking, the law of reciprocity recedes before the law of superabundance. The love of the enemies to which the Nazarene exhorts is already exemplified in an Old Testament story.

But the "Jonah" in us wishes, rather, to regress to the motherly womb, to a stage *before* an existential decision must be made. "Jonah" wants to "kill time," not to "redeem time"; he wants to reduce human life to deterministic formulas (What has been will be; Nineveh will always remain Nineveh). He prefers the uncertainty of a perilous escape to "Tarshish," to the *mysterium tremendum* of God's revelation. Rather, to die than to become "other." Rather, the hatred of Ninevites than the love of God; the former is comprehensible and all too fathomable, the latter is the unknown and hence a threat to security.

The author of Jonah had the amazing boldness to show the "anti-Jonah," the anti-man-for-nothing in the persons of the wicked Ninevites. To the Jonah who hungers for certainty they opposed the ultimate uncertainty of "perhaps." They thus opened an immense possibility, namely, that God might choose extravagance over determinism, that a human person might be a gerundive rather than an animate puppet manipulated by genetics and other laws.

The author of Jonah was an Israelite. He chose to give his story a double ending: the wager of the Ninevites was vindicated; God, according to Israel, gives victory to those who risk everything on an open future. And as for Jonah himself, he is pondering until today whether or not it is advantageous to side with extravagance.

APPENDIX:
Jonah, a Milestone to Apocalypse

The problem of the passage from prophecy to apocalypse in Hebrew literature is notoriously difficult. Contemporary scholars have, however, contributed to a better understanding of this topic, particularly through analyzing the transitional shaded area where documents still belong to prophecy but announce already the advent of the apocalyptic genre.[1] The aim of the appendix is to advance further the research in the postexilic evolution of prophecy. Jonah, as a matter of fact, is such a forgotten milepost *on the way* to apocalypse.

A forgotten milepost, for conspicuous reasons. The dating of the book too close to the time of return from exile in Babylon was not conducive to a comparative study with late developments in Israel's oracular literature. We have shown at length in chapter 2, above, that the date of Jonah is the third century B.C.E., a time when full-fledged apocalypses were in existence, to wit, parts of the Enochian traditions and even the book of Jubilees (beginning of the second century). The parallels that we have drawn earlier with Third Isaiah, particularly with chapter 60, point to the same direction. As P. Hanson has shown, Third Isaiah contributes to the "dawning" of Jewish apocalyptic. Similarly, from an ideological point of view, we have repeatedly indicated that Jonah finds its place among postexilic subversive writings, and precisely among those polemicizing works written in opposition to the Second Temple institutions. They eventuate in an eschatological cataclysmic vision, characteristic of the apocalypse. At the point of departure of the evolutive line, Third Isaiah contends that the exilic promise of the prophets must be understood as referring to the future, not to the present of an alleged "restoration" in the sixth century (see Isa. 59:1, 9–15; 63:1–6; 63:7–64:11). The point of arrival, in the Bible, is of course Daniel 7–12.

Of particular importance is the increasingly embarrassing problem, for the former exiles, of the nonfulfillment of the promises. One enters the dangerous pass of sifting true from false in the oracles preserved by tradition. The process had been initiated by the prophets themselves (Jeremiah, esp. 28:8f.; 28:15–17; 44:28–30; see Deut. 18:21f.; Amos 7:17; Isa. 7:16; 37:30; 38:1ff.).

Jeremiah contrasts oracles of bliss and oracles of doom (see chap. 28). Each kind has sundry warrants, but both kinds can be legitimate. Indeed, the exiles, especially after the "restoration" of the sixth century, considered that their trials in Babylon had totally and definitely[2] fulfilled the oracles of doom as far as they were concerned.[3] The prophetic threats were from now on directed either to the nations or to the apostates in Israel. By the same token, the oracles of bliss had found their point of impact in history with the return to Zion after 538.

But there is the still more radical attitude of those who do not even mention Cyrus' edict and the return from exile in 538. In a definitely polemical stance, they consider the event as just relative. From Third Isaiah to Second Zechariah, the whole prophetic literature of resistance looks toward the future and bypasses the former events. It expects the eschatological advent of the kingdom of God, a situation fully illustrated later by all Jewish apocalypses. So, in the second century C.E., 2 Baruch and 4 Esdras punctuate history down to their own days with decisive events, among which the sixth-century restoration finds no room!

With the apocalypse, the cosmic dimension of events is particularly emphasized. As we said above, Hellenistic universalism had changed the minds. This facilitated a strong reentry of the cosmological myths that the prophets so strenuously attempted to eradicate in Israel. It is, among other things, the presence of that very mythical element that characterizes the apocalyptic genre.

Universalism and myth mix harmoniously in Jonah. The book divides easily into two parallel parts. The sea monster in "Jonah A" finds a replica in the perverted city of Nineveh of "Jonah B." The prophet is engulfed in the former and the latter; in both cases it is a descent to hell. The Ninevite mass, presented here as almost undistinguishable from animals, corresponds to the ship deck with its variegated crew in which it seems that each one has a particular divinity to pray to. The Ninevites are 120,000 and their number figures the whole universe. Their fundamental ignorance, their moral "illiteracy," their "Barbarian" mindset, the outcome of the distance between them and the knowledge of the living God, even the animals with which they are associated—all stress their cosmic symbolism.

Consequently, the prophetic threat against Nineveh must be understood as having a bearing upon the world at large. And this is exactly the situation envisaged by apocalyptic literature. All the more so as the mode of judgment is here and there a cataclysm, total and end-all destruction that amounts to an end of the world, as in the case of Sodom and Gomorrah.

Cosmological elements are found already in "Jonah A." In the prayer of chapter 2, Jonah describes himself as discovering the "roots" and secrets of the universe (see 2:4–7). He speaks of his ordeal in terms of a generalized catastrophe on the model of the flood. He is tossed around by cataracts. In "Jonah B," however, the imagery changes although the substance remains. Under the influence of Parsiism, as a matter of fact, the aquatic typology leaves room for the igneous one. Hence, in Israel, there is a shift from Noah's myth to Sodom and Gomorrah's destruction by heavenly fire. Such should be the fate of Nineveh; it should be "overthrown" as Sodom and Gomorrah were (see Gen. 19:21, 25; Deut. 29:22; Amos 4:11; Jer. 20:16; Lam. 4:6).

Similarly, as Sodom and Gomorrah are full of *hamas* ("violence"), according to Psalm 11:5, so Nineveh is condemned for the *hamas* in its midst, a characteristic of the Assyrians in the eyes of Israel's prophets (see Isa. 10:13–14; Nah. 2:11–12; 3:1; etc.).

True, Nineveh is not destroyed, so the prophetic oracle amounts to a theoretical evocation of a mere possibility. There occurs no "deluge" or return to the origins, so a new humanity would start a new history. But, if the catastrophe does not come literally, there is at the minimum a liturgical and symbolic return to the pre-formal at Nineveh's court and in town. There occurs a voluntary regression to a time of beginning, to a time of *renovatio*. The king, the court, the "great" and the "small," people and animals go back to a stage that antedates all diversification and distinction, that is, a return to chaos before cosmos. That liturgical pause makes superfluous the other kind of chaos announced by Jonah that would associate Nineveh with Sodom and Gomorrah in a tragic trilogy.

Jonah himself is not exempt from passing through death, a prerequisite to the newness of life especially in Mystery religions. In "Jonah A," he is symbolically put to death and buried, drowned and swallowed by the monster of the netherworld. He comes out transformed from the tomb and "goes to Nineveh." In "Jonah B," he undergoes the "falling out" of the fire that he called upon the Assyrian city. In a striking parallel with Nebuchadnezzar's servants burned by the flame of the overheated oven in Dan. 3:22, Jonah is hit by a scorching east wind, and the sun hammering on his head brings him to the point of passing out and of begging for death (Jon. 4:8). Thus, ironically, Jonah has the foretaste of the "apocalypse" he wanted to unleash upon others. Such an irony perfectly becomes divine dialectic according to chapter 4: Jonah must understand that one is judged after one's norms in judging others.

Jonah is not isolated. Behind him are all the well-meaning of Jerusalem. Through Jonah, a whole group is criticized. For, according to them, ever since the return from Babylon and the "restoration" of 538, the "chips are down." All the preexilic and exilic oracles have been fulfilled. Israel is restored for good in its convenanted prerogatives and the nations are condemned because of the role they played in Israel's punishment, for they went way overboard with their "flogging" of a culprit whose insignificant fault is soon more than paid for (cf. Isa. 40:2) and who becomes an innocent martyr. On that basis, the "integrists" in Jerusalem develop a theocratic ideology and interpret in a triumphalist way the old prophecies.

J. D. Crossan has shown how Jonah responds to the complacent theory.[4] In a hermeneutical perspective, Jonah and others of the same "party" strike a negative balance. The bliss and happiness of the return is absent; and the doom and woe of the nations does not occur either. Even "Nineveh" may be spared by divine compassion in the eighth century, although the city is destined to become, a few decades later, a thorn in Israel's flesh. This proved to be true of the Babylonian and the Persian empires; it is as true today of the Macedonian regime. What conclusion must one draw? That the exilic promises are unreliable? No. But the "orthodox" hermeneutics of the theocratic party in Jerusalem is to be fundamentally reassessed. Its terms must even be reversed. The oracles of bliss are not necessarily for the exclusive benefit of Israel, and the oracles of doom only for the non-Jews. The actual situation dictates the following schema:

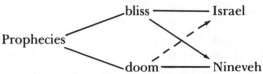

This diagram indicates that the prophecy of bliss, which is normally directed to Israel, is now directed to Nineveh, and the prophecy that should normally be for Nineveh is *by implication* addressed to Israel.

One can take this a step further. Jeremiah 36:12–20 served as a model for Jonah 3:6. From such a connection, however, emerges a taut paradox. Where no one appears receptive to Jeremiah's oracle in chapter 36 that humans and beasts would be destroyed (see vss. 29–31), the terse prediction of Jonah to the Ninevites stirs a general repentance that means for them salvation, not only of humans but also of beasts (see Jon. 3:6–8, 10; 4:11). We can, therefore, draw a second schema:

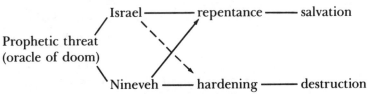

The diagram is read as follows: while the prophetic threat normally brings Israel to repentance and hence to salvation, the same oracle of doom should harden the heart of the Ninevites and bring them to destruction. But instead, the book of Jonah shows that the prophetic threat brings the Ninevites to repentance and hence to salvation. The implication is that if addressed to Israel, the same oracle would harden their hearts and bring about their destruction (cf. Isa. 6:9f.; Matt. 11:23, 12:41).

It would be wrong to see here Jonah taking exception to the ideology of Jeremiah-Ezekiel. We have seen above (chap. 1) what to think of such an opposition. The exilic prophets have, to the contrary, paved the way to Jonah's subversive logic according to which, in the words of Crossan, "the hearer expects prophets to obey God and pagans, such as the Ninevites especially, to disobey God. But the speaker tells a story in which a prophet disobeys and the Ninevites obey beyond all belief."[5] It is by divine extravagance (see above, chap. 8) that the city that was predicted to destroy Israel[6] is spared. Were Nineveh destroyed, Israel would be safe.[7] But through Jonah's mission the enemy of Israel is paradoxically kept in reserve for further evil-doing against Jerusalem. It was in order to avoid this that Jonah had proclaimed the inevitable doom of the wicked city, on the model of Sodom in Genesis 19. But, in Jonah, Sodom is not destroyed!

As with a parable, there is here present a collision of the "structure of hearer expectation" with the "structure of speaker expression," to quote Crossan again. If we call the former *(A),* and the latter *(B),* we have the following tableau: *(A)* The Structure of Hearer Expectation:

approves $(+) \rightarrow$ the destruction of wicked city $(-)$
$\rightarrow$ announced by good prophet $(+)$
God $\rightarrow$ who lives $(+)$.

disapproves $(-) \rightarrow$ the salvation of wicked city $(+)$
$\rightarrow$ announced by bad prophet $(-)$
$\rightarrow$ who dies $(-)$.

This schema becomes, according to *(B)* The Structure of Speaker Expression:

approves $\rightarrow$ destruction $\rightarrow$ good prophet $\rightarrow$ lives.
God
disapproves $\rightarrow$ salvation $\rightarrow$ bad prophet $\rightarrow$ dies.

So for *(B):*

$$\text{God} \rightarrow (+) \rightarrow (+) \rightarrow (+) \rightarrow (+).$$

Such a structure presents a resolution of all contradictions into a constant positive,[8] a solution that clashes with Jonah's intimate conviction that

$$God \rightarrow \text{wrongly approves}$$
$$\rightarrow \text{salvation of wicked city}$$
$$\rightarrow \text{not announced by a good prophet}$$
$$\rightarrow \text{who wishes to die.}$$

Hence:

$$God \rightarrow (-) \rightarrow (-) \rightarrow (-) \rightarrow (-),$$

or, the resolution of all contradictions as proposed by Jonah would put each term of the structure in the negative and thus reflect negatively upon God.

The exploration of further contrasting "structures" (of expression versus expectation) will allow us, at this point, to indicate the far-reaching and pioneering role of the book of Jonah in the development of Israel's reflections and modes of discourse. For this purpose, we first go back to the motif of the forty days' delay of the destruction of Nineveh. Forty is the number that accompanies a test in the Bible (forty days and nights of the flood; forty years in the desert; forty days of Jesus' temptations; etc.). But the outcome of the test for Israel is the antipode of its outcome for the "nations": the inheritance of Eretz Israel, or the whole world at peace. But, for the nations, the test proves lethal, as in the time of Noah the universe is destroyed, or in the time of Moses Egypt meets its fate (cf. Exod. 24:18; 24:28; 1 Kings 19:8, in contrast with Gen. 7:4 etc.; Ezek. 29:11–13; Jon. 3:4).

In the tale of Jonah, the terms of the syllogism are reversed. The test brings the Ninevites to repentance, to mourning over their past way of life, and to entering a new existence (a parallel to the Promised Land after the desert). If so, by implication, the customary role played by the "nations" has now become Israel's!

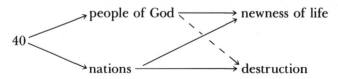

Appendix

Other schemas are possible. But already we must ask whence comes this structural reversibility, and whither this new mode of discourse takes us. As is well known, the style or the literary genre is meant to correspond in depth to the ideology it conveys. Any change in the literary expression is symptomatic of a change in the philosophical or theological reflection. Witness here the evolution inaugurated by the great pioneer and prophet Ezekiel. Let us take, for example, the text of Ezekiel 29:12–16. Here an astonishing transformation of the "normal" structure of discourse occurs. The central event of Israel's history, the exodus complex with its actualizing reinterpretation providing a typology for the return from the Babylonian exile, undergoes, in the prophet's vision, a radical shift of reference. Now the Egyptians are exiled and scattered "for forty years." The test, as seen above, should destroy them. But, "at the end of forty years," they are "gathered." Both terms, "scatter" and "gather," are technical. They specifically designate the Israelite experience in Egypt, then in Babylon. At this point, therefore, one is tempted to prolong the line drawn by the prophet and to conclude, by implication, that Israel will see the restoration of her enemy and be endangered in the process.

It is, anyway, the method adopted by Jonah in the third century. As for Ezekiel, however, he cut short that type of speculation, but what is significant is that he felt the necessity to do so. He says that Egypt will be restored, but "diminished," meaning that it will be unthreatening for Israel. "It shall be the most lowly of the kingdoms, and never again exalt itself above the nations" (vs. 15). Besides, it will not be the delusive ally in political or military adventures. "It shall never again be the reliance of the house of Israel" (vs. 16).

Such a changing of wolves into lambs, so to speak, is clearly *eschatological*. It goes beyond a mere historical change of fortune. Ezekiel, rather, inaugurates a logic that we find developed in Jewish apocalyptic. It is a logic of the definitive and irreversible. Quite understandably, a new mode of expression must be created that fits that unusual vision of things. Not that classic prophecy was not at times teleological, but it is *history* that brings about the unexpected. The proclamation "yet forty days and X will be destroyed" means, in fact, for the prophets: as history is now oriented, or rather, disoriented by human sinfulness, it is headed straight to catastrophe. Therefore, it is necessary to repent and, so, reorient the course of history toward its redemption.

Not so in apocalyptic literature. The time for reorientation is over. It is now too late. The chips are down. After a protracted delay granted by God, history comes to its conclusion: the wicked will utterly and irremediably be destroyed by divine justice. Whereas in prophetic literature, "forty days" might be the sign of gracious delay (see, e.g., Ezek. 29:12 analyzed earlier), the apocalyptic discourse does not count any longer on the impossible possibility of human turning about. "Forty days" means that, by divine computation, the eschatological event will come at that time no matter what, bringing the destruction of the wicked, foreigners and apostate Jews, and the salvation of the People of the Saints (cf. 2 Bar. 76:4–5; 4 Esdras 14:23ff.; Acts 1:3).

One recognizes here Jonah's attitude and the inexorability of his message. But, in the book of Jonah, something highly unusual occurs: the message is addressed not to Israel but to a foreign nation. For, if we bring the classic prophecies against foreign nations to bear here, two of their characteristics must be noticed, one is ideological, the other literary. The oracles against the nations find their justification in that they denounce their role as enemies of God's people.[9] Furthermore—and this is the literary point—the prophet speaks *indirectly* only to Tyre or Edom, to Egypt or Assyria. Even when the discourse is direct, its audience is solely composed of Jews, and it is for them in the first place that the oracle is uttered. In Jonah, however, the terms are reversed. It is here, for the first time ever in the Old Testament, that a message that is indirectly destined for Israel is directed to Nineveh.

It is more than a peculiarity of the book of Jonah. This phenomenon emphasizes once more that Jonah constitutes a link between prophecy and apocalyptic in Israel. If we designate by *A* the call to repentance, a prophet's characteristic, and by *B* the announcement of capital punishment (which, when it becomes the inexorable forecast of the final catastrophe, is an apocalyptist's characteristic), we have something like this:

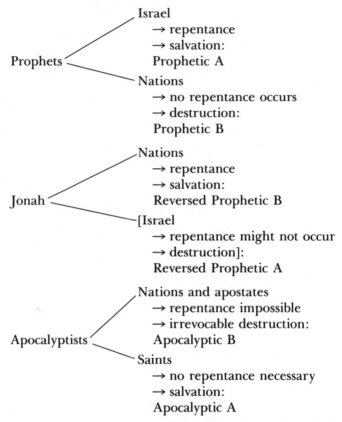

Prophets
- Israel
  → repentance
  → salvation:
  Prophetic A
- Nations
  → no repentance occurs
  → destruction:
  Prophetic B

Jonah
- Nations
  → repentance
  → salvation:
  Reversed Prophetic B
- [Israel
  → repentance might not occur
  → destruction]:
  Reversed Prophetic A

Apocalyptists
- Nations and apostates
  → repentance impossible
  → irrevocable destruction:
  Apocalyptic B
- Saints
  → no repentance necessary
  → salvation:
  Apocalyptic A

Our analysis has shown that Jonah is a hinge in the ideological and literary history of Israel. On the one hand, it is a confirmation of our dating for the book (see chap. 2, above); furthermore, the original and subversive identity of the tale is thus underlined. Jonah is a *sui generis* piece; it is no longer prophetic and not yet apocalyptic. This transitional character is further strengthened by its literary genre, namely the Menippean satire, as we have insisted early in this book. As always in literary history, a transitional, hybrid genre signals the end of a brand of classicism.

JONAH, A MILESTONE TO APOCALYPSE

Jonah innovates; it is pioneering. This means that, like Moses standing on Mount Nebo (Deut. 32:48–52), he sees and makes us contemplate the whole of a Promised Land before others enter it and settle there. The absence of an end to the tale is far-reaching. There is no "after." The parameters of classic prophecy are crossed over. Jonah already signals the advent of the heir to the prophet, the apocalyptist. But, for a while at least, Nineveh's destruction is postponed. Who knows, however, what the future is made of? The apocalypse will fill the void left by this question and bring an "end" to the tale of Jonah. Nineveh shall indeed be overthrown, and with it all the nations, and all the apostates, all the wicked and the world as a whole. Only the Saints of the Most High will remain. To them is reserved the glory of eternal life.

NOTES

1. See O. Plöger, *Theocracy and Eschatology* (Richmond Va.: John Knox Press, 1968); P. Hanson, *The Dawn of Apocalyptic* (Philadelphia: Fortress Press, 1980); J. J. Collins, ed., *Semeia*, no. 14; also A. LaCocque, *Daniel in His Time* (Columbia: University of South Carolina Press, 1988).

2. See Isa. 40:2.

3. Hence the reaction of "subversive" prophets such as Joel and Second Zechariah, who forecast the coming of a still greater catastrophe "in the last days." This oracle must have sounded particularly cruel to those who had experienced the exile in Babylon.

4. J. D. Crossan, *The Dark Interval* (Niles, Ill.: Argus, 1975).

5. Ibid., p. 76.

6. See Hos. 9:3; 11:5, 11; Amos 5:27; Ps. 137:7–9.

7. See Nah. 3 celebrating Nineveh's fall.

8. About Jonah, J. Steinmann wrote these somewhat overstated words: "Blessed be the author who, at the time when Ezra was creating racism, responded in the name of God with laughter. This was the only effective retort to save the prophets' message!" (*Le livre de la consolation d'Israël et les prophètes du retour de l'Exil* [Paris: Cerf, 1960], p. 290).

9. Even Amos 1–2 must be seen from this standpoint; see A. Neher, *Amos, Contribution à l'Étude du Prophétisme* (Paris: Vrin, 1950, 1981).

ABBREVIATIONS

Add.	*Additions to the Book of Daniel*
Altoriental. Forsch.	*Altorientalische Forschung*
ANET	*Ancient Near Eastern Texts Relating to the Old Testament*, ed. J. B. Prichard
Ant.	Josephus, *Jewish Antiquities*
A.T.	Ancien Testament; Altes Testament
ATD	Das Alte Testament Deutsch (series)
Bibl. Sacra	*Biblia Sacra*
BJ	*Bible de Jerusalem* (*The Jerusalem Bible*)
BK	Biblischer Kommentar (series)
BQ	*Baba Qamma*
BZ	*Biblische Zeitschrift*
BZAW	*Beihefte zum Alten Testament Wissenschaft* (q.v.)
CAT	Commentaire de l'Ancien Testament (series)
CBQ	*Catholic Biblical Quaterly*
DB	*Dictionary of the Bible*
EB	Etudes Bibliques (series)
EThR	*Etudes Théologiques et Religieuses*
FRLANT	Forschungen zur Religion und Literatur des Alten und Neuen Testaments (series)
HAT	Handbuch zum Alten Testament (series)
Hist.	*Histories* (Herodotus)
HUCA	*Hebrew Union College Annual*
IB	*Interpreter's Bible*, 12 vols.
ICC	International Critical Commentary (series)

ABBREVIATIONS

IDB	*Interpreter's Dictionary of the Bible,* 4 vols.
IDBSup.	*IDB Supplementary Volume*
Interp.	*Interpretation*
JBL	*Journal for Biblical Literature*
JE	*Jewish Encyclopedia*
Jer.	Jerusalem Talmud
J. of Psy. and Theol.	*Journal of Psychology and Theology*
JQR	*Jewish Quarterly Review*
JSOT	*Journal for the Study of the Old Testament*
KAT	Kommentar zum Alten Testament (series)
Kl. Schr.	*Kleine Schriften*
LXX	Septuagint
NICOT	The New International Commentary on the Old testament (series)
N.T.	New; Nouveau Testament
O.T.	Old Testament
PG	J. Migne, Patrologia graeca
PL	J. Migne, Patrologia latina
PRE	*Pirqe de Rabbi Eliezer* (ed. Friedlander)
Q	Qumran
1QH	Hodayot from cave 1 of Qumran
RB	*Revue Biblique*
RGG	*Die Religion in Geschichte und Gegenwart* (3d ed.)
RHPR	*Revue d'Histoire et de Philosophie Religieuse*
SBT	Studies in Biblical Theology (series)
Scott. J. of Theol.	*Scottish Journal of Theology*
SDB	*Supplément au Dictionnaire de la Bible*
Strack-Billerbeck	Strack and Billerbeck, *Kommentar zum Neuen Testament aus Talmud und Midrasch*
Syb. Or.	Sybilline Oracles
Test. XII Patr.	Testaments of the Twelve Patriarchs
Tg.	Targum

ABBREVIATIONS

ThWNT (ThDNT)	*Theologisches Woerterbuch zum Neuen Testament (Theological Dictionary of the New Testament)*
ThEH	*Theologische Existenz Heute*
Theol. St. u. Krit.	*Theologische Studien und Kritiken*
ThR	*Theologische Rundschau*
ThZ	*Theologische Zeitschrift*
TOB	*Traduction Oecuménique de la Bible*
Vlg.	Verlag (edition)
VT	*Vetus Testamentum*
VTSup.	*Vetus Testamentum Supplement*
War	Josephus, *Jewish War*
ZAW	*Zeitschrift für die Alttestamentliche Wissenschaft*

BIBLIOGRAPHY

Ab Arnim, Hans. *Stoicorum Veterum Fragmenta.* 4 vols. Leipzig: G. B. Teubner, 1903–24; Stuttgart: G. B. Teubner, 1968.

Ackerman, James S. "Satire and Symbolism in the Song of Jonah." In *Traditions in Transformation: Turning Points in Biblical Faith* (F. M. Cross 60th Birthday Festschrift). Ed. B. Halpern & J. O. Levenson. Winona Lake, Ind.: Eisenbrauns, 1981.

Ackroyd, Peter R. *Exile and Restoration.* Philadelphia: Westminster Press, 1968.

———. *Israel under Babylon and Persia.* London: Oxford University Press, 1970.

Adler, Alfred. *The Education of Children* (first pub. 1930). Chicago: Henry Regnery Co., 1970.

———. *The Practice and Theory of Individual Psychology* (first pub. 1925). Totowa, N.J.: Littlefield, Adams & Co., 1969.

———. *Problems of Neurosis* (first pub. 1929). New York: Harper & Row, 1964.

———. *The Science of Living.* Garden City, N.Y.: Garden City Publishing Co., 1929.

———. *Social Interest: A Challenge to Mankind* (first pub. 1933). New York: G. P. Putnam's Sons, 1964.

———. *Superiority and Social Interest.* Ed. H. & R. Ansbacher. Evanston, Ill.: Northwestern University Press, 1964.

———. *What Life Should Mean to You* (first pub. 1931). New York: Capricorn Books, 1958.

Adorno, Theodor. *Der Jargon der Eigentlichkeit: Zur deutschen Ideologie.* Frankfurt: Suhrkamp Vlg., 1964. *(The Jargon of Auhenticity.* Trans. K. Tarnowski and F. Will. Evanston: Northwestern University Press, 1973.)

———; Else Frenkel-Brunswick; Daniel J. Levinson; & R. Newitt Sanford. *The Authoritarian Personality.* New York: Harper & Row, 1950.

Allen, Leslie C. *The Books of Joel, Obadiah, Jonah, and Micah.* (NICOT.) Grand Rapids: Eerdmans, 1976.

Allport, Gordon W. *Becoming.* New Haven: Yale University Press, 1955.

Alt, Albrecht. *Die Ursprünge des israelitischen Rechts.* Leipzig: S. Hirzel, 1934.

BIBLIOGRAPHY

Alter, Robert. *The Art of Biblical Narrative.* New York: Basic Books, 1981.

Anderson, Erika. *The Schweitzer Album.* New York: Harper & Row, 1965.

Angyal, Andras. "Evasion of Growth." *American Journal of Psychiatry* 110 (1953–54): 358–62.

——. *Neurosis and Treatment: A Holistic Theory.* New York: John Wiley, 1965.

Ansbacher, Hans L. "The Concept of Social Interest." *Journal of Individual Psychology* 24 (1968): 131–49.

——, & Rowena Ansbacher, eds. *The Individual Psychology of Alfred Adler.* New York: Harper Colophon Books, 1956.

Asch, Solomon E. "Studies in Independence and Conformity. A Minority of One against Unanimous Majority." *Psychological Monographs,* 70 no. 9 (1956).

Assagioli, Roberto. *The Act of Will.* Baltimore: Penguin Books, 1973.

——. *Psychosynthesis.* New York: Viking Press, 1971.

——. "The Synthetic Vision: Conversation with Roberto Assagioli." In *Voices and Visions.* Ed. Sam Keen. New York: Harper & Row, 1974.

Atkinson, John W., & N. T. Feather, eds. *A Theory of Achievement Motivation.* New York: John Wiley, 1966.

——, & J. O. Raynor, eds. *Motivation and Achievement.* Washington, D.C.: V. H. Winston, 1974.

Auerbach, Erich. *Mimesis: The Representation of Reality in Western Literature.* Trans. W. R. Trask. Princeton: Princeton University Press, 1953.

Bakhtin, Mikhail. *Problems of Dostoevsky's Poetics.* Ann Arbor: Ardis, 1973.

——. *Rabelais and His Work.* Cambridge, Eng.: Cambridge University Press, 1968.

Bardwick, Judith, ed. *Readings on the Psychology of Women.* New York: Harper & Row, 1972.

Barth, Karl. *Die Protestantische Theologie in 19. Jahrhundert.* Zurich: Evangelischer Vlg., 1952.

Barthes, Roland. *S/Z.* Paris: Seuil, 1970.

Becker, Ernest. *The Denial of Death.* New York: Free Press, 1973.

——. "The Heroics of Everyday Life." In *Voices and Visions.* Ed. Sam Keen. New York: Harper & Row, 1974; pp. 175–98.

Bellak, Leopold, "The Emergency Psychotherapy of Depression." In *Specialized Techniques in Psychotherapy.* Ed. E. Bychowski & J. L. Despert. New York: Grove Press, 1952.

Berscheid, Ellen, & Elaine H. Walster. *Interpersonal Attraction.* New York: Addison-Wesley, 1978.

Bettelheim, Bruno. "The Decision to Fail" (first pub. 1961). In *Surviving.* New York: Vintage Books, 1979; pp. 142–68.

——. *The Informed Heart.* New York: Free Press, 1960.

——. *Love Is not Enough.* New York: Avon Books, 1950.

BIBLIOGRAPHY

──── . *The Uses of Enchantment*. New York: Alfred A. Knopf, 1976.

──── , & Karen Zelan. *On Learning to Read: The Child's Fascination with Meaning*. New York: Alfred A. Knopf, 1982.

Bewer, Julius A. *The Book of the Twelve Prophets*. ICC series. Edinburgh: T. & T. Clark, 1949.

Bickerman, Elias. "Les deux erreurs du Prophète Jonas." *RHPR* 45 (1965): 232–64.

──── . *Four Strange Books of the Bible: Jonah, Daniel, Koheleth, Esther*. New York: Schocken Books, 1967.

Blank, Sheldon H. "Doest Thou Well to Be Angry? A Study in Self-Pity." *HUCA* 26 (1955): 29–41.

Blenkinsopp, Joseph. *A History of Prophecy in Israel*. Philadelphia: Westminster Press, 1983.

Boehme, W. "Die Komposition des Buches Jona." *ZAW* 7 (1887): 224–84.

──── . "Die Komposition des Buches Jona." *ZAW* 25 (1905): 285–310.

Bonhoeffer, Dietrich. *Letters and Papers from Prison*. Ed. E. Bethge. Trans. R. H. Fuller. New York: Macmillan, 1972 (enlarged edition).

Booth, Wayne. *A Rhetoric of Irony*. Chicago: University of Chicago Press, 1974.

Brockington, Leonard H. "Jonah." *Peake's Commentary on the Bible*. Ed. M. Black & H. H. Rowley. London: Nelson, 1962; pp. 627–29.

Brown, Norman O. *Life against Death*. New York: Vintage Books, 1959.

Brown, Walter A. "The Meaning of Success in a Person with a 'Success Phobia.' " *Psychiatry* 34 (1971): 425–30.

Buber, Martin. *Eclipse of God*. New York: Harper & Row, 1952.

──── . "Guilt and Guilt-Feelings." *Psychiatry* 20, no. 2 (May 1957): 114–29.

──── . *I and Thou*. New York: Charles Scribner's Sons, 1970.

──── . *Knowledge of Man*. New York: Harper & Row, 1965.

──── . *The Prophetic Faith*. New York: Harper & Row, 1960.

──── . *The Way of Man*. New York: Citadel Press, 1967.

──── . *The Way of Response*. New York: Schocken Books, 1966.

Budde, Karl. "Jona." *JE* 7 (1916): 225–30.

Bugental, James F. *The Search for Authenticity*. New York: Holt, Rinehart, & Winston, 1965.

Bulka, Reuven P. "Death in Life—Talmudic and Logotherapeutic Affirmations." *Humanitas* 10, no. 1 (February 1974): 33–34.

Burrows, Millar. "The Literary Category of the Book of Jonah." In *Translating and Understanding the Old Testament: Essays in Honor of Herbert G. May*. ed. H. T. Frank & W. L. Reed, Nashville: Abingdon, 1970; pp. 80–107.

Bychowski, E., & Louise J. Despert, eds. *Specialized Techniques in Psychotherapy*. New York: Grove Press, 1952.

Calvin, John. *Opera Selecta.* 6 vols. Ed. P. Barth & G. Niesel. Munich: Kaiser, 1926–36.

Campbell, Joseph. *The Hero with a Thousand Faces* (first pub. 1949). New York: Pantheon Books, 1968.

———. *The Mythic Image.* Princeton: Princeton University Press, 1974.

Camus, Albert. *La peste.* Paris: Gallimard, 1947.

Canavan-Gumpert, Donnah; Katherine Garner; & Peter Gumpert. *The Success-Fearing Personality.* Lexington, Mass.: D. C. Heath, 1978.

Carroll, Robert P., *When Prophecy Failed.* New York: Crossroad, 1979.

Cason, H. "The Learning and Retention of Pleasant and Unpleasant Activities." *Archives of Psychology* 21, no. 134 (1932): 5–10.

Cervantes, Miguel de. *Don Quijote de la Mancha* (first pub. 1615). *The Adventures of Don Quixote de la Mancha.* New York: Cuneo Press, 1936.

Chaplin, James P. *Dictionary of Psychology.* New York: Dell Publishing Co., 1968.

Cheyne, Thomas K. "Jonah, A Study in Jewish Folklore and Religion." *ThR* 57 (1877): 211–19.

———. "Jonah." *Encyclopedia of the Bible,* vol. 2. London: Adam & Charles Black, 1901; cols. 2565–71.

Childs, Brevard S. *Introduction to the Old Testament as Scripture.* Philadelphia: Fortress Press, 1979.

———. "Jonah: A Study in Old Testament Hermeneutics." *Scott. J. of Theol.* 11 (1958): 53–61.

Chomsky, Noam. "Recent Contributions to the Theory of Innate Ideas." In *Boston Studies in the Philosophy of Science.* Ed. R. Cohen & M. Wartofsky. Vol. 3. Dordrecht: Reidel, 1968.

Christian, James L. *Philosophy: The Art of Wondering.* San Francisco: Rinehart Press, 1973.

Cioran, E. M. *La tentation d'exister.* Paris: Gallimard, 1956.

Cirlot, Juan Eduardo. *A Dictionary of Symbols.* New York: Philosophical Library, 1962.

Clements, R. E. "The Purpose of the Book of Jonah." *Congress Volume* 1974. *VTSup.* 28. Leiden: Brill, 1975; pp. 16–28.

Cohen, S. H. "A Growth Theory of Neurotic Resistance to Therapy." *Journal of Humanistic Psychology* 1 (Spring 1961): 48–63.

Cohn, Dorrit. *Transparent Minds.* Princeton: Princeton University Press, 1978.

Cohn, Gabriel H. *Das Buch Jona im Lichte der biblischen Erzählkunst.* Assen: Van Gorcum, 1969.

Collodi, Carlo. *Pinocchio, the Story of a Marionette.* Trans. M. A. Murray. New York: E. P. Dutton, 1956.

Combs, Arthur, & Donald Snygg. *Individual Behavior: A Perceptual Approach to Behavior.* New York: Harper & Row, 1969.

BIBLIOGRAPHY

Crawford, Helen M. *A Reluctant Missionary.* Chicago: Board of Christian Education, United Presbyterian Church, 1965.

Crenshaw, James L. *Prophetic Conflict: Its Effect upon Israelite Religion,* BZAW 124, Berlin, 1971.

Crossan, John D. *The Dark Interval.* Niles, Ill.: Argus Communications, 1975.

―――. "Parable, Allegory, and Paradox." In *Semiology and Parables.* Ed. D. Patte. Pittsburgh: Pickwick Press, 1976.

―――. ed. "Paul Ricoeur on Biblical Hermeneutics." *Semeia* 4 (1975).

Darley, J. M., & Ellen Berscheid. "Increased Liking as a Result of the Anticipation of Personal Contact." *Human Relations* 20 (1967): 29–40.

Delatte, A. "Le cycéon, breuvage rituel des mystères d'Eleusis." *Bulletin Classe des Lettres,* Académie Royale de Belgique, 5e. sér. 40 (1954): 690–752.

Detweiler, Robert. *Story, Sign, and Self.* Philadelphia: Fortress Press, 1978.

Deutsch, Helen. *The Psychology of Women.* New York: Grune & Stratton, 1944.

de Wette, W. M. L. *Lehrbuch der historisch-kritischen Einleitung in kanonischen und apokryphen Bücher des Alten Testaments.* Berlin: G. Reimer, 1817.

Dodds, E. R. *The Greeks and the Irrational.* Berkeley: University of California Press, 1951.

Dostoevsky, Feodor. *Crime and Punishment.* New York: E. P. Dutton, 1933.

Dowling, Colette. *The Cinderella Complex: Women's Hidden Fear of Independence.* New York: Simon & Schuster, 1981.

Edinger, Edward F. "The Tragic Hero: An Image of Individuation." *Parabola* (1976): 66–75.

Eissfeldt, Otto. "Amos und Jona in Volkstümlicher Überlieferung." In *Festschrift für Ernst Barnikol.* Berlin, 1964; pp. 9–13; also in *Kl. Schr.* 4 (1968): 137–42.

―――. *The Old Testament: An Introduction.* Trans. P. R. Ackroyd. New York: Harper & Row, 1965.

Eliade, Mircea. *Birth and Rebirth.* New York: Harper & Row, 1958.

―――. "The Cult of the Mandragora." In *Zalmoxis, the Vanishing God.* Chicago: University of Chicago Press, 1972; pp. 204–25.

―――. *A History of Religious Ideas.* 3 vols. Chicago: University of Chicago Press, vol. 1, 1978; vol. 2, 1982; vol. 3, 1984.

―――. *Images and Symbols.* New York: Sheed & Ward, 1969.

―――. "La mandragore et les mythes de la 'naissance miraculeuse.'" *Cahiers Zalmoxis* 3 (1940–42): 3–48.

―――. *Myth and Reality.* New York: Harper & Row, 1963.

―――. *Myths, Dreams and Mysteries.* New York: Harper & Row, 1960.

―――. *Patterns in Comparative Religion.* New York: Sheed & Ward, 1958.

―――. *The Quest.* Chicago: University of Chicago Press, 1969.

BIBLIOGRAPHY

——— . *The Sacred and the Profane*. New York: Harper & Row, 1961.

——— . "Sacred Tradition and Modern Man: A Conversation with Mircea Eliade." *Parabola* 1, no. 3 (1976): 74–80.

——— . *The Two and the One*. Chicago: University of Chicago Press, 1965.

——— , & Joseph Kitagawa. *The History of Religions*. Chicago: University of Chicago Press, 1959.

Ellul, Jacques. "Le livre de Jonas." *Foi et Vie* 50 (1952): 81–184.

Erikson, Erik H. *Identity, Youth and Crisis*. New York: W. W. Norton, 1968.

——— . *Insight and Responsibility*. New York: W. W. Norton, 1964.

——— . *Life History and the Historical Moment*. New York: W. W. Norton, 1975.

——— . *Young Man Luther: A Study on Psychoanalysis and History*. New York: W. W. Norton, 1961.

——— , & R. I. Evans. *Dialogue with Erik Erikson*. New York: E. P. Dutton, 1969.

Evelyn-White, Hugh G., trans. *Hesiod, the Homeric Hymns and Homerica*. New York: Macmillan, 1914.

Eysenck, H. J. *Behavior Therapy and the Neuroses*. New York: Pergamon Press, 1960.

Farson, Richard. "Carl Rogers, Quiet Revolutionary." In Richard I. Evans, *Carl Rogers: The Man and His Ideas*. New York: E. P. Dutton, 1975; pp. xxviii–xliii.

Feifel, Herman. "Death-Relevant Variable in Psychology." In *Existential Psychology*. Ed. Rollo May. New York: Random House, 1960.

Fenichel, Otto. "The Dread of Being Eaten" (first pub. 1928). In *The Collected Papers of Otto Fenichel*, vol. 1. New York: W. W. Norton, 1953; pp. 158–59.

——— . *The Psychoanalytic Theory of Neurosis*. New York: W. W. Norton, 1945.

Ferenczi, Sandor. *Thalassa, A Theory of Genitality*. New York: Psychoanalytic Quarterly Inc., 1938.

Ferguson, Marilyn. "Yankelovich: Another Critic of the Inner Journey." *Leading Edge Bulletin* 1, no. 14 (1981): 3.

Feuillet, André. *Études d'Exégèse et de Théologie Biblique: Ancien Testament*. Paris: Gabalda, 1975.

——— . "Le livre de Jonas." *BJ* (Paris: Cerf, 1951).

——— . "Le livre de Jonas." *DBS*, vol. 4, cols. 1104–31.

——— . "Les sens du livre de Jonas." *RB* 54 (1947): 340–61.

——— . "Les sources du livre de Jonas." *RB* 54 (1947): 161–86.

Fingert, H. H. "Psychoanalytic Study of the Minor Prophet Jonah." *Psychoanalytic Review* 41 (1954): 55–65.

Frankl, Viktor E. *The Doctor and the Soul*. New York: Alfred A. Knopf, 1955.

——— . *Man's Search for Meaning*. Boston: Beacon Press, 1962.

BIBLIOGRAPHY

————. "Meaninglessness: A Challenge to Psychologists." In *Theories of Psychopathology and Personality.* Ed. T. Millon. Philadelphia: W. B. Saunders Company, 1973.

————. *Psychotherapy and Existentialism.* New York: Washington Square Press, 1967.

————. "Self Transcendence as a Human Phenomenon. *Journal of Humanistic Psychology* 6 (1966): 97–106.

————. *The Unconscious God.* New York: Simon & Schuster, 1975.

————. *The Will to Meaning.* New York: New American Library, 1969.

Frazer, Sir James G. *The Golden Bough* (first pub. 1922). London: Macmillan, 1967.

Freud, Sigmund. *Civilization and its Discontents* (1930). New York: W. W. Norton, 1961. (Also in *The Complete Psychological Works of Sigmund Freud* [=Standard Edition], vol. 21, London: Hogarth Press, 1961; pp. 64–145.

————. "Contributions to the Psychology of Love," Parts 2 and 3, (First publ. 1912, 1918). In Standard Ed., vol. 11, London: The Hogarth Press, 1957, pp. 179–208.

————. "Inhibitions, Symptoms and Anxiety" (1926). In Standard Ed., vol. 20. London: The Hogarth Press, 1959, pp. 87–172.

————. *The Psychopathology of Everyday Life* (1901). New York: W. W. Norton, 1965. (Also in Standard Edition, vol. 6).

————. "Some Character-Types Met With in Psychoanalytic Work" (1916). Standard Ed., vol. 14. London: The Hogarth Press, 1957, pp. 309–333.

————. "Totem and Taboo" (1913). Standard Ed., vol. 13. London: The Hogarth Press, 1955, pp. 1–161.

Friedlander, Gerald, ed. *Pirke de Rabbi Eliezer.* New York: Hermon Press, 1965.

Friedman, Maurice. "Aiming at the Self: The Paradox of Encounter and the Human Potential Movement." *Journal of Humanistic Psychology,* 16, no. 2 (1976): 5–33.

————. "Introductory Essay." In M. Buber, *Knowledge of Man.* New York: Harper & Row, 1965, pp. 11–58.

————. *To Deny Our Nothingness: Contemporary Images of Man* (1967). Chicago: The University of Chicago Press, 1978.

Frobenius, Leo. *Das Zeitalter des Sonnengottes.* Berlin: G. Reimer, 1904.

Fromm, Erich. *The Art of Loving.* New York: Harper & Row, 1956.

————. *Escape from Freedom.* New York: Rinehart & Winston, 1941.

————. *The Forgotten Language.* New York: Grove Press, 1951.

————. *Man for Himself.* Greenwich, Conn.: Fawcett, 1947.

————. *Psychoanalysis and Religion.* New Haven: Yale University Press, 1950.

BIBLIOGRAPHY

—— , & R. I. Evans. *Dialogue with Erich Fromm*. New York: Harper & Row, 1966.

Frye, Northrop. *The Great Code: The Bible and Literature*. New York: Harcourt, Brace, Jovanovich, 1982.

Gadamer, H. G. *Reason in the Age of Science*. Cambridge, Mass.: M.I.T. Press, 1981.

Gaster, Theodor H. *Festivals of the Jewish Year*. New York: William Sloane, 1953.

—— . *Myth, Legend, and Custom in the Old Testament* Vols. 1–2. New York: Harper & Row, 1975.

Geller, Leonard. "The Failure of Self-Actualization Theory: A Critique of Carl Rogers and Abraham Maslow." *Journal of Humanistic Psychology* 22, no. 2 (1982): 56–73.

Gelman, David. "Finding the Hidden Freud." *Newsweek*, November 30, 1981; pp. 64–70.

Ginzberg, Louis. *The Legends of the Jews*. 7 vols. Philadelphia: Jewish Publication Society, 1955.

Girard, René. *La violence et le sacré*. Paris: Bernard Grasset, 1972.

Goldenson, Robert M. *The Encyclopedia of Human Behavior*. Garden City, N.Y.: Doubleday, 1970.

Goldstein, Kurt. *The Organism*. New York: American Book Co., 1939.

—— . "Effects of Brain Damage on Personality." In *Theories of Personality and Psychopathology*. Ed. T. Millon. Philadelphia: W. B. Saunders, 1973; pp. 54–62.

Good, Edwin M. *Irony in the Old Testament*. Sheffield: Almond Press, 1981.

GrosLouis, K. R. R., ed. *Literary Interpretations of Biblical Narratives*. Nashville: Abingdon, 1974.

Hadas, Moses. *Hellenistic Culture: Fusion and Diffusion*. New York: Columbia University Press, 1959.

Haller, Eduard. "Die Erzählung von dem Propheten Jona." *Theologische Existenz Heute*, n.s. 65 (1958): 5–54.

Hamilton, Edith. *Mythology: Timeless Tales of Gods and Heroes*. New York: New American Library, 1942.

Handelman, Susan. *The Slayers of Moses: The Emergence of Rabbinic Interpretation in Modern Literary Theory*. Albany: State University of New York Press, 1982.

Harlow, Harry F. *Learning to Love*. San Francisco: Albion Publishing Co., 1971.

Haronian, Frank. "Repression of the Sublime." In *The Proper Study of Man*. Ed. F. Fadiman. New York: Macmillan, 1971.

—— . "The Repression of the Sublime." *Synthesis* 1 (1977): 125–36.

BIBLIOGRAPHY

Harris, J. R. *The Odes and Psalms of Solomon*. Cambridge, Eng.: Cambridge University Press, 1909.

Hartmann, Heinz. *Ego Psychology and the Problem of Adaptation*. New York: International Universities Press, 1958.

Hengel, Martin. *Judentum und Hellenismus, Studien zu ihrer Begegnung*. J. C. B. Mohr, *(Judaism and Hellenism*, 2 vols. J. Bowden. Trans. Tübingen: 1973². Philadelphia: Fortress Press, 1974).

Heschel, Abraham. *The Insecurity of Freedom*. New York: Farrar, Straus & Giroux, 1966.

———. *Man Is Not Alone* (first pub. 1951). New York: Farrar, Straus & Giroux, 1976.

———. *The Prophets* (first pub. 1962). New York: Harper Torchbooks, vol. 1 (1969), vol. 2 (1971).

———. *The Wisdom of Heschel*. Ed. Ruth M. Goodhill. New York: Farrar, Straus & Giroux, 1970.

Hitzig, F. *Die Zwölf Kleinen Propheten*. Leipzig: S. Hirzel, 1863.

Holbert, John G. " 'Deliverance Belongs to YHWH': Satire in the Book of Jonah." *JSOT* 21 (1981): 59–81.

Hoonacker, A. van. *Les 12 petits prophètes*. (EB.) Paris: Gabalda, 1908.

Horner, Matina. "The Motive to Avoid Success and Changing Aspirations in College Women." In *Readings on the Psychology of Women*. Ed. J. Bardwick. New York: Harper & Row, 1972; pp. 62–68.

———. "Sex Differences in Achievement Motivation and Performance in Competitive and Noncompetitive Situations." Unpublished doctoral dissertation, University of Michigan, 1968.

———. "Toward an Understanding of Achievement Related Conflicts in Women." *Journal of Social Issues* 28 (1972): 157–75.

Horney, Karen. *The Neurotic Personality of Our Time*. New York: W. W. Norton, 1964.

Hower, J. T. "The Misunderstanding and Mishandling of Anger." *J. of Psy. and Theol.* 2 (1974): 269–75.

Jacobi, Jolande. *Complex, Archetype, Symbol*. Princeton: Princeton University Press, 1959.

———. *The Psychology of C. G. Jung*. New Haven: Yale University Press, 1962.

Jahoda, Marie. *Current Concepts of Positive Mental Health*. New York: Basic Books, 1958.

James, William. *The Varieties of Religious Experience* (first pub. 1902). New York: New American Library, 1958.

Jeremias, Joachim. "Ionas." *ThDNT.* Vol. 3, pp. 406–10.

Jerome, Saint. *Selected Letters of St. Jerome*. Trans. F. A. Wright. Loeb Classical Library series. London: Heinemann, 1933.

241

BIBLIOGRAPHY

Johnson, Aubrey R. "Jonah 2:3–10: A Study in Cultic Fantasy." *Studies in Old Testament Prophecy.* Ed. H. H. Rowley and T. H. Robinson. New York: Charles Scribner's Sons, 1950.

Jourard, Sidney M. *The Transparent Self* (first pub. 1964). New York: D. Van Nostrand, 1971.

Joy, Charles R., ed. *See* Schweitzer, Albert.

Jung, Carl G. (The complete works were published in German by Walter Vlg. AG, Olten, Germany, and in English by Princeton University Press, Bollingen Series 20, Princeton, N.J.) The year of original publication in German follows the title.

——— . *Aion: Researches into the Phenomenology of the Self* (1951). Princeton: Princeton University Press, 1959. (Collected Works, Bollingen Series 20, vol. 9ii).

——— . *Symbolik des Geistes* (1948) = *Alchemical Studies.* Princeton: Princeton University Press, 1967. (Collected Works, Bollingen Series 20, vol. 13).

——— . *Analytical Psychology: Its Theory and Practice* (1935). New York: Vintage books, 1968. (Collected Works, Bollingen Series 20, vol. 18).

——— . *The Archetypes and the Collective Unconscious* (1959). Princeton: Princeton University Press, 1968. (Collected Works, Bollingen Series 20, vol. 9i).

——— . *Civilization in Transition* (collected articles). Princeton: Princeton University Press, 1964. (Collected Works, Bollingen Series 20, vol. 10).

——— ."Concerning Rebirth" (1939). In *The Archetypes and the Collective Unconscious.* Princeton: Princeton University Press, 1968; pp. 113–47. (Collected Works, Bollingen Series 20, vol. 9i).

——— . *Critique of Psychoanalysis* (1910). Princeton: Princeton University Press, 1975. (Collected Works, Bollingen Series 20, vol. 4).

——— . *C. G. Jung Letters.* Vol. 2, letters of 1951–61. Princeton: Princeton University Press, 1975.

——— . *Memories, Dreams, Reflections.* New York: Random House, 1961.

——— . *Modern Man in Search of a Soul* (1933). New York: Harcourt, Brace & World, 1933. (Collected Works, Bollingen Series 20, vol. 11).

——— . *Psychological Reflections.* Eds. J. Jacobi and R. F. C. Hull. Princeton: Princeton University Press, 1970.

——— . *Psychological Types* (1921). Princeton: Princeton University Press, 1971. (Collected Works, Bollingen Series 20, vol. 6).

——— . *Psychology and Alchemy* (1944). Princeton: Princeton University Press, 1968. (Collected Works, Bollingen Series 20, vol. 12).

——— . *Psychology and Religion* (The Terry Lectures, 1938). New Haven: Yale University Press, 1978. (Collected Works, Bollingen Series 20, vol. 11).

BIBLIOGRAPHY

—— . *The Psychology of Transference* (1946). Princeton: Princeton University Press, 1966. (Collected Works, Bollingen Series 20, vol. 16).

—— . "Religion and Psychology: A Reply to Martin Buber" (1952). In *The Symbolic Life.* Princeton: Princeton University Press, 1976; pp. 663–70. (Collected Works, Bollingen Series 20, vol. 18).

—— . *The Structure and Dynamics of the Psyche* (1960). Princeton: Princeton University Press, 1969. (Collected Works, Bollingen Series 20, vol. 8).

—— . *The Symbolic Life: Miscellaneous Writings.* Princeton: Princeton University Press. 1976. (C.W., vol. 18).

—— . *Symbols of Transformation* (1912). New York: Pantheon Books, 1967. (Collected Works, Bollingen Series 20, vol. 5).

—— . *Two Essays on Analytical Psychology* (1953). Princeton: Princeton University Press, 1966. (Collected Works, Bollingen Series 20, vol. 7).

—— . *The Undiscovered Self* (1957). New York: New American Library, 1958. (Collected Works, Bollingen Series 20, vol. 10).

—— , & Carl Kérényi. *Essays on a Science of Mythology.* (1951). Princeton: Princeton University Press, 1963.

Kafka, Franz. *The Trial* (first pub. 1915). New York: Schocken Books, 1968.

Kant, Immanuel. *Fundamental Principles of the Metaphysical Morals* (first pub. 1785). New York: Liberal Arts Press, 1949.

Karpe, M. "The Origins of Peter Pan." *Psychoanalytic Review* 43 (1953): 104–10.

Kaufmann, Yehezkel. *The Religion of Israel.* Trans. and abridged by M. Greenberg. Chicago: University of Chicago Press, 1960.

—— . *Toldot ha-emunah ha-yisraelit.* Vol. 4 Tel Aviv: Bialik Institute, 1963.

Keel, O. *The Symbolism of the Biblical World.* New York: Seabury, 1978.

Keen, Sam, ed. *Voices and Visions.* New York: Harper & Row, 1974.

Keller, C. A. *Joël, Abdias, Jonas.* CAT 11a. Neuchâtel: Delachaux & Niestlé, 1965.

—— . "Jonas, le portrait d'un prophète." *ThZ* 21 (1965): 329–40.

Keniston, Kenneth. *The Uncommitted: Alienated Youth in American Society.* New York: Dell, 1965.

Kérényi, Karl. "Epilegomena: The Miracle of Eleusis" (first pub. 1949). In C. G. Jung and K. Kérényi, *Essays on a Science of Mythology.* Princeton: Princeton University Press, 1963; pp. 178–83.

Kiley, Dan. *The Peter Pan Syndrome: Men Who Have Never Grown Up.* New York: Dodd, Mead & Co., 1983.

Kitagawa, Joseph M. & Charles H. Long, eds. *Myths and Symbols: Studies in Honor of Mircea Eliade.* Chicago: University of Chicago Press, 1969.

243

BIBLIOGRAPHY

Klein, Melanie. *Envy and Gratitude and Other Works.* New York: Dell, 1975.
———. "Love, Guilt and Reparation" (first pub. 1937). In M. Klein and Joan Riviere, *Love, Hate and Reparation.* New York: W. W. Norton, 1964; pp. 57–119.
———. "Notes on Some Schizoid Mechanisms" (first pub. 1946). In *Envy and Gratitude,* pp. 1–24.
———. "On Mental Health" (first pub. 1960). In *Envy and Gratitude,* pp. 268–74.
———. "On the Termination of a Psychoanalysis" (first pub. 1950). In *Envy and Gratitude,* pp. 43–47.
Knight, George A. F. *Ruth and Jonah.* Torch Bible Commentaries. London: SCM Press, 1950.
Kohut, Heinz. *The Analysis of the Self.* New York: International Universities Press, 1971.
———. *How Does Analysis Cure?* Chicago: University of Chicago Press, 1984.
———. *The Restoration of the Self.* New York: International Universities Press, 1977.
Komlos, O. "Jonah Legends." *Études Orientales: À la mémoire de Paul Hirschler.* Budapest, 1950; pp. 41–61.
König, E. "Jonah." *DB.* New York: Charles Scribner's Sons, 1911; pp. 744–53.
Kotchen, Theodor A. "Existential Mental Health: An Empirical Approach." *Journal of Individual Psychology* 16 (1960): 174.
Kraeling, Emil. *Commentary on the Prophets.* Camden: Nelson, 1966.
LaCocque, André. *But as for Me.* Atlanta: John Knox Press, 1979.
———. *Daniel in His Time.* Columbia, S.C.: University of South Carolina Press, 1988.
———. "Date et milieu du livre de Ruth." *RHPR* 59, nos. 3–4 (1979): (*Mélanges Edmond Jacob*): 583–93.
———. "De l'individu à la personne" In *Martin Buber: L'homme et le philosophe.* Bruxelles: Ed. de Institut de sociologie de l'Univ. de Bruxelles, 1968; pp. 59–71.
———. "Job or the Impotence of Religion." *Semeia* 19 (1981): 33–52.
———. "A Return to a God of Nature?" *Sources of Vitality in American Church Life.* Ed. Robert L. Moore. Chicago: Exploration Press, 1978.
———. "Sin and Guilt." In *Encyclopedia of Religion.* Ed. Mircea Eliade. New York: Macmillan, 1987; vol. 13, pp. 325–31.
———. "II Zacharie." CAT XI*b*. Neuchâtel: Delachaux & Niestlé. 2nd ed. Geneva: Labor et Fides, 1988.
Lacocque, Pierre-Emmanuel. "Desacralizing Life and Its Mystery: The Jonah Complex Revisited." *Journal of Psychology and Theology,* 10, no. 2 (1982): 113–19.

BIBLIOGRAPHY

——— . "Fear of Engulfment and the Problem of Identity." *Journal of Religion and Health* 23, no. 3 (1984): 218–28.

——— . "On the Search for Meaning." *Journal of Religion and Health* 21, no. 3 (1982): 219–27.

Laing, R. D. *The Divided Self.* Baltimore: Penguin Books, 1965.

Landes, George M. "Jonah, Book of." *IDBSup.* Nashville: Abingdon, 1976; pp. 488–91.

——— . "Jonah: A Mashal?" In *Israelite Wisdom: Theological and Literary Essays in Honor of Samuel Terrien.* ed. J. G. Gammie. Missoula, Mont.: Scholars Press, 1975; pp. 137–58.

——— . "The Kerygma of the Book of Jonah." *Interp.* 21 (1967): 3–31.

——— . "Linguistic Criteria and the Date of the Book of Jonah." *Eretz-Israel* 16 (1982): 147–70.

——— . "The 'Three Days and Three Nights' Motif in Jonah 2:1." *JBL* 86 (1967): 446–50.

Langs, Robert. *The Bipersonal Field.* New York: Jason Aronson, 1976.

Lethbridge, David. "A Marxist Theory of Self-Actualization." *Journal of Humanistic Psychology* 26, no. 2 (1986): 84–103.

Leeuw, G. van der. *Religion in Essence and Manifestation: A Study in Phenomenology.* New York: Harper & Row, 2 vols., 1938/1963.

Lods, Adolphe. *Histoire de la littérature hébraïque et juive.* Paris: Payot, 1950.

——— . *The Prophets and the Rise of Judaism.* Trans. S. H. Hooke. London: Routledge & Kegan, 1950.

Lohfink, N. "Und Jona ging zur Stadt hinaus (Jon. 4, 5)." *BZ*, new series, 5, no. 2 (1961): 185–03.

Lorand, S. "Success Neuroses." *Clinical Studies in Psychoanalysis.* New York: International Universities Press, 1931.

Lord, Albert. *The Singer of Tales.* Cambridge, Mass.: Harvard University Press, 1973.

Loretz, O. *Gotteswort und menschliche Erfahrung: Eine Auslegung der Bücher Jona, Rut, Hohes Lied und Qohelet.* Freiburg: Herder, 1963.

——— . "Herkunft und Sinn der Jona Erzählung." *BZ*, new series 5 (1961): 18–29.

Lowen, Alexander. *Fear of Life.* New York: Macmillan, 1980.

Lubac, Henri de. *Aspects du Bouddhisme,* Paris: Seuil, 1951.

Maddi, Salvatore R. "The Existential Neurosis." *Journal of Abnormal Psychology* 72 (1967): 311–25.

Magness, J. L. *Sense and Absence.* Chico, Calif.: Scholars Press, 1986.

Magonet, J. *Form and Meaning: Studies in Literary Techniques in the Book of Jonah.* Bern and Frankfurt: H. & P. Lang, 1976.

Mahler, Margaret S. *On Human Symbiosis and the Vicissitudes of Individuation.* New York: International Universities Press, 1968.

BIBLIOGRAPHY

———. *The Selected Papers of Margaret S. Mahler.* Vol. 2.: *Separation-Individuation.* New York: Jason Aronson, 1979.

Mankowitz, Wolf. "It Should Happen to a Dog." *Religious Drama* Vol. 3. Selected and introduced by M. Halverson. Meridian, N.Y.: Living Age Books, 1959.

Mann, Thomas. *The Magic Mountain* (first pub. 1924). Trans. H. T. Lowe-Porter. New York: Modern Library, 1927.

Martin, A. D. *The Prophet Jonah, the Book and the Sign.* London/New York: Longmans, Green Co., 1926.

Maslow, Abraham H. *The Farther Reaches of Human Nature.* New York: Penguin Books, 1971.

———. *Motivation and Personality.* New York: Harper & Row, 1970.

———. "Neurosis as a Failure of Personal Growth." *Humanitas* 3 (1967): 153–69.

———. *The Psychology of Science.* Chicago: Henry Regnery Co., 1966.

———. "Self-Actualizing People: A Study of Psychological Health" (first pub. 1950). *Motivation and Personality.* New York: Harper & Row, 1970; pp. 149–80.

———. *Toward a Psychology of Being* (first pub. 1962). Princeton: D. Van Nostrand, 1968.

———, & H. M. Chiang. *The Healthy Personality.* New York: Van Nostrand, Reinhold Co., 1969.

Masterson, James F., & David Rinsley. "The Borderline Syndrome: The Role of the Mother in the Genesis of Psychic Structure of the Borderline Personality." *International Journal of Psychoanalysis* 56 (1975): 163–78.

May, Rollo. *The Courage to Create.* New York: W. W. Norton, 1975.

———. *Existential Psychology.* New York: Random House, 1960.

———. "Existential Psychology and Human Freedom." *Chicago Theological Seminary Register* 52 (October 1962): 11–19.

———. *Existential Psychotherapy.* Toronto: Bryant Press, 1967.

———. *Love and Will.* New York: Dell, 1969.

———. *Man's Search for Himself.* New York: W. W. Norton, 1953.

———. *The Meaning of Anxiety.* New York: W. W. Norton, 1977.

———. "Modern Man's Image of Himself." *Chicago Theological Seminary Register* 52 (October 1962): 1–11.

———. *Power and Innocence.* New York: W. W. Norton, 1977.

McClelland, David C.; John W. Atkinson; Russell A. Clark; & Edgar L. Lowell. *The Achievement Motive.* New York: Appleton-Century-Crofts, 1953.

McGuire, William, "The Freud/Jung Letters." *Psychology Today* 7, no. 9 (1974): 37–42, 86–94.

BIBLIOGRAPHY

Mednick, M. T., & G. R. Puryear. "Motivational and Personality Factors Related to Career Goals of Black College Women." *Journal of Social and Behavioral Sciences* 21 (1975): 1–30.

Meisel, Frederick. "The Myth of Peter Pan." *The Psychoanalytic Study of the Child* 32 (1977): 545–63.

Melville, Herman. *Moby Dick or the Whale.* New York: Holt, Rinehart & Winston, 1957.

Meserve, Harry C. "Nobody Here but Us Humanists."*Journal of Religion and Health* 21, no. 2 (1982): 179–83.

Miles, John A. "Laughing at the Bible: Jonah as Parody." *JQR* 65 (January 1975): 161–81.

Milgram, Stanley. *Obedience to Authority.* New York: Harper & Row, 1979.

Montaigne, Michel de. *Oeuvres.* Paris: Pléiade, 1976.

More (Muggia), Joseph. "The Prophet Jonah: The Story of an Intrapsychic Process." *American Imago* 27 (1970): 3–11.

Morgan, G. Campbell. *The Minor Prophets.* London: Pickering, 1960.

Moustakas, Clark E., ed. *The Self: Explorations in Personal Growth.* New York: Harper & Row, 1956.

Murdoch, Iris. "Against Dryness." *Encounter.* January 1961.

Nabert, J. *Éléments pour une éthique.* Paris: P.U.F., 1943.

Nachtigal, J. C. *Eichhorn's allgemeine Bibliothek der biblischen Literatur.* Vol. 9. Lips: Weidmannschen Buchhandlung, 1799.

Neher, André. *Amos, contribution à l'étude du prophétisme.* Paris: Vrin, 1950.

——— . *L'Exil de la Parole.* Paris: Seuil, 1970 (*The Exile of the Word: From the Silence of the Bible to the Silence of Auschwitz.* Philadelphia: Jewish Publication Society of America, 1981).

——— . *The Prophetic Existence.* Trans. W. Wolff. South Brunswick, N.J.: A. S. Barnes, 1969.

Neuman, Mildred & Bernard Berkowitz. *How to Be Your Own Best Friend.* New York: Ballantine Books, 1971.

Neil, William. "Jonah. Book of." *IDB* vol. 2. Nashville: Abingdon, 1962, pp. 964–67.

Neumann, Erich. *The Great Mother* (first pub. 1953). Princeton: Princeton University Press, 1963.

Nilsson, M. P. *Geschichte der griechischen Religion.* Munich: Beck, 1941.

——— . "Götter und Psycholgie bei Homer." *Archiv für Religionswissenschaft* 22 (1925): 363ff.

Nock, Arthur D. *Conversion.* Oxford: Clarendon Press, 1933.

Nord, Walter. "A Marxist Critique of Humanistic Psychology." *Journal of Humanistic Psychology* 17, no. 1 (1977): 75–83.

Orwell, George. *Inside the Whale and Other Essays.* London: Victor Gollancz, 1940.

Otto, Rudolf. *The Idea of the Holy* (first pub. 1929). London: Oxford University Press, 1958.

Otto, Walter F. "The Meaning of the Eleusinian Mysteries" (first pub. 1944). In *The Mysteries* (Papers from the Eranos Yearbooks, vol. 2). Ed. Joseph Campbell. New York: Pantheon Books, 1955; pp. 14–31.

Ouaknin, M. A., & E. Smilévitch, *Pirqé de Rabbi Eliézer*. Paris: Verdier, 1983.

Ovesey, Lionel. "Fear of Vocational Success." *Archives of General Psychology* 7 (1962): 82–92.

Parrot, André. *Ninive et l'Ancien Testament*. Neuchâtel: Delachaux et Niestlé, 1953.

Patte, Daniel, ed. *Semiology and Parables*. Pittsburgh: Pickwick Press, 1976.

Patterson, C. H. *The Therapeutic Relationship: Foundations for an Eclectic Psychotherapy*. Monterey, Calif. Brooks/Cole, 1985.

Pederson, J. E. "Some Thoughts on a Biblical View of Anger." *J. of Psy. and Theol.* 9 (1974): 210–15.

Perls, Frederick. *Gestalt Therapy Verbatim*. Lafayette, Calif.: Real People Press, 1969.

Pohlenz, Max. *Die Stoa*. 2 vols. Göttingen: Vandenbroeck & Ruprecht, 1948–49.

Rad, Gerhard von. *Der Prophet Jona*. Nürnberg: Laetare, 1950.

Rank, Otto. *Beyond Psychology*. New York: Dover Books, 1958.

———. *The Myth of the Birth of the Hero*. Vienna: F. Denticke, 1909.

———. *Will Therapy and Truth and Reality*. New York: Alfred A. Knopf, 1964.

Redfield, James M. *Nature and Culture in the Iliad: The Tragedy of Hector*. Chicago: University of Chicago Press, 1975.

Reitzenstein, Richard. *Hellenistische Wundererzählungen*. Darmstadt: Wissenschaftliche Buchgesellschaft, 1963.

Reymond, Philippe. *L'eau, sa vie et sa signification dans l'Ancien Testament*. *VTSup.* 6. Leiden: Brill, 1958.

Ricoeur, Paul. *The Conflict of Interpretations*. Ed. D. Ihde. Evanston: Northwestern University Press, 1974.

———. *Interpretation Theory: Discourse and the Surplus of Meaning*. Fort Worth: Texas University Press, 1976.

———. *The Symbolism of Evil*. (first pub. 1960). Boston: Beacon Press, 1967.

———. *Time and Narrative*. 3 vols. trans. K. McLaughlin and D. Pellauer. Chicago: University of Chicago Press, 1984–88.

Riesenfeld, Harald. "La tradition sacramentelle du baptème johannique." *Dieu Vivant* 13 (1949): 29–37.

Robinson, Theodore H. *Prophecy and the Prophets in Ancient Israel*. London: G. Duckworth, 1953.

BIBLIOGRAPHY

————, & F. Horst. *Die Zwölf Kleinen Propheten*. HAT 1/14. Tübingen: Mohr-Siebeck, 1964.

Rofé, A. "Classes in the Prophetical Stories: Didactic Legenda and Parable." *Studies on Prophecy*. VTSup. 26. Leiden: Brill, 1974; pp. 143–64.

Rogers, Carl R. *Client-Centered Therapy*. Boston: Houghton Mifflin, 1951.

————. "The Necessary and Sufficient Conditions of Therapeutic Personality Change." *Journal of Consulting Psychology* 21 (1957): 95–103.

————. *On Becoming a Person*. Boston: Houghton Mifflin, 1961.

Rohde, Erwin. *Der griechische Roman und seine Vorläufer*. 4th edn. Hildescheim: Georg Olms, 1960.

Rowley, Harold H. *The Missionary Message of the Old Testament*. London: Carey Press, 1945.

Royce, James E. *Personality and Mental Health*. Milwaukee: Bruce, 1955.

Rudolph, Wilhelm. *Joel-Amos-Obadja-Jona*. KAT 13/2. Gütersloh: Mohn, 1971.

Sartre, Jean-Paul. *Les mouches*. Paris: Gallimard, 1947.

Sasson, Jack. *Ruth: A New Translation with a Philological Commentary*. Baltimore: Johns Hopkins University Press, 1979.

Schachter, Stanley. "Deviation, Rejection and Communication." *Journal of Abnormal and Social Psychology* 46 (1951): 190–207.

Scheler, Max. *On the Eternal Man*. Garden City, N.Y.: Doubleday Anchor Books, 1972.

Schmidt, Hans. *Jona, eine Untersuchung zur vergleichenden Religionsgeschichte*. FRLANT 9. Göttingen: Vandenhoeck & Ruprecht, 1907.

————. "Die Komposition des Buches Jona." *ZAW* 25 (1905): 285–310.

Schmidt, L. *"De Deo" Studien zur Literarkritik und Theologie des Buches Jona*. BZAW 143. Berlin: De Gruyter, 1976.

Schneidau, H. *Sacred Discontent: The Bible and Western Tradition*. Berkeley: University of California Press, 1976.

Scholes, Robert & Robert Kellogg. *The Nature of Narrative*. London: Oxford University Press, 1966.

Schuster, Daniel B. "On the Fear of Success." *Psychiatric Quarterly* 29 (1955): 412–20.

Schweitzer, Albert. *Albert Schweitzer: An Anthology*. Ed. Charles R. Joy. New York: Harper & Row, 1947.

————. "The Ethics of Reverence for Life." *Christendom* 1 (Winter 1936): 225–39.

————. *Kulturphilosophie*. Vol. 1: *Verfall und Wiederaufbau der Kultur* (first pub. 1923). Munich, 1946. Vol. 2. *Kultur und Ethik* (first pub. 1923). Munich, 1946 (*Civilization and Ethics*. London: Adam & Charles Black, 1946).

————. *Ma vie et ma pensée* (first pub. 1931). Paris: Albin Michel, 1960 (*Out of My Life and Thought*. New York: Henry Holt, 1933).

————. *Reverence for Life*. New York: Harper & Row, 1969.

————. *Souvenirs de mon enfance* (first pub. 1926). Paris: Albin Michel, 1984. (*Memoirs of Childhood and Youth*. New York: Macmillan, 1931).

————. *The Wit and Wisdom of Albert Schweitzer*. Ed. Charles R. Joy. Boston: Beacon Press, 1949.

Scott, R. B. Y. *The Relevance of the Prophets*. New York: Macmillan, 1969.

————. "The Sign of Jonah." *Interp.* 19 (1965): 16–25.

Searles, Harold F. "Anxiety Concerning Change, as Seen in the Psychotherapy of Schizophrenic Patients—With Particular Reference to the Sense of Personal Identity" (first pub. 1961). *Collected Papers on Schizophrenia and Related Subjects*. New York: International Universities Press, 1965; pp. 443–64.

Sellin, E. *Das Zwölfprophetenbuch*. KAT 12. Leipzig: A. Deichert, 1922.

————, & G. Fohrer. *Introduction to the Old Testament*. Trans. D. E. Green. Nashville: Abingdon, 1968.

Sherwin, Byron L. *Abraham Joshua Heschel*. Atlanta, Ga.: John Knox Press, 1979.

Simon, Ulrich. *Story and Faith*. London: SPCK, 1975.

Smart, James D. "Jonah." *IB*, vol. 6. Nashville: Abingdon, 1956.

Smith, Brewster. "On Self-Actualization: A Transambivalent Examination of a Focal Theme in Maslow's Psychology." *Journal of Humanistic Psychology* 13, no. 2 (1973): 17–33.

Smith, George A. *The Book of the Twelve Prophets*. Vol. 2. Garden City, N.Y.: Doubleday-Doran & Co., 1929.

Smith, Sir Grafton Elliot. *The Evolution of the Dragon*. Manchester: Longmans, Green & Co., 1919.

Snygg, Donald, & Arthur W. Combs. *Individual Behavior: A Perceptual Approach to Behavior*. New York: Harper & Row, 1959.

Solovine, M. *Démocrite, doctrine philosophique et réflexion morale*. Paris: Alcan, 1928.

Speiser, Ephraim A. "Nineveh." *IDB*, vol. 3. Nashville: Abingdon, 1962, pp. 551–53.

Staiger, Emil. *Die Kunst der Interpretation*. Zurich: Atlantis Vlg. 1955.

Stanton, G. B. "The Prophet and His Message." *Bibl. Sacra* 108 (1951): 237–49, 363–76.

Steinbeck, John. *The Pearl*. New York: Bantam Books, 1945.

Steiner, George. *The Death of Tragedy*. New York: Oxford University Press, 1980.

Steinmann, J. *Le livre de la consolation d'Israël les prophètes du retour de l'exil*. Paris: Cerf, 1960.

Strack, Hermann L., & Paul Billerbeck. *Kommentar zum Neuen Testament aus Talmud und Midrasch*. Vol. 1. Munich: Beck, 1926.

BIBLIOGRAPHY

Sullivan, Harry Stack. *The Psychiatric Interview.* New York: W. W. Norton, 1954.

Swift, Jonathan. *Gulliver's Travels.* New York: Modern Library, 1931.

Szekely, Lajos. "Success, Success Neurosis, and the Self." *British Journal of Medical Psychology* 33 (1950): 45–51.

Tec, Leon. *The Fear of Success.* New York: Reader's Digest Press, 1976.

Thoma, A. "Entstehung des Büchleins Jona." *Theol. St. u. Krit.* (1911): 479–502.

Thompson, W. I. *At the Edge of History.* New York: Harper & Row, 1972.

Tillich, Paul. *The Courage to Be.* New Haven: Yale University Press, 1952.

––––––. *The Eternal Now.* New York: Charles Scribner's Sons, 1963.

––––––. *Morality and Beyond.* New York: Harper & Row, 1963.

––––––. *Religious Perspective.* New York: Harper & Row, 1963.

Travers, P. L. "The World of the Hero." *Parabola* 1, no. 1 (1976): 42–51.

Tresmer, David. *The Fear of Success.* New York: Plenum Press, 1977.

Trible, Phyllis. "Studies in the Book of Jonah." Ph.D. dissertation. New York: Columbia University, 1963.

Uspenski, Boris. *A Poetics of Composition: The Structure of the Artistic Text and Typology of a Compositional Form.* Berkeley: University of California Press, 1973.

Vaccari, Alberto. "Il Genre Letterario del Libro di Gioni in Recenti Publicazioni." *Divinitas* 6 (1972): 231–52.

Vischer, Wilhelm. "Jonas." *EThR* 24 (1949): 116–19.

Weinreb, F. *Das Buch Jonah, der Sinn des Buches Jona nach der ältesten jüdischen Uberlieferungen.* Zurich: Orgo Vlg., 1970.

Weiser, A. *Das Buch der Zwölf Kleinen Propheten,* vol. 1. ATD, no. 24. Göttingen: Vandenhoeck & Ruprecht, 1959.

Weiss, M. "Einiges über die Bauformen des Erzählens in der Bibel." *VT* 13 (1963): 456–75.

––––––. "Weiteres über die Bauformen des Erzählens." *Biblica* 46 (1965): 181–206.

Weiss, Raphael. "Al sepher Yonah." *Mahanayim* 47 (1961): 45–48.

Welleck, René. *A History of Modern Criticism: The Romantic Age.* New Haven: Yale University Press, 1955.

Weston, P. & M. T. Mednick. "Race, Social Class, and the Motive to Avoid Success in Women." *Journal of Cross-Cultural Psychology* 1 (1970): 284–91.

Wheelis, Allen. "How People Change." *Commentary* 47 (May 1969): 56–66.

White, Robert W. "The Concept of the Healthy Personality." *The Counseling Psychologist* 4, no. 2 (1973): 3–12, 67–69.

Wiesel, Elie. *Five Biblical Prophets.* Notre Dame, Ind.: University of Notre Dame Press, 1981.

Bibliography

Williamson, E. G. "A Concept of Counseling." *Occupations* 29 (1950): 182–89.

Winckler, H. "Zum Buche Jona." *Altoriental. Forsch.* Leipzig: E. Pfeiffer, 1900.

Winnicott, Donald W. *The Maturational Processes and the Facilitating Environment.* London: Hogarth Press, 1965. See esp. "The Theory of the Parent-Child Relationship" (first pub. 1960): pp. 37–55; "Ego Distortions in Terms of True and False Self" (first pub. 1960): pp. 140–52., and "The Development of the Capacity for Concern" (first pub. 1963): pp. 73–82.

————. "Transitional Objects and Transitional Phenomena" (first pub. 1951). In *Collected Papers: Through Pediatrics to Psychoanalysis.* London: Tavistock Publications, 1958; pp. 229–42.

Wolff, H. W. "Jonabuch." *RGG.* Tübingen: Mohr-Siebeck, 1959, vol. 3, cols. 854–55.

————. *Studien zum Jonabuch.* Biblische Studien 47. Neukirchen-Vluyn: Neukirchener Vlg., 1947. (Köln, 1965).

Wolpe, Joseph. *Psychotherapy by Reciprocal Inhibition.* Stanford, Calif.: Stanford University Press, 1958.

Wright, Charles H. H. "The Book of Jonah Considered from an Allegorical Point of View." *Biblical Essays, or Exegetical Studies on the Books of Job and Jonah.* Edinburgh: T. & T. Clark, 1886.

Wright, G. Ernest. *God Who Acts: Biblical Theology as Recital.* Studies in Biblical Theology, First Series, no. 8. London: SCM Press, 1952.

Yalom, Irwin. *Existential Psychotherapy.* New York: Basic Books, 1980.

Yankelovich, Daniel. *New Rules in American Life: Searching for Self-Fulfillment in a World Turned Upside Down.* New York: Random House, 1981.

Zeigarnik, Bluma. "Uber das Behalten von erledigten Handlungen." *Psychologie Forschung* 9 (1927): 1–85.

Zeligs, Dorothy F. "A Psychoanalytic Note on the Function of the Bible." *American Imago* 14 (Spring 1957): 57–60.

Index of
Authors Cited

INDEX

INDEX

INDEX

Topical Index

INDEX

Index

INDEX

INDEX

Index

INDEX

Respect
    of life, 203f.
    of the Person, 188f.
Responsibility, 60, 71, 79, 176, 186, 190, 197, 210, 213n26
Resurrection. *See* Birth/Rebirth
Reticence/Reluctance, xxii, 8f., 34, 186ff., 195ff.
Ricinus Communis. See *Qiqayon*
Rites (of Initiation). *See* Rebirth
Roman, 36, 186
Rupert of Deutz, 144
Ruth, xxii, 48n45, 78

Sacredness/Sublime, 188, 202
Sailors, 8, 17, 80, 86, 88f., 92n38, 92n48, 97, 123, 136n37, 216
Saktideva, 55
Samson, 54, 64n14
Sarcasm, 49n7
Satire, xxii, 22, 26ff., 39ff., 46n7, 49, 62, 77, 99, 105, 119, 123, 126,
    138, 141, 147, 165n2, 215, 217, 228
Schweitzer, Albert, 203ff.
Sea, 8, 17, 31, 32, 59, 63n21, 71f., 76ff., 80, 89, 92n20, 92n38, 101f., 110n5, 111n18, 112n36, 115, 126, 166n14, 221
Sea of Reeds, 102
Second Time, 114ff., 134n3
Selective Inattention (Sullivan), 87, 203
Self-actualization/Potentialities, *chapters 8 and 9*, 214n4
Self-decentralization, 185
Self-oblivion, 185ff.
Self-realization. *See* Maslow, Abraham H., in Index of Authors Cited
Self-transcendence, 69ff., 74, 106, 109, 174, 180f.
Seneca, 47n40, 47n43
Shakespeare, William, 29
Shammai, 165
Shark. *See* Fish
Siduri, 112n36
Silence, 147, 154, 157
Sinope, 36
Siracide/ben Sira, 20, 22
Sitz im Leben (of Narrative), xxi, 159
Sleep, 80ff., 89f., 104

Snake, 143, 155, 158
Socrates, 192, 202
Sodom/Gomorrah, xxi, 23n10, 32, 39, 118f., 134n9, 140, 146, 148, 161, 221f., 224
Solipsism, 116, 118, 139, 173ff., 177, 185ff., 202, 208, 213n26, 216, 218. *See also* Inner Voice
Solitude. *See* Isolation
Sophocles, 114, 189
"Sorge," 213n26
Storm, 32, 60, 69ff., 79f., 88, 151. *See also* Sea
Soul/Psyche, 29, 38, 44, 49, 50, 60, 63n21, 72, 82, 94, 109, 124, 146, 169n68, 175, 182, 185, 186
Stage
    of the "Authentic-Self," 110n9, 184ff.
    of the "Prior-Self," 110n9, 184ff.
Stalin, 189
Stoa/Stoicism, 38ff., 42, 161f., 186, 193n33
Subversion/protest, 19, 27f., 35, 44, 78, 109, 144, 215, 220, 228
Success. *See* Failure
Succoth/Feast of Booths, 41, 90n4, 127
Suffering, 54, 56, 163f., 199, 201, 204
Suicide, 75, 88f., 190. *See also* Death
Sukkah, 105, 137ff., 153ff., 157ff., 167n30, 167n35
Sun, 32, 78, 92n27, 148f., 156ff., 167n30, 222
Survival (Instinct of), 105, 157, 165
"Suspension of the Ethical," 76
Symbol/Symbolism, xviii, xx, xxivn3, 11f., 19, 23n12, 39f., 35, 45, 48n53, 49f., 53f., 56ff., 60, 63n21, 63n23, 64n25, 64n31, 64n33, 64n34, 71, 73, 78, 80f., 87, 95, 99ff., 109, 111n27, 117ff., 153ff., 158f., 163, 168n52, 169n61, 174, 178, 208f., 221f.
Symptom, 58, 71, 134n12, 226
Syndrome (of Jonah), xxi, xxii, 70, 201ff

Tammuz, xviii
Tarphon, Rabbi, 101
Tertullian, xiii

263

INDEX